AND YOU SHALL TELL YOUR CHILDREN

A Chronicle of Survival:
Lessons of Life for Today

By Ida Akerman-Tieder

DE**V**ORA
PUBLISHING
NEW YORK◆JERUSALEM◆LONDON

And You Shall Tell Your Children
A Chronicle of Survival: Lessons of Life for Today

Published by Devora Publishing Company

Text Copyright © 2011 Ida Akerman-Tieder

Translated from French by David Maisel

Previously published in French as *Et Tu Raconteras à tes Enfants* by Editions Erez, Jerusalem (1995) and in Hebrew as והגדת לבנך by Erez, Sifriat Beth-El (2002).

COVER DESIGN: Shani Schmell
TYPESETTING: Daniella Barak
EDITORIAL AND PRODUCTION DIRECTOR: Daniella Barak
EDITOR: Shirley Zauer

Soft Cover ISBN: 978-1-934440-40-7

First Edition
Printed in Israel

Distributed by:

Urim Publications
POB 52287
Jerusalem 91521, Israel
Tel: 02.679.7633
Fax: 02.679.7634
urim_pub@netvision.net.il

Lambda Publishers, Inc.
527 Empire Blvd.
Brooklyn, NY 11225, USA
Tel: 718.972.5449
Fax: 718.972.6307
mh@ejudaica.com

www.UrimPublications.com

❧❧❧❧❧❧❧

To my husband Fred,
who vanished too soon,
without whom
I would not have been able
to make this out of my life.

May his soul be bound in the bond of life!

❧❧❧

In memory
of my parents
who in dying
commanded me to live.

May the Lord avenge their blood!

❧❧❧❧❧❧❧

TABLE OF CONTENTS

POEMS

PREFACE

A book of life, an opening towards life: Ida Akerman's book is a fascinating and moving account, which she does not turn into an autobiography. It is a kind of "resonator" (I do not know if the word exists, but it suits this book). In her personal journey from her childhood in Berlin to setting up house in Jerusalem, it is hardly a "me" that comes to light. It is a "you" through a "me," so little is the author focused on herself.

She is a doctor, a pediatrician, a psychoanalyst, but one feels she is more of a midwife. She tries to bring out the whole potential for being and living of the person who reads her book. She has not written to give an account of herself. Well, perhaps a trifle, but so little! Just enough to let the world know, so that the curtain should not be drawn following the rejoicings on the fiftieth anniversary of the end of the Second World War, so that satisfaction at the victory over Hitler should not cause the nightmares of "children of silence" like her to be forgotten. She has made a tremendous effort to speak, but in reality it is not of herself that she has spoken.

She has spoken for "the others," for all those she ran into and continues to run into and who do not have the gift that she has to express their feelings. Bearing the most tragic of wounds – the arrest of her parents, their dreadful absence, their definitive non-return from the death-camps – suddenly transported to France, forced to adjust to a new present totally disconnected from the warm recent past, she succeeded through sheer willpower in overcoming these overwhelming obstacles. The entire book carries the implicit message, which is stated openly only towards the end: "You, reader, can also do it, since I have done it." "You, reader" is not only the child of deported parents but also those today who have lost their way in life, the disorientated refugee, the victim of troubles in the family. You will undoubtedly find an "angel" to help you on your life's path if you are able first of all to help yourself. This "angel" will be someone who knows how to listen.

To know how to listen! A rare virtue, of which my father, also a doctor, gave me an example. My husband, André Neher, one day received a splendid compliment from a university colleague of great intelligence but out of step with real life: "*You* at least know how to listen." Indeed, listening is easy if you have good hearing, but to "know" how to listen is to listen in order to give the right answer; it is to have, so to speak, one's heart and one's brain in one's ear. This anatomical peculiarity Ida Akerman possesses in the highest degree. She also found it in my husband, who encouraged her warmly to write this book to provide food for reflection for those who would like to listen but do not "know how." They will find here plenty of examples of hurtful behavior to avoid. She also, from her "Moissac days" onwards, found this faculty of "knowing how to listen" in Régine Lehmann, an outstanding woman whose exceptional friendship has enriched those who have had the privilege to find her on their path, and whose attentive presence still brings together Ida and myself long after her death.

In this book, there is no self-pity, no dwelling on misfortunes. No, one builds, one struggles to build – to construct a life, a real human life. Jewish tradition in its purest form helped Ida Akerman tremendously to regain the roots that persecution had torn away from her. One feels on every page of the book a wonderment before Jewish teachings on life, for it is not only a matter of words, precepts, prayers but a moment-by-moment commitment in the most day-to-day activities, which then become a vehicle of light. This is a book, which it does one good to read. It is a book that cost the writer a great deal, but which gives the reader still more. It is one of those too rare books that remind one of men's wickedness, but at the same time paradoxically reconcile one with humanity. It is a book that makes one want to be a "*ben-adam*," to use the fine but untranslatable Hebrew expression.

Rina Neher-Bernheim, Iyar 5755, May 1995

This book was published thanks to the person who is concealed under the title of Keren Isaac. He does not want his tremendous generosity to be merely inconspicuous, but prefers it to be secret.

FOREWORD

This book was the product of a long maturation. Its starting point was the wish to reply to questions put by young people born just before, during or after the *Shoah*, (the Holocaust). The same questions always recurred, whatever the age of the questioner and his or her social, family or religious status. The questioners all wondered about our history, asking me about it, about the meaning of that history and how one should situate oneself in relation to the values and heritage of our people and its prophetic vision of life.

While being unconscious vehicles of our experience, these young people did not have the basic data to grasp it in its reality.

In the face of these questionings, this perplexity, this crisis of identity, I agreed to reply on a tape-recorder to the questions put successively by two people who seemed to me to be representative.

This explains the essentially oral nature of this narrative and the presence of traces of the dialogue in its "you" form of address.

The oral narrative, which emerged some twenty years ago, was then transcribed and reworked. In view of the painfulness of these events, which can never be mourned sufficiently, one can understand the difficulty of working on such a text, for to relate these things is to live through them again.

This explains the very long period that elapsed between the original form and the final draft of the text.

For a very long time I was incapable of re-reading these pages alone, and it was just as difficult for someone else to assist me, or to do it instead of me. Finally, helped by the lapse of time, the enterprise reached its conclusion. At each stage, someone sitting next to me sustained me in my effort, helping me to make the modifications needed to render the text more accessible, while respecting the spirit of the narrative.

After the various stages described in these pages, we are now finally settled in Jerusalem, where we are very happy and enjoy every moment of our lives in the land of Israel. Our children are married, have children of their own and have work that they like. They are occupied in helping others and are fully engaged in the adventure of reconstructing the life of our people true to its identity in its land.

This text is thus not only a reply to questions. I also wanted my children and grandchildren to know the truth about my life-experience, of which they have inherited both the horror and the "lesson" it has to teach.

Nor did I want others to speak for us and fabricate books of "history" that have nothing to do with what we really remember and our forever-wounded souls.

Finally, it was important for me to convey the Jewish and collective "meaning" of what each of us has borne on his or her solitary and helpless shoulders in a state of total, inhuman exile.

I wished to show that even though we have been for so long and so cruelly pursued and exterminated, we have the good fortune to be the possessors of an invaluable treasure of life and wisdom: the Jewish heritage we have received and which has enabled us to overcome all adversities.

May the children of my people
leave the petrifying skins of the onions of all the Egypts
they have passed through,
find the original splendor of their authenticity
and together bring it back to life each day in our recovered land!

ৡৡৡৡৡৡৡ

PART I

ৡৡৡৡৡৡৡ

Childhood and Destruction

Give Thanks...

Dear children of yesterday and today
who have the good fortune to be alive,
Give thanks...
thanks at every moment
that you have your parents
who say goodbye to you
in the morning
and who nevertheless
wait for you in the evening...
Give thanks
that you can sleep in your bed
and have a piece of bread
to calm your hunger.
Give thanks
that you have a sheet
and also
a roof
to shelter you
from cruel enemies
who snatch you from your nest,
maltreat you and kill you.
Give thanks
that when you are in the street
you are not the target of a thousand boots
and rifles.
Give thanks
that you have someone who runs up
when you call for help
and who is there to reassure you
when you are frightened.
Give thanks at every moment

that your brothers, sisters
parents,
uncles, aunts, grandparents,
teachers, cousins,
friends, neighbors
are not taken from you
once and for all.
Give thanks that you have clothes
and shoes
so that you do not shiver
and tear your feet,
tremble in your heart and soul
because you are cast aside,
exposed to the shame
of not being one of theirs...
to absolute helplessness
and to the fear
that never leaves you,
of being at the mercy
of the whims of others,
recognized by the first passerby
who is not always tenderhearted
because you have a hooked nose
or a slight accent,
or at best
are saved
by decent strangers
whom you have to submit to
nicely
and say thanks,
thanks continually,
and – whatever your age –
you are obliged to be good!
Give thanks again
that, for you, suitcases mean
holidays,
trains and stations,
the chance of going on journeys,

and when you go off with a group of children
it is only
to have a good time.
And finally give thanks
when the war is over
and you have survived,
that all these memories
buried
so that life can go on
do not explode in your face
unexpectedly
like underground mines
which suddenly blow up
– like unwanted guests
sitting down at your table –
taking you to other times,
to camps...
making you tremble
in the present,
shaking the house
and all your constructions
because you react
in an "unsuitable"
totally disproportionate manner
incomprehensible to the uninitiated
to little daily hitches,
and often for no reason at all.
Give thanks
that if someone is a little late
it is not always "too late"
and that the slightest threat
does not mean
that there is no longer
any place for you at all.

I could go on and on
listing the symptoms of this "illness"
inflicted by their infamy,

and above all its infinite variants
according to the past and nature
of each individual,
of each of these children of Israel
whom they wished to efface
down to their very names
because they were sparks of the light
of these bearers of the Divine Name!

And all this would be as nothing
if our little ones
(two generations already)
were not seized
by these same demons.
Our tribulations
experienced
yesterday
and, which live for them
today,
even if "imaginary,"
are very real,
at least
in their unconscious,
without their knowing
how to protect themselves,
especially as the parents
in most cases
could only keep silent,
as to relate them
would be to go through them again.
But tell me,
is this some diabolic machination
on our path,
a unique, tragic event,
or is it
the nations' final attempt
to foil
the divine plan

for humanity
that Israel is called
to proclaim
and carry out,
so that each time
we take a step forward
they band together against us
to prevent it from coming to pass?

But we have no choice:
either the values of the Torah
regulate our lives
or murderous
absolute inhumanity,
the darkness of yesterday
like that of Hitler
who knows only the force of his arm
and thinks all is allowed him
because he does not believe
in anything
above himself.

So give thanks
that we are a remnant that survived.
Give thanks
that you have regained your plot of earth,
where you can bury your parents
decently at the proper time
and where your children
can sing in Hebrew freely
in the streets...
where you can raise your head
and celebrate your feasts,
where it is your son
who defends you
and not foreign police
eager to give you a kick
while taking you away

to camps...
Give thanks
that you are able
openly
to call yourself
Levi
(even if you are still over there
for a moment),
and have no illusions:
we are but a straw in the wind
among the nations,
and especially outside our home in Zion!

Paris, November 23, 1983

ORIGINS

Shall I tell you about my family?

It's quite a usual history, fairly typical. Just in myself, I embody several quarter-centuries of Jewish history.

My parents, *Ostjuden*,[1] left Poland for Berlin, where I was born.

In Poland life was wretched, so everyone tried to leave in the hope of eating *fisch*[2] instead of having to make do with the head of a herring. Those who could went to America; the more courageous ones went to Australia.

You had different types of people: on the one hand there were the tailors, the road menders, the coachmen, the *balagoules*.[3] These were not afraid to forge a new life in Israel, the Far West or anywhere else. And then you had the others.

In that Poland, where there was nothing to do, where one was not recognized as fully human, where one could not take part in society-at-large, what in fact did they do? They did what they were able to: they withdrew and concentrated on studying, *lernen*, perpetual study of the Torah.

Was this a simple defensive reflex? Possibly, but it was a positive reflex: cultivating one's own field, one's own values for lack of a field to cultivate in the world of the others.

And strangely enough, I felt this in my "guts" when I returned to the *gola* (Diaspora), from Israel: if you don't have a country, you carry your landscape within yourself. It's your language, your world, your whole conception of things, your way of living, everything that is bound up with your history, your geography, and without it you perish.

My parents, then, came from Poland. It was a huge family, as was often the case in that milieu (my great-grandfather had a hundred grand-

---

1. Eastern European Jews.
2. Yiddish for fish, especially carp.
3. *Baal agala*, literally, in Hebrew, "owner of a wagon"; "wagon-driver" in Yiddish.

children). The bad side was that while the men studied, the women had to keep things going. My maternal grandparents had an *Eisengeschäft*.[4]

One day, when I was very small, my mother took us to Poland to meet our grandmother (our grandfather had already died in 1923). I have an unpleasant recollection of that journey and a terrible fear of that country. We crossed a lake, and on the other side, in front of her house above a flight of steps, stood a severe-looking old woman dressed entirely in black.

I remember that my sister didn't want to kiss her, that she frightened her. She was one of those strong women who have to keep life at arm's length at all costs.

So much for my mother's side. On my father's side, almost the whole family – my grandfather, aunts and uncles – came from Hungary and had settled in Berlin.

My mother and one of her brothers ran a shop together. At the beginning they sold eggs and later fabrics; they did what they could. It's the story of an exile already begun before our birth. You will see how exile has been influential in my life to the nth degree.

My mother was very alone in Berlin, far from her people. These Jews from the East, who did not have German as their mother tongue and who spoke Polish or Yiddish among themselves, were not at all integrated. They were neither Western intellectuals, nor assimilated Jews or *wichtige Menschen*.[5] Nobody had any special need for them, but they tried to find some sort of acceptance as human beings.

At the same time, there were the German Jews. Already very "Germanized," they were disdainful of these Polish Jews, these "easterners" whom they viewed as primitive and uncultured. They, for their part, saw themselves as "civilized," as "cultured," as *feine Menschen*[6] who knew how to live.

Who were these shabby types, these down-at-heels from the other side of the Danube who spoke a ridiculous German with a strange accent, went about with beards and *payes*,[7] lived like primitives, celebrated *Shabbat* (the Sabbath) on Saturday instead of Sunday, refused to eat pork and retained all their peculiarities?

---

4. Ironmonger's shop.
5. Important people, notables.
6. Refined, civilized people.
7. Sidelocks, which in the case of men were never cut. Pl. *payes*.

These peculiarities in my opinion had a great power of life. Because, as far as I am concerned, these Polish Jews from the Chasidic *shtetl*[8] in that Western Europe created by Napoleon with its consistories and emancipations, were perhaps the only ones who had succeeded in maintaining something very warm and living both in their family lives and in their lives as human beings and as Jews. They were not assimilated; just a bit contaminated, because Poland is a very Christian and somewhat superstitious country.

I have not forgotten the stories my mother told me. When I thought about it later on, it was hard for me to disentangle the element of tradition they contained from folklore or *Aberglauben* (superstitious beliefs). It's hardly surprising: in that part of the world it was very cold, one got lost in the forest, one floundered in mud. Constantly threatened by drunken peasants who hated them or by big landowners who had power over them and their possessions, the Jews knew neither security nor serenity.

So one can say that one was devalorized before one was even born, inasmuch as one's parents lived in a country that was strange to them and where they counted for nothing. They were merely refugees who tried to earn a living while respecting certain essential principles: not to work on Shabbat, not to eat *treif*[9] and to take off religious holidays.

They could thus neither be officials nor work for non-Jews. And there was no money for the long course of study needed for access to the liberal professions. First of all, one had to eat every day.

My father was an oldest son, and his mother died in 1917 at the end of the First World War. He worked with *his* father. Together they sold *postiches* (wigs). It was the great fashion at that time.

In Hungary, my grandfather had been a *Rav* (rabbi). He had studied in a yeshiva and had been recognized by his teachers as being qualified to teach in turn. He had married and founded a family. With his wife he ran a *schenke*, a kind of inn-cum-grocery-store, somewhere on the borders of Hungary and Poland, an area that was later part of Czechoslovakia. It changed owners in accordance with peace treaties.

I remember a story my father told us. One day his parents had gone away somewhere, and he was alone with his brothers and sisters who were crying from hunger. Then he went out and brought them back some

---

8.　Jewish village in central or Eastern Europe.
9.　Non-kosher.

snow, which he gave them with some spirits. Two minutes later they were all asleep!

Of Berlin, I have many memories. The apartment (I can visualize it very clearly) gave onto the *Weinstrasse*.[10] Surprisingly, my father at that time was no longer working with his father. He had a wholesale wine business, the *Rheinische Weinkellerei*.[11]

Earlier, I think we lived in the Palissadenstrasse, where my mother kept a shop with her brothers. In this shop, when I knew it (I can't quite distinguish between what I've been told from what I remember) they sold eggs; they candled, sorted and arranged them.

Later, they measured and sold lengths of material. My older sister, who had character, placed herself on the counter and made *pipi* on the fabrics in order to attract attention! It was when I was born; she was fifteen months old. My poor mother must have had a hard time of it!

All I personally remember is a shop giving onto the street. There was my father, my mother, my sister, my brother and myself. I can't say I can recall my brother's birth. I remember the five of us in an apartment in a certain neighborhood and the quality of the light.

In the Palissadenstrasse, the entire family lived behind the shop; we must have been very small. Then my parents had to manage to find an apartment with the right number of rooms and plenty of sunlight. At the corner of the street from this new apartment there was a huge park called the *Friedrichshain*, where we children spent most of our time. At the drop of a hat, we would go and play in the street or run around in the park.

How shall I describe my parents? My father was a Jew, a Jew... What shall I say? You see, I cry when I think of him and I shall still be crying in the next world.

So, how was it? I was telling you about the park. My father is connected with all the memories I have of the park. He spent his life playing with us, or, at least, in a manner of speaking, because he was far from us during the week. This, too, was something of a paradox: in order to earn a living, he ran a business of non-kosher wines of which he never drank a single drop.

---

10. Wine Street.
11. Rhenish Wine-cellar.

He left to sell his wine on Mondays or Tuesdays. He must have had vines in Alsace or somewhere in the Rhineland. And he had a cellar to which he took us on Sundays in a cart drawn by a big, white horse. The cellar was full of barrels of wine, wooden boxes and all sorts of things.

When we were allowed inside, it was a joy. We saw the wines being put in the bottles, and then their "*Spedition*" (expedition) when they were sent off. For us children, it was like magic. A stick of flaming sulphur was run around the inside of the bottles (was it to sterilize them?), and when the bottles were full, labels were stuck on plus shiny pieces of paper in various colors. Then the boxes were marked with pre-cut-out letters and a brush dipped in black ink. We watched all this: it was extraordinary. I have often thought that children who are able to go and see their father at his place of work and help a little are very fortunate.

I see my father as a great child, a poet. What did he live for? He lived for his Shabbat; he lived for his wife whom he adored; he lived for his children who were his whole life, and he also lived in order to help others. You know that the work I am doing today is probably not a matter of chance.

In the First World War, my father refused to bear arms: he was a medical orderly. He had always dreamed of studying medicine and playing the violin, but who would pay for his studies? Who would have bought him a violin? And then, learning the violin meant entering into a milieu where one assimilated, and that was totally out of the question. So he managed to be taken on as a medical orderly. I have photos of him in uniform, which I obtained after the Second World War.

I imagine him going about his work, making his way through the countryside, but I'm quite sure that at every farmstead he visited, he assisted people both physically and morally. He helped them and then he left, bringing back eggs and honey for his dear children, and that's how it went.

Do you think it was amusing to make these journeys every week and to have to deal with non-Jewish peasants with whom he couldn't sit down and eat or drink wine?

He went around with his *Aktentasche*, his briefcase, his familiar briefcase, which was the only thing he kept during the exodus of 1940, containing his *tallit*, his prayer shawl; his *tefillin*, his phylacteries (see glossary); and his prayer-book. It was all that was left... I imagine that his life during the week, far away from his family, was no joke. And on Sundays he was so happy to be able to take us to the cellar or to the park, and finally be able to take charge of his children.

On Thursday nights, we children were like crazy. It was impossible to send us to bed. We waited to hear the sound of the key in the lock, and then suddenly, even if it was midnight, everyone was up and all three of us were on him at once before he even had time to take off his coat. The fun had started, and if the fun had started it was because he was at least as happy as we were that we had come together again.

We had a comfortable home with fairly large rooms. There was a room for the children, a diningroom, a kitchen, my parents' room, and a long corridor at the end of which there was a rather mysterious room where they stored postiches, a relic of the time when my father was working with my grandfather.

This room was special. It was where we put the *chametz*[12] during *Pesach.*[13] I kept my doll there, the doll my father had given me and on whose head he had placed a wig with ringlets. This doll was a dream! The apartment was bright, spacious and clean.

My mother was a woman with a rare personality. In my family, they say she was a princess, an aristocrat, and it's true. She never said anything, she always did everything without seeming to; she watched, she observed, she registered, and in all situations showed great, quiet courage.

Life can't have been easy for her. She was alone half the week in that hostile Berlin with three small children, her husband away, her family in Poland, facing a clan of in-laws who can't have been too well disposed towards her because she had taken away the oldest brother. I have been told it was a love match; they adored and respected one another.

It was fine in that apartment, where I don't remember being hampered in my movements at all. There were beds and we danced on them. On the lintel of the door they had set up a swing and we fought one another to take turns on it.

Everything was made to our measure. I suppose they had chosen this apartment because it was near the park so that we children could play there. There was a little balcony; we went down into the street to play at the slightest sign of sunshine; we spent nearly all our time out of doors. At the front of the house, the windows gave onto the Weinstrasse, a quiet

---

12. The yeast-based products, which could not be eaten during Passover.
13. Passover, the holiday celebrating the exodus from Egypt.

street, which led into the park, and at the back there was a large courtyard with chestnut trees, enormous chestnut trees, which still live among my memories of light, sunshine, trees, birds.

Even today, I am a person who cannot live without trees. Quite recently, I realized how much this need for trees can be decisive. When you spend your life, as I do, in trying to find the key to your actions, one day you realize that you work in such-and-such a school because of the chestnut trees in the courtyard. Or else you notice that you have chosen the pediatric department in such-and-such a place and have stayed there for three or four years – in contrast to other places, where you couldn't stay – because the head resembles your grandfather. The only person with whom I have been able to truly establish a trusting professional relationship had something of my father about him. Do you think it is mere chance?

So there we were, the three children and my mother. When we were small, a woman called Lene came to help her look after us. We came into the world in quick succession, and it must have been a difficult task for my mother, especially as she probably still had to run her shop.

We found this Lene later in Israel. She spoke to us about our childhood, gave us photos. She was a Polish Jewess, and when she spoke to us about our mother, it was with adoration. I know that she had come from the same village in Poland. When a woman has worked for someone and speaks about that person as that woman spoke about my mother, I now know from my experience what that means.

So she helped my mother a great deal and had to look after my sister, virtually taking charge of her at the time I was born. My sister appears to have been very "oppositional" in her behavior; she vomited, she didn't want to eat. There was only fifteen months' difference between the two of us, and she was no doubt terribly jealous. She threw sand in my eyes and tried in a thousand little ways to annoy me. One day, when my mother's back was turned, she bit me in the stomach. She couldn't help it, poor thing.

My brother was the youngest child, so, rightfully speaking, I should have been jealous of him, but in fact we got on very well. I always played with him. Against my sister, who represented a certain danger, I had to defend myself. She was stronger and bigger than I was, and everything I did seemed wrong. You see, it's difficult to make a place for oneself and be the newcomer in someone else's territory, and yet my brother was smaller

14

than me and I don't think I gave him any trouble. His birth was no doubt an occasion for joy.

I suppose that for Jewish parents, having a son was very important. My sister was the first one, but she wasn't a boy. However, my parents accepted it. But the birth of a second daughter must have been a problem for them. Nevertheless, people tell me I was so sweet that everyone loved me. I probably hadn't much choice!

So, in this apartment we took turns on the swing. On days that we were sick, we stayed at home. After school, after playing in the garden, my mother prepared us our dinner. One should have seen the comings and goings between the kitchen and the diningroom, each one carrying his plate, because she made us things we liked – for instance, *Kartoffel Puffer*,[14] fritters or French toast! Servings of these things had to be prepared just at the time one ate them, and everyone went to get his ration as quickly as possible.

Apart from that, I have hardly any memories... Ah, yes! I remember *Sukkot* (the Feast of Tabernacles), when we ate on the terrace: that's to say, on the balcony. It's strange how memories are selective. I don't, for example, recall a table in the diningroom, although there must have been one. We were always on the floor. On the other hand, I remember that we stayed up very late with my mother doing our homework, as she tried to help us.

I didn't go to a German school. I went to a Jewish school, for two reasons: because, for my parents, the most important thing was to remain Jewish, and because Hitler was already in power, which meant that we didn't have the right to go to a German school.

I was born in 1927. Not far from our home lived one of my father's sisters with her husband and son. This aunt, Aunt Ida (we both had the same name, no doubt in honor of some common ancestor) worked in the kindergarten we went to. It was nearby, opposite the park, two minutes away.

In the same building, on Shabbat, there was an *Oneg Shabbat*[15] in the afternoon. There was a rabbi who got us to sing and pray and who gave us something for tea. I don't know what work Aunt Ida did, but the

---

14. Grated potato pancakes.
15. The "joy of the Sabbath," was a festivity given for children on Sabbath afternoons.

fact is that, thanks to her, we were always under some sort of protection in that kindergarten.

The food we were given didn't please us because it was cooked in the German manner: Brussels sprouts with white sauce, fish with parsley, and so on. It disgusted us.

We were not used to eating in that way, because my mother cooked in the Polish manner or in her own style: light, unfussed, dairy products, fish, fresh vegetables, the best there was. Our parents gave us the best they could find.

I don't know whether my mother ate properly every day, but as for us... It's remarkable, this lack of egoism: she never asked anything for herself. She never complained, or, at least, I never heard her complain. You know what it's like to have three little redheads full of life. When we went somewhere it was a reign of terror because the other children would join us and suddenly start doing things that they would never have dared to do on their own.

We were facetious and always had some new idea in our heads. When people came to the house, in two seconds we were all three under the table. We pinched one another, laughed, gave them all nicknames, saw exactly the little thing that made them ridiculous. That was it – they had entered into our folklore – but for my mother, it can't have been easy. She had to run the house, prepare the meals and deal with everything alone. When father returned, it was a joy: he was like God to us.

He arrived, sat down, took all three of us on his lap and began to play and sing. He told stories: he always had stories to tell. I don't know where he got them from. All my life I've tried to find the origin of these stories, but I haven't really succeeded. I think they were *midrashim*, stories from the Talmud or the *Chumash*, the Bible, or Chasidic tales. He bounced us on his knees, he sang, he got us each in turn to sing *traurigen nigen* and *lustigen nigen*.[16] He taught us these Chasidic melodies, we laughed together, and I don't recall that he was ever at home without being completely with us. I now realize the strength that such a presence gives in life.

In winter, he took the toboggan and brought us to a little hill in the Friedrichshain. He put the three of us on the sledge, and there you go!

---

16. Sad and happy melodies. A *niggun* is a melody; *lustig* and *traurig* are happy and sad.

This could continue for days on end. I suppose that this was in order to keep us out of the way, so that my mother could get ahead with her work and enjoy a little peace.

On Shabbat mornings, we would leave with him for *shul*.[17] This shul was a long way off, in the Grenadierstrasse, a center of Jewish life, somewhat like the rue des Rosiers in Paris. It was a *shtiebel*[18] where he would find people who prayed in the same way as he did and sang the same melodies.

These shuls did not have names but were known by their number in the street. When people asked "Where do you pray?" one would reply, "I pray at number twenty-six." I forget the number of our shtiebel.

Whenever we went with our father, we savored life to the full. On Shabbat, we would walk at least three quarters of an hour together. We were very small, but I didn't find it at all burdensome. If I love walking today, I'm sure that's where the taste comes from. And as we went, he would tell us stories. Whether going there or coming back, the walk never seemed to us long enough.

During prayers, the children stayed outside, or wandered around among the men who would give us a *knip*[19] as we passed. After prayers, we would sometimes be given some herring. And on Yom Kippur we would eat our slice of bread in the courtyard, after taking it unobtrusively from our mother's bag.

The *Shochet*,[20] who was a friend of my parents, lived a little further away, and my mother had a sister in that famous Grenadierstrasse. Coming back from shul, we would visit one or the other. The Shochet would offer us *kiddush*.[21] There was also an aunt of my father's who lived on the way back, and we would eat a little fisch there as we passed by. The parents exchanged their stories.

They got on well together. The great-aunt was my grandfather's sister on the paternal side. There we also met my father's female cousin, her

---

17. Yiddish term for synagogue.
18. Yiddish term for small place of worship.
19. Pinch on the cheek.
20. Ritual slaughterer of animals for butcher's meat.
21. Blessing over wine, followed by refreshments. It is an opportunity to come together on Shabbat and the Jewish holidays and hear short teachings on the *parshiot*, the weekly Torah readings.

husband and their two sons, second cousins of our own age who are still alive in Belgium. So, when we arrived, we jumped on the beds or hid beneath them. The cousins, for their part, were more reserved in their behavior. The family was already comfortably off: they had *grosse Sessel*, big leather armchairs. We turned up there like savages.

On our return from shul, we ate and slept a little, and then my father sat down with us to study the *sidra*[22] of the week or the *Pirkei Avot*[23] and then he took us into the park to wait for Shabbat to end. Other Jewish parents living in the same neighborhood joined us. The adults talked together and the children played.

Years later, my brother, who had just settled in Israel, was sitting in the shul nearest to his home. Someone put his hand on his shoulder and asked: "Isn't your name Tieder? Aren't you from Berlin? When I was small, your father asked my father if I could lend you my "*Roller*" (scooter)."

This was our Shabbat. And you see, what has remained with me is Shabbat and the Jewish holidays.

School was already associated with fear. In 1933 I was six years old, and it was on our way to be registered for school that I had the first shock of my life. It was at the time when Hitler seized power. School, especially in Germany, was given great importance.

There was the custom of giving children the *Zucker-Tüte*. On their first day at school, parents gave their children a sort of enormous cornet wrapped in multicolored paper decorated with all sorts of designs. The Zucker-Tüte, which was pointed at the bottom and widened towards the top, was filled with various sweets. This tradition was a way of giving small children the taste to go to school.

For us, at any rate, it was a joyful event: we had been prepared for it. Studying was a real pleasure. Even without the Zucker-Tüte, it was like being together with my father. It is no accident that all of us have studied: it has been our refuge and at times the only way for us to live.

It happened on the day my father went to register me and my sister at the school. The three of us were on our way back. I don't know what happened, exactly: perhaps a march-past of Nazis in the street. I only

22. Weekly portion of the Torah.
23. The *Ethics of the Fathers*, a tractate of the Talmud.

remember the fear that seized us. Suddenly, my father grabbed us by the arm and dragged us into a house, behind the front door. What was terrible was that the top half of this door was made of glass, and I saw my father bending down in order to hide. One is haunted by a thing like that: your father, who is like God to you, crouching down to hide! It was only later that I understood why he didn't want to be seen behind the glass. If the S.S. found a Jew in the street, they trampled upon him with their boots and he would be ripped open; they crushed him, and that was that. If they had seen us, it would have been the end of us: no escape was possible. My father was in modern dress, he had no beard; he didn't have a kaftan and payes and he wore a hat, but he still looked like a foreigner. So you see, that was my first experience of school!

We went to a Jewish school. It was splendid, but in the street it was something else. As you'll see, all the time there was this dichotomy between the world within and the world outside. So we went to this Jewish school, which was quite far away. Since then, I have met many people who went to this school, the Rykestrasse.

This primary school, where boys and girls were together, took half to three-quarters of an hour to reach on foot. There was no public transportation, and we were half dead from fear all the way. In Berlin, night came in quickly: there was sometimes an atmosphere like that in certain frightening tales. Many decades later, I still had nightmares where I was bathed in this light from some world of witchcraft.

Only once did I find this strange light again, on Monte Baldo in Italy, when we were in the clouds. Everything is gray, the atmosphere is palpable and one can't see ahead. It's a state of anxiety.

Moreover, these were crisis years in Berlin, when one heard all sorts of stories such as those of Dr. Mabuse: stories of kidnappings, disappearances... Such fear! And together with this there were other fears, which were superimposed in layers: fear of the Nazis, the fear, which everything exuded, the cold, which made you weep, the fear when one came home in the evening or even in the afternoon. (I can't remember what time we came back from school).

There was a hunchback who followed us. Was he following us or was he simply going the same way? We were frightened: we ran like mad.

One day, when we got home, we went through the big front door and were in the hall, which led to the courtyard. In the dim corner beneath the staircase on the right there was a great dark mass: the fright I had! It was a man sleeping.

And then, when you played in the park, the Friedrichshain, it was forbidden to go on the grass. If by any chance your ball fell on the lawn, a great strapping fellow, the keeper came up, who wasn't too friendly to us little Yids. He arrived with a nasty superior air, which struck fear into us. Only recently, I've had nightmares in which he pursued me. He'd become the prototype of the persecutor.

At school we had the good fortune to have an outstanding teacher. He was called Herr Neumann and we adored him.

Luckily for us, the school was excellent. It was a religiously observant Jewish school, but modern Hebrew was taught there as well. Every morning we began with an hour of Hebrew. Fantastic!

Herr Neumann was very fond of us. I later learned that he was also a friend of my uncle Jacob, Aunt Ida's husband, who was also a teacher. They lived very near to us and we were very close.

My sister was in the same class as me, as she had had a primary tubercular infection. She had to go to a preventorium[24] and had lost a year, and we consequently ended up in the same class. It was just what should have been avoided, but did they have any choice?

As a result, she was always first in class and I was second, with rare exceptions, which made my sister very angry. This fixed state of affairs pursued me; it was impossible to get rid of it. But perhaps this has helped me in life, if only because it gave me a better understanding of my own children and a better grasp of their problems and those of my young patients.

My sister, as I saw it, was good at everything and everything came to her easily. She was a good pupil, and she was also able to sew, to knit, to select colors, to draw, to embroider. Next to her, I felt like a *shlemazel*.[25] I used to say, "I don't know how to do it, and I never will. I don't know anything!" If I had to draw a bird, I didn't know how to hold my pencil. They said I wrote very badly: "*Idele schreibt azoi vi a hindl krazt mit die fiess.*"[26] So in the evening I begged my mother to draw the pictures for me, and she, poor dear, was so overburdened. We received a new dress for Yom Kippur and at Pesach with a little white collar, and every evening she washed the collar, and in the morning it was impeccable, neat, ironed, sewn on. We

---

24. An institution for patients infected by tuberculosis who did not yet have an active form of the disease.
25. Clumsy creature who does everything wrong.
26. "Ida writes as a chicken scratches with its feet."

always looked spick and span as if we were the children of the lord of the manor, but nobody suspected how much work that required.

Throughout practically the whole of my school years in Berlin, Herr Neumann was my teacher. I remember that one day he came into the class and announced, "I've got a son!" He was radiant, as our father probably was when we were born. We felt that day that perhaps the most extraordinary thing in life was the arrival of a child. What is a course of sex education next to the joy that man communicated to us?

There was a boy who was the dunce of the class: I can't remember his name. In Germany at that period, in every class the teacher had a *Nachsitzebank*, a "punishment bench," which didn't face in the same direction as the others but was placed in the corner against the wall, and those who didn't conform were relegated there. I think that this boy spent a good part of his school career on that bench. His hands were always stained with ink. He was held up to us as an example of all one shouldn't be!

Years later, I met him in Tel Aviv. He told me how he managed to survive the war. I said to myself, "You see, he didn't conform. He was full of life and imagination, and thanks to that he got through the war." I can no longer remember his adventures: it was like a novel. At any rate, he didn't let himself be caught.

We were very happy. We liked this school very much, apart from the fact that, personally, I had the feeling that I wasn't good at anything. How can one think otherwise when one's model is perpetually someone bigger than oneself and who is therefore already physiologically more mature? Moreover, it was as if it were "forbidden" to overtake my sister. It would have been a treacherous act, as if I'd robbed her of her birthright. These are universal problems.

My parents were probably not too aware of these considerations. They always dressed us both in the same way, so we were a bit like twins. They did what they could in the way that they could, in accordance with the norms of the period. I don't judge them in any way.

So here we were in the primary school, and the school was full of life. On *Lag Ba'omer*,[27] which falls in the spring, Herr Neumann took us to Grünewald, a wooded area close to the city. The place was a pine forest, which we thought enchanting. These *Ausflüge* (class excursions) were a

---

27. *Lag ba'omer* is the thirty-third day of the counting of the *Omer*, the day that interrupts the period of mourning that follows *Pesach*.

21

real joy. We took our slices of bread and butter and went with the teacher and the whole class. We also went to do gymnastics in the heart of nature and we sang songs. It was glorious! And of course Herr Neumann also taught us to write: he taught us German and Hebrew.

And here we come to a problem of special importance to me: that of language, which is finally that of having the right to one's own peculiarity.

Our mother tongue was Yiddish, but our parents sometimes spoke Polish between themselves, especially when they didn't want us to understand what they said. We nevertheless understood, as all children understand when one speaks about them in another language. However, when they spoke to us, they addressed us in Yiddish, the language of the heart.

Hebrew, for my father, was *loschen koidesh*, the Hebrew of the sacred texts. At school and in the outside world we spoke German. One had to know that language if one didn't want to be considered an *Untermensch*[28] and if one didn't want to be laughed at.

While my father pronounced Hebrew in a certain way (he prayed and sang with the accent and intonation of the Polish Jews), at school we were taught to pray in a Germanized Hebrew: "*au bau mau schmau.*" It seemed to us so cold! And to this was added modern Hebrew with a Sephardi accent. This linguistic panoply I have inherited goes back to my childhood, and I was particularly fond of Hebrew, which I have continued to learn throughout my life, and I'm still working at it.

My mother – I don't know where she'd learnt it – wrote German very well. I will never know if it's true, but I have the impression that my father knew it less well. My mother, who grew up in Galicia under Austro-Hungarian rule, had learned German at school. My father, on the other hand, had learned Torah in his *cheder*.[29] My mother always said: "Your father hasn't been to university, but he's nevertheless a man who has read a great deal." One felt she wanted to upgrade him.

If one tries to show up somebody's worth...perhaps her ideal was to have a husband with a fine academic diploma and a good position in the society in which they lived, who looked like everyone else and corresponded to the norm. That, rather than to be appreciated only by a little circle of outsiders, of alien exiles who try to preserve around them

---

28. Subhuman.
29. Jewish religious primary school.

But to us children it was all the same. Nothing equaled Shabbat with my father; nothing can ever replace that. And it is perhaps because of this dual presence of Shabbat and my father that we have never gone astray, or at least that is true where I am concerned.

The Tieder family in Berlin, 1911 (Ida's grandparents, uncles and aunts).

Yaacov and Sarah Tieder (Ida's grandparents), Berlin.

Yehoshua Tieder (Ida's father), medical orderly in the Austro-Hungarian army, World War I.

Yehoshua Tieder as a young man. Before 1914.

Brucha Salpeter (Ida's mother) as a young woman.

Ida, Martin and Sarah Tieder. Berlin, about 1930.

Ida and Sarah Tieder holding the Zucker-Tüte on the first day of school. Berlin 1933.

Rav Yaakov Tieder (Ida's grandfather) on his visit to Eretz Yisrael, 1935.

Victor Tieder (Ida's uncle) and his window-cleaners. Haifa 1933.

Yaacov Leisner (Ida's uncle). London 1948.

Ida, Martin and Sarah Tieder after their arrival in France, 1940.

Brucha Salpeter-Tieder, born January 28, 1892, deported to Auschwitz on September 16, 1942.

Yehoshua Tieder, born February 18, 1892, deported to Auschwitz on September 9, 1942. Identification photos in profile, showing the ears in accordance with the racial requirements of the Vichy Government. Le Sablet 1942.

(These photos were miraculously preserved throughout the war by Ida, who sowed them into the collar of her coat.)

Memory

Memories
are only part
of past
reality
which the subconscious
has picked out.
That's how life protects itself...
But one must
remember certain events
consciously
if one wants
to go forward
and not be
simply
the passive object
of one's repressions.

January 8, 1984

FIRST ALARMS

Where was I? My first feelings of fear, I can tell you about them. The Nazis came in, and it started. Before that, we went down into the street to play on the pavements like kids the world over. On sunny days in winter and in summer when it didn't rain we played outside.

What did we play at? We didn't have mechanical or electrical toys; we didn't have much. So we spun tops, we played ball, we skipped with skipping ropes, played marbles, leapfrog, hopscotch, played with hoops for days on end!

I don't know if at the beginning we played with our little neighbors in the area, but I do remember that at a certain moment they begun to call us "dirty Jews," throwing bits of wood at our heads – the pieces of wood with which one lit fires – and spitting in our faces, saying we were "*dreckische Juden.*"[1] And as all three of us were redheads, they also made fun of us because of the color of our hair. They shouted "*Rotkopf, die Ecke brennt, Feuerwehr kommt angerennt*"[2] or "*Dachstuhlbrandt*,"[3] and other little catchwords about redheads. One may laugh about it now, but you know how vulnerable children are where this sort of thing is concerned, as indeed adults are also.

It is not without cause that foreigners try to assimilate. Nobody likes to be different from others and to be an object of rejection and criticism. There's a type of conformism, a gregarious instinct, a sort of psychological law, and to be able to resist it requires a complete education.

I am increasingly of the opinion that Jewish education is one of the most powerful pedagogical instruments for building up such a resistance, and my entire story – this story of continual persecutions – eventually proved to be positive in this respect.

---

1. Dirty Jews.
2. "Redhead, there's a fire at the corner of the street, the firemen are coming."
3. "The roof's on fire!"

People began to leave Berlin. I know for example that my father's youngest brother married in 1933, and on the very night of his wedding left for Israel, which was then called Palestine.

We had just learned a charming Chanukka song at school and our mother had sewn us two pretty little pink dresses. All three of us standing on a table sang "*Agudal miyamin, agudal mismol, shnei nerot li yesh,*"[4] and we ran through all our fingers with accompanying gestures. We were the great attraction on that occasion, and that day we were even given permission to drink brown beer from a little cask.

Then, letters arrived. What was uncle doing in Israel? He was a *Fensterputzer*, a window-cleaner, almost the worst possible comedown! It was enough to curb any desire to join him. But the matter was probably being considered: so why don't we also leave?

Next, it was Aunt Dora who left by ship for Argentina. In 1937, she had to pack her bags from one day to the next. A maid had denounced her for throwing a non-kosher egg in the dustbin, saying it was "wasting the resources of the nation."[5] They were summoned to the Gestapo. When they succeeded in getting out of there alive, they left for Paris as tourists without delay. At the last minute, two friends brought them a few suitcases at the railway-station (the neighbors were on no account to know what was happening). From Paris, they succeeded in acquiring a visa in return for payment and managed to get to Argentina.

There was no lack of frightening stories...

Nearly every Sunday we went to my grandfather's. The whole family, all the little cousins, the aunts, the uncles, gathered around this grandfather, an impressive-looking man, very learned, seated in his dining-room next to a wonderful library. He was really rather patriarchal: he was the Father. When I think of it, I imagine my own father must have felt himself to be a little boy compared to him.

The grandmother had also been a personality. Unfortunately, she had died in 1917. Legend has it that when my father and grandfather were mobilized in the First World War, she didn't hesitate for a moment: she followed them to the front lines, left her whole brood of kids in the hands of her eldest daughter and accompanied her men to the front. She did this because they couldn't eat the army food as they ate kosher, and

---

4. "A thumb to the left, a thumb to the right - that gives me two candles."
5. A fertilized egg with a blood-spot in its yolk is not kosher.

they couldn't fight, as one is not allowed to kill except in self-defense, and what were they to do if they faced another Jew in the opposing army?

Thus, they always had to arrange things so that they didn't have to shoot, and it was not for lack of courage, for perhaps it needs far more courage to resist and remain true to one's values. My father managed to become an orderly and my grandfather returned home.

My grandmother made such a great effort; she pestered people so much that in the end she succeeded in bringing the men home, inventing stratagems beyond imagination. For goodness knows how many months she wandered around on the front from place to place, eventually arriving in Hungary where she had lived and where she still had family.

She went to see the colonel's wife, telling her that my grandfather was old and in a few days would no longer be eligible for military service, and that there were still small children at home. It's unbelievable... Our *imahot*[6] were truly heroes!

It is said that as a result of all these tribulations she was so worn out that she died. Her absence weighed upon the family for a long time. Each of her children wanted to give her name to their eldest daughter. I never knew her. I know only that she is buried in the cemetery of Weisensee, a name that says something to me, but that's all.

After her death, my grandfather married someone else, who of course nobody in the family liked. She was, nevertheless, quite nice: we called her "Aunt Mania." We couldn't meet on Shabbat as we lived too far away, so we all gathered at grandfather's on Sundays. The men sat together and studied; they talked about business, about things that had happened, about decisions to be taken.

We children began to become boisterous and lark about; we were just happy to see one another again. We would act wild, we would run down-stairs, outside, into a square we called the "Billianzplatz," where we played. Later, when I learnt French, I realized it was the "Belle Alliance Place." In the center of the square stood the statue of one of the Fredericks; I don't know which one.

Grandfather lived in the Friedrichstrasse, at the other end of Berlin from us. So every Sunday we crossed the whole of Berlin by tram, going over the Spree in both directions, on our way out and on our way back, and in the evening we would return dead tired, half asleep despite the jolts of the journey.

---

6. Mothers in Hebrew.

We thought up all sorts of pranks. For example, you'd take two chairs, you'd blindfold somebody, you'd stretch a towel between the two chairs, supposedly a seat. Two people would sit on the chairs tucking the ends of the towel under their buttocks; you'd say to the blindfolded person, "Come on, sit with us, between us two!" He'd sit on the stretched-out towel, the two others would get up, and wham, he'd be on the floor, and the laughter wouldn't stop until we began to prepare the next game.

We would say, "Do you want to play 'captain?,'" "Yes, yes..." "Do you see the sky?" "Yes, yes... " "Do you see the stars?" "Yes, yes... " Then, we'd make a telescope with the sleeve of a jacket, the other person said "yes," and during that time we'd bring up a bowl of water and throw it in his face.

This was the sort of nonsense that kept us happy in childhood. It shows you that despite all the threats and dangers, it is not easy to restrain the life force of children, their desire to play. All this was wrenched away from us.

So Aunt Dora left. A great many people left, and they often spent their last night in Germany in our home. I remember that one of my mother's cousins, Uncle Goldsand, came to see us: he was good-looking, like all my mother's family, or at least he appears so in my memory. They all had something about them that we envied, perhaps because we hardly knew them.

I saw more of my father's family. Uncle Jacob, who was a teacher and lived nearby, helped my father with his bookkeeping. He was rather an extraordinary personality for children like us. He never came to our house without bringing a little box of chocolate and coffee-flavored sweets for each of us. I can still see that orange-colored cone-shaped little box with coffee-grains incorporated in its design.

It was a little thing, but it showed that in coming to your house he had thought of you, he had tried to find something that would make you happy. For him, you were someone who counted. I think that's what is important for children. He didn't come only for your parents; he was also aware that you existed.

After the war, he was the only person with whom we were able to renew contact. He was the one who spent the money he needed to buy bread on buying stamps and attempting to trace the entire family. He was the one who wrote to each and every member of the family to find out who had survived. He was the only person to whom one could speak. He was quite simply human. He had the faculty of putting himself into your skin for a moment. It must be said that he, too, had had a rough time.

For example, when later on, invited by some families, we got away from Moissac for a few weeks' holiday in London, he, living in London, was terribly unhappy not to be able to receive us in his home as he was so poor.

One day, he dragged my brother into a shop in order to buy him a pair of shoes. At that time we wore rough shoes of a special wartime model. He said: "What's this? I'm your uncle; surely I can buy you a pair of shoes!" My brother responded: "No thanks, I'm quite alright. I don't need it," because he knew that our uncle was as poor as a church mouse. In making this gesture, however, our uncle had turned the world on its head.

So every Sunday we would go to visit this grandfather who was re-married to this woman we didn't really like. At that time, there was a crisis situation in Berlin: there was a shortage of everything. There was a campaign for *Eintopfsgericht*[7] – "putting everything into one pot." One could find neither butter nor meat, and still less kosher meat, as kosher slaughtering was forbidden. On Sunday evenings, Aunt Mania would give us slices of bread and butter. She spread the butter on thickly for her own daughters (my grandfather had three daughters with her), but for us she scraped the butter. We weren't long in finding a nickname for her: "Aunt Mania *kratzt* (scrapes)."

For us children, my mother's family presented a contrast with that of my father's. We knew Uncle Goldsand, my mother's good-looking cousin, who came to see us in Berlin. He was dark-haired, and we little redheads dreamt of being dark-haired with big black eyes like our mother. We would often make ourselves disguises from the stock of wigs and postiches, which remained with my father.

Uncle Goldsand brought each of us a fountain pen of a type just like those they are making again today. They seemed to be made of horn or tortoiseshell, in bright colors – red, green – with shades that melted into one another in a spiral pattern. To us they were dream pens. We took them to school, like idiots; they were stolen the very same day! It was the tragedy of our lives, not so much because of the pens but because of this uncle.

---

7. A single, economical dish.

A short time later, we received a card from that same uncle, from a concentration camp. Was it Dachau, Oranienburg or somewhere else? On the card were only written the words *behomer u vilvenim*.[8] Read the Passover Hagaddah; read what it says about all the Israelites had to go through in Egypt. It's written *homer* – matter, clay – and *levanim* – bricks. We understood immediately; he didn't have to say any more.

How did he manage to get out? I don't know. At any rate, he did get out, but he didn't get very far. He reached France, from where he was deported once again.

At that time, one began to hear all sorts of rumors. One fine day, they would come to arrest someone at his home, and three days later his family would receive an envelope containing his ashes.

The Jews were not the only ones to be affected: the communists were also in the line of fire. In our street, the Weinstrasse, a little further up, there was a prison, which for us children was an advantage because in front of the prison there was a wide pavement without shops or anything in the way where we could go roller-skating without hindrance. But when we came home at nightfall, we made a point of walking noisily – you know how children do. I tried to imitate my mother's walk to give the impression it was a grownup walking in the street. This didn't reassure anyone except myself, and even that is doubtful!

The fear increased from day to day. It was said that the prison was full of Jews and communists, that they had their flesh cut into and salt poured onto the wound and had other tortures inflicted on them. Passing in front of that prison had become a real nightmare. I no longer knew if I really heard screams or if I imagined I heard them.

It became very difficult to get enough to eat. Every Thursday, my father brought a chicken back from the countryside, and this chicken would be kept at home until the following Wednesday. Then my mother would put it in a shopping bag with its legs tied together, and she would take all three of us to the Shochet in the Grenadierstrasse. We trembled all the way at the thought that somebody might hear the chicken squawking. Imagine if we were caught! It was thanks to this, however, that we had "meat" on Shabbat. I don't remember that I was really short of food, but if we ever got a slice of sausage it was a real feast.

The heart, the backbone of our existence was provided by the Jewish holidays, which filled it with light. Shabbat was extraordinary, I can

---

8. "With clay and bricks," Exodus 1:4

hardly describe it. My father sang, we all sang together; we sang *zemirot,*[9] we went to shul and my mother made some nice cakes and a fish dish; she prepared all kinds of good things. The more I tell you about it, the more our home comes back to me, with its great porcelain stoves at the corner of each room at which we warmed ourselves. You felt warm just looking at them. She made *cholent,*[10] which simmered gently inside the stove, and she also made *hallot.*[11] She made noodles herself: she knew how to do everything. She was able to embroider, to draw, to knit and to sew. Nothing was beyond her capacity.

Met hot sie nicht gehert, met hot sie nicht gesehn.[12] Always "on the go," she didn't make much noise. Fascinated, we would watch her for hours on end cutting noodles and baking cakes, impatiently waiting for the moment when we could lick the bowls like children throughout the world, and we fought amongst ourselves to get a bit more.

Chanukkah I liked because my birthday fell at that time. I was born on the Shabbat of Chanukkah. We lit candles in front of the window, and as it was dark outside, the contrast was striking. My father sang well.

It was a very simple holiday without elaborate décor, but it had such an intimacy that we were conscious of its serene power. The feast of Chanukkah lasted for eight days, and it was a joy. However, in that Berlin, for the non-Jews, Christmas was in full swing, with Father Christmases and Christmas trees. You could see them everywhere, and my father took us to visit the great stores and look at Father Christmas and the shop windows and anything else we might like to see.

The Germans, for their part, ate sausages and all sorts of delicacies, which made us terribly envious, but we never touched these things. Then my father bought us some red toffee apples and we were as happy as kings!

He took us on his shoulders and showed us the toys, the people, the crowds, the illuminations. What was our little Chanukkah next to such spectacles! You lit a few candles at home, you ate some potato pancakes, you spun a top around the table in the company of your parents and won

---

9. Traditional songs sung by the family at table on Shabbat.
10. A dish whose name is derived from the mediaeval French *chault* (hot), which is put on the stove before the Sabbath begins and is eaten for the Sabbath lunch the next day. Another possible derivation: *chaud-lent,* meaning "hot-slow."
11. Kneaded loaves for the Sabbath table.
12. "One didn't hear her, one didn't see her."

some sweet things to eat. Yet with this one had everything. We would not have exchanged our holiday for their brilliant decorations for anything in the world.

Our neighbors, with whom we were on good terms, would invite us in to see their Christmas tree, and we always brought them a present: a pair of gloves, a tie. They were well disposed towards us. But on the other floor there was a horrible old woman who looked like a witch, surrounded by cats. She terrified us. I don't know why, but when one is a child one senses people, strange atmospheres. We didn't want to go there...

Heritage

Tatteleh...
No, he wasn't a fearsome father
or a drunken spouse.
He had the art
of loving
and of telling stories,
to amuse and elevate
his children.
He went down with us on the sledge
speaking of the Deluge.
We were three
contending for the arms
and lap
of this so gentle man
with his crazy love
of God and his own family.
No, his pockets he did not fill:
a poet-musician was he,
who made us dance and sing,
play, listen, dream,
laugh and cry
with Avraham, Yitzhak, Yaakov and Yosef,
Moses and the prophets,
the midrashim
and the sad and gay *niggunim*
of the Chasidim
together with their tales...

He left in despair,
bequeathing us as our sole heritage
a final message:

"The Sabbath keep
and do not desecrate,
rebel not against God
and help ye one another."
A gentle visionary?
No, all he was able to give us
before at Auschwitz he was slain
empowered us to struggle
against wind and tide
a true life to extract,
that of the sages
throughout the ages
of the eternal
Israel.

November 7, 1981

THE HERITAGE

I have spoken of fears and now we have arrived at the holidays. *Pesach* – what can I tell you about it? The house was completely clean, as if it were quite new. There was the special set of dishes, pots, cutlery, glass-ware, etc., set aside in a particular place. It was all carefully packed in newspaper and kept in boxes. It was never touched during the year and was taken out only for Pesach.

Everything was cleaned, polished, rubbed. Everything had been thought of: the wooden boards, the metal sheets to cover the stove, all the equipment necessary for the operation. Not a minute was lost and no effort was spared – but the result was like a rebirth.

It was forbidden to eat bread and we waited impatiently for the *Seder*. We were repeatedly told to go and lie down, but how could one sleep? We were excited by the thought of the coming feast. When evening came, my father presided over the Seder. He put on his *weissen kittel*, the white garment which is worn on Yom Kippur and which also serves as a shroud.

You see, Judaism associates death with whatever is alive, but never as a final end. On the Seder table at Pesach there is a burnt egg to remind one of the destruction of the Temple, but at the same time one prays for the reconstruction of the Temple.

In our civilization, there is a tendency to ignore death, to spirit it away, and people accumulate gadgets: having in place of being. If death is not taken into account, life is no longer possible.

Life is what renews itself constantly. It is true that where death is concerned, we have had our share, but our history has taught us the meaning of life, and that was our advantage over assimilated Jews.

Take Stefan Zweig, for example. A good German, he was thrown out of Germany. When he reached South America, he committed suicide. Why? Because life no longer had any meaning for him.

But we've imbibed with our mother's milk the idea that to be Jewish is to have a history with a meaning, even in exile. This exile continually recurs. One day it's Egypt and another it's Persia, another it's Greece and yet another it's Rome. And one day Amalek[1] is Hitler, and the next day it will be the Russians or the Arabs or the Chinese.

My father said to me one day during the war: "You'll see, there will be the war of Gog and Magog, and then the time of the Russians will come, and then that of the Chinese." He knew...

Children though we were, we also knew there was persecution ahead; we knew what awaited us. We knew it was nothing new – we were aware of all this.

It was part of our collective historical consciousness. One had to continue, to live, to survive. One had to continue even in the worst situations. Do you know what our parents said to us in the last letter they wrote? "We are going off in an unknown direction... Don't rebel against God, keep Shabbat, help one another."

Did I accept this? Do you think one can receive a message of this kind delivered in such circumstances without rebelling? I accepted nothing whatsoever; but since then I've made some progress. You can't accept such a thing just like that. It isn't possible.

Today I know I can admire my parents and respect them deeply. They were heroes, and when I think that people have dared to say that they were cowards, that they didn't know how to fight, that they let themselves be led like sheep to the slaughter, it makes me furious. When I hear little Israeli kids allowing themselves to speak in that way, I explode. They didn't resist? Would I have been able to hold out as they did?

In wartime, when you have nothing to eat, and the little you find you don't eat because it isn't kosher, isn't that a supreme example of human fortitude? And if they allowed themselves to be taken away, it's because they had no choice. They knew what to expect: it represented total despair of humanity They had learnt it to their cost through bitter experience.

One day in the camp at Agde, a fire broke out. There was panic. All the occupants of the camp succeeded in breaking down an entrance gate with their hands: they could all have escaped into nature. But nobody left. Where would you have gone in that winter of 1941 with three little kids, without knowing a word of French, without a penny to your name, without papers? Where could you have gone? What could you have done? Who would have bothered about you? Nobody!

---

1. A descendant of Esau, whose declared aim was to annihilate Israel.

We knew nobody in that accursed country, nobody at all. Where could you have run to? You would be caught once again; the *gendarmes* (policemen) would get hold of you and bring you back to the camp. Or you'd be killed on the spot.

I was speaking of the Jewish holidays, and here I am at the camp. It's like Seder-night: you celebrate the exodus from Egypt and you describe the slavery. It was at Agde; we were taken there one fine morning. We passed through the town at five a.m. We had come out of the cattle-cars; some shutters were opened a little: "What's happening? Oh, it's only some Jews!" The shutters were closed again. That was it. What can one do after that?

I was speaking to you about Berlin, about the Seder, and here I am at Agde. Everything is jumbled together. Pesach, the exodus from slavery, the Seder, Egypt – we lived through the whole thing. You will understand now why throughout my life I have fought to pass on this treasure to my children. There was such a richness, such a warmth, such a – what shall I say? – transmission of the meaning of *life*. And although I've knocked about the world I have never found anything to replace it either in its content or in its pedagogic value.

For children, when their parents sit down at table, celebrate the feast, read the Hagaddah, eat with them, drink the cups of wine, it's a true festivity. In the modern world, everybody chases after pleasures and festivities, but the festive spirit eludes them, because what they get every time is a false festivity – artificial, meretricious, commercial.

This difference in the concept of celebration and life I have experienced with my children and I experience it with their friends. I have experienced it with certain members of my family. For decades now it has been my daily bread.

Against this background of anxiety and persecution, one needs points of reference, one needs to know the criteria and values according to which one's life should be constructed, and how to recognize and neutralize one's "phantoms."

These "phantoms" are unbearable, but once you know they are merely the image of something which was once a reality, of something which can return in another form, but for the moment is only an obsessive fantasy, it's quite different. When people tell me I have "persecution mania," I say no, for I have really been persecuted by a mania! By the mania of the others, the persecutors.

Someone who has been persecuted drags around with him all his life something in his shadow. Worse still, so does his child, without even knowing what it is. And this shadow lengthens and reproduces itself. It is not by chance that the nations have associated Zionism with Nazism and that young Jews consciously or otherwise follow suit. Because in a sense there is only one image. Once the prototype-image has been established, one takes it and re-uses it somewhere else.

I've got my own ideas concerning the proposition: "The persecutor, the person who has persecuted you, is internalized by you to such a degree that you end up seeing yourself with his eyes and judging yourself solely according to his criteria. And little by little you destroy yourself." The whole phenomenon of assimilation-as-an-escape can be stated psychologically in the form of an alternative: either you're the wolf or the lamb.

This dilemma is to be found in the Diaspora as well as in Israel, where one has these reflexes of ill-adapted adaptation. I hope it's only a matter of a single generation. The problem will be superseded provided a work of clarification is carried out, a collective therapy for all Jews – a task that seems to me increasingly urgent.

For two thousand years we have been the victims, and we've internalized the executioner. And today, some people remain stuck with this pattern, which has been imposed on us: either you're the executioner or you're the victim. The victim generally goes to the crematorium. As you can no longer bear to be the victim, you identify with the executioner. You dream of being tall, fair, with blue eyes and of crushing the other, feeling that otherwise it is he who will reduce you to ashes. This reaction is sometimes to be found in Israel. For my part, I feel it to be an unconscious defensive reaction, which sooner or later proves to be ineffective in real life and leads to self-hatred.

You can find the same process at work in the life of couples: "If I don't want him to devour me, I'll have to devour him." The same applies to relations between teacher and pupil, doctor and patient, and to any little clerk in the National Health Service. Some little bureaucrat sitting on his *benkel*,[2] protected by his screen, faces the other person, and puffed up with his superiority uses it to overpower him. What has happened to our messianic dream of the tiger grazing with the lamb?

---

2. Small bench or chair.

Moreover, this isn't all that is written. It is also written that swords will be turned into ploughshares: that is to say, that life will be possible without our having to make war, to devour one another.

I no longer know whether it's the panther or the leopard that will graze side by side with the lamb, or whether it's the wolf, because the wolf is really the prototype of the devourer intoxicated with his own strength, with his big mouth and big teeth. And the lamb is the poor defenseless little lamb, the *chad gadya*.[3]

Why does the wolf devour the lamb? Because he has the physical superiority. When the wolf grazes with the lamb it will be a different time, a time when both of them will feed on the grass of the field. One is strong, the other weak, but if one of them is strong, it is not in order to destroy the other! It is in order to possibly cultivate life together. This side of things (the practice of mutual aid, the concern for one's relationship with others, etc.), has always been emphasized in traditional circles, particularly in Israel.

Can this perception explain certain aspects of *kashrut*?[4]

Take, for instance, the precept: "You shall not boil a kid in its mother's milk" (Exodus 23:19). One should not confuse life and death. With her milk, the mother gives life to the kid, and this milk shouldn't be its grave. If the mother is strong, if she has milk, it is not in order for her to use it against the child for her own benefit in a quasi-incestuous manner, making him into a "thing." He wasn't born to serve his mother, whose task is, on the contrary, to make him grow up.

The prototype of this perversion, the mother-who-devours, is Egypt. The word *mitzrayim* (Hebrew for Egypt) contains the idea of confinement (*tzar*, Hebrew for narrow), as though in a womb, associated with the memory of the onions of Egypt hankered after by the children of Israel in the desert, but which can never be anything else than a series of superimposed envelopes.

The womb is made to give life, and not to suffocate the child to be born by retaining him for one's own pleasure once the time for birth has arrived. Thus, the exodus through the Red Sea is like a grandiose delivery, an exit into the open air through the long tunnel of the vagina.

---

3. A small lamb that symbolized the people of Israel in a liturgical song in the Passover Seder.
4. The Jewish dietary laws.

And in order for the delivery to result in a new being, one needs the *yad hazaka u'zro'a netuya*, the "strong hand and outstretched arm" – a third force, which biologically is the father, the guarantor of identity. He gives the name, he recognizes the child, he is the third element thanks to which the child can have a life of his own and go his own way, far from his mother's apron strings. One doesn't have to be a doctor, an analyst or a great expert in order to be familiar with these problems.

But in order to be a father, it is not enough to simply be a fellow with male biological characteristics; one has to be recognized as a father, especially by the mother, and to recognize oneself as such – that is to say, as a bearer of values. The father is the intermediary who helps the child to detach himself from the mother, to become a being capable of thinking for himself, with a moral consciousness, capable of autonomous action in a world whose rules he does not yet know but of which the father is the guarantor. He needs points of reference, a law.

To the degree that the father is able to be the depository of that law, he becomes the vehicle of God's presence in the world. With a father worthy of the name, the child can become himself, and no one else can impose on him a model extraneous to himself.

"You shall make yourself no other images before Me, before My face." That is absolute monotheism. Each person must find in himself the imprint of that which caused him to be born unique.

And why are you persecuted? Because your nose does not conform to the accepted model! What did the Nazis decide? You're not an Aryan, you're not fair-haired, you haven't got blue eyes, you're not as I want you to be, so you've got to disappear. If you were Aryan, muscular, marching in step, you'd have the right to live, but in that case you'd be the absolute anti-human, a copy of Amalek.

It would not have been worth leaving Egypt, being born as a people, if we did not also have Mount Sinai and the giving of the tablets of the Law. How do they begin? *Anochi*, "I am." I am, so you can also be. I am your guarantor. But nobody knows the full potential you have within you: even you don't know, and your entire life is nothing else than your adventure in discovering this until the day of your death. You don't know it, because it is something to be realized at every moment of your existence on the model of the Eternal One who revealed Himself to Moses under the name of *"Eh'yeh asher eh'yeh"* ("I shall be Him whom I shall be.")

This is the father, as against the mother represented by the sea: the Red Sea, the *Yam Suf. Suf* means reeds, but also end (*sof*). The children of Israel were there facing the sea, pursued by the Egyptians, the *mitzrim* — those who keep one confined, those who use others.

We had been their slaves. What is a slave? He is a person who has been made totally into a thing, reduced to a number, which they have gone so far as to inscribe on his skin.

He no longer has any freedom, any choice, any gesture of his own. He has become a sort of machine, made to subject himself to the all-powerful desires of those who utilize him for their own benefit, and who terrorize him.

This fear I know well. I'd sow panic in a whole army in a second, sometimes for less than nothing, and as soon as the panic overtakes me I'm paralyzed. At the slightest threat my heart gives way. I can say that the fear penetrates every cell in my body; I just can't help it. It is as it is described in Emile Ajar's book *La vie devant soi*, where it is so well said that Madame Rosa was frightened, so frightened that she was even much more frightened than that!

"And among these nations you shall find no ease, and there shall be no rest for the sole of your foot; but there the Lord will give you a trembling heart and failing eyes and an anguished soul; your life shall hang in doubt before you; night and day you shall be in dread, and have no assurance of your life. In the morning you shall say, 'If only it were yesterday evening!' and in the evening you shall say, 'If only it were this morning!' because of the dread that you will have in your heart, and the sights that your eyes shall see." (Deuteronomy 28:65–67)

If I get up every morning to face the day, the least of my actions is a real miracle: I have so many obstacles to surmount. What a weight of death I have to overcome every day simply to stay on my feet, to do anything whatsoever, to make the slightest gesture of life!

Would I have done better to repress the paralyzing past? No, I think that if I had kept it in my unconscious, I wouldn't have been able to live. Why did I first decide to psychoanalyze myself? I'd finished my exams, I was a graduate. I only had to open an office and wait for my clients. Can you imagine my panic at the arrival of my first patients? What was I to do? Why were they coming to me? Already, when I first stood in for another doctor, my husband went along with me. I brought along all my books; I checked everything, even things I knew by heart.

How can I get rid of this fear? I'd gladly make a present of it; I offer it to anyone who wants it, but I think I shall die with it. All I can do is to recognize it and to give it a name when it takes me by surprise.

For instance, there was the time when I arrived at a splendid place with my children and husband. It was holiday time. It was Shabbat, a marvelous Shabbat amongst young people full of life, together with a rav – a real one – but as for me, I had the blues, I couldn't sleep, I was once again in the children's home. I'd again lost my father and mother; I no longer had a home, I was back once more; I was about to be killed.

Or else, when I go away on holiday, go skiing, I can no longer sleep, I have the blues again. What's happening? The woman who runs the place sends me back to the manageress of the children's home. It's crazy!

Every day one has to make this effort, every day, in connection with anything whatsoever, over the merest trifle. You can't imagine the amount of energy one has to put into this perpetual readjustment, in order to face situations that for anyone else would be perfectly ordinary. Because it was a miracle that I wasn't taken in 1942, in the roundup, in the village of Le Sablet, where we landed after we succeeded in getting out of the concentration camp at Agde in the south of France.

They had tricked us, we were "had," because we had been brought to the hayloft with the refugees and were then put on a train going to this camp. And today, in the midst of my holidays, in this wonderful chalet in the mountains, all of a sudden I wake up in the night in a state of anguish until I realize that the wooden boards of the walls around us remind me of the cattle-car and the shacks of the camp. Okay, the fear subsides... until the next time.

So one must identify the source of one's fear, one must realize that it is a memory of a different place and a different time and it has no connection with the present.

When one understands this, it's as if one had been relieved of an enormous weight. What oppressed you disappears as though by magic. But as long as one doesn't know what the matter is, one can't get rid of it – it sticks to one. It's what could be described as a "dybbuk";[5] it's as though some parasite has gotten hold of you; you're possessed. In effect, you're possessed by yourself in a different time, in a different place. It's the essence of neurosis, the very prototype of alienation. That is the reason why this experience, which I went through, is a kind of neurosis char-

---

5.   From the Hebrew root *dbk*, to stick.

acteristic of three generations of Jews (and goodness knows how many other people).

And if the Jewish people didn't become psychotic from being morally and physically penned up in the ghettoes of the peoples of the world, it was because it was able to ceaselessly cultivate the memory of its original "House" and the faith that it would be restored.

For what other reason did I begin to psychoanalyze myself? It was because one day I agreed to see a woman I had known in a students' home and who was a survivor of the Warsaw ghetto. She had asked to see me as a pediatrician for her son, and she began to tell me her story.

I said to myself: I haven't the right to take her on without myself being analyzed. I also thought I ought to keep ahead of her. And if I didn't die while listening to her, it's because I am strong.

She related among other things how her uncle, the last survivor of the family, who had succeeded in escaping to the forests, was finished off with an axe by a Polish partisan while the Germans were on his trail.

The hostility of the outside world was thus already familiar to us. We knew that there were, so to speak, two worlds, and there always remained to us the inner world – the family, the haven, the home – which one had constantly to build up and maintain in good and solid condition. Even during the war, nothing was lost as long as I was with my parents.

What is Left?

My mother
so proud, a
princess in Israel,
so beautiful and
true,
with her fairy hands
knew how to enchant us,
draw birds,
embroider pictures and
show off
our clothes to best advantage.
With nothing, she could make
all the dishes we loved,
our favorite cakes,
run a home,
love our father,
look after us,
receive the Shabbat
and work to help us make a living.
From the Gestapo she escaped,
remaking our home
when we were refugees,
and in the camp created
a corner to protect us,
clean, decent, respected.
When all crumbled around her
she remained erect,
foreseeing the future
yet unable to escape.
What a crazy tale!
Naught remains but her ring;

the rest is ashes.
Tender image
(such absurdity),
so difficult to forget...
I seem to hear her crying out
and calling for help,
and I run up,
but where to?
There's nothing to be done.
It only remains
the memory to repress
or to weep incessantly
and, like her, continue bravely
on the path of life
and follow her example,
that of a devoted
Jewish mother.

November 7, 1981

THE STRANGLEHOLD TIGHTENS

B y the way, I haven't yet told you about Marienbad, the day the Sudetenland was invaded. Marienbad was a place where the Jews of
Germany used to go on holiday, and they strolled around there, treating
it as "the garden for the Jews who lived in Germany."

On the day of the Nazi invasion of the Sudetenland in 1938, in the
space of a second, the entire population of the town without exception
switched allegiance, brought out flags with swastikas (which must have
been prepared beforehand!), and began chasing the Jews and insulting
them.

You ran to the station, you caught the last train that moved off, in
the midst of an incredible panic and turmoil.

On that day, we were officially on holiday in Marienbad, but in reality we were already there to prepare for our departure from Germany. My
mother had gone there first with my brother, and when she returned, my
father left with my sister and me. It was a way of taking out money. We
were thus able to entrust someone with some foreign currency. However,
we never heard of the man again.

When we got to Marienbad, we found our grandfather, and we were
full of amazement, because we had just left a place, the Germany of 1938,
where life wasn't so funny, and not only for the Jews. There were already
food restrictions for all.

In Marienbad, it was beautiful: mountains, forests, natural scenery.
We stayed in a large hotel overlooking the mountains, and we had our
meals in a restaurant where we were served meat. Until that time, I didn't
know the taste of either beef or veal. Chicken, and sometimes if we were
very lucky, a slice of "dry" sausage, were the only kinds of meat on the
menu at home. So we ate, we were free!

You know what freedom is? Not to be afraid to go out into the street
and... to have your father near you all the time.

All of a sudden we found ourselves with all the other Jews at the station in Marienbad, trying to catch the last train to Prague in the midst of shouting and pandemonium, out of our wits at having lost our father in the general panic. I was afraid we were going to be left on the platform without him. Happily, we found each other again.

The train took us to Prague, and it was our first experience of becoming refugees. Stuck in Prague, condemned to wander round and round in the city, there we were, a wretched father and two kids, cut off from the rest of the world. In a little hotel, father cooked us *fisch* on a small petrol stove he had bought. He gave us slices of bread and butter in the way that he himself liked them: slices of tomato on bread with little onions. Even today, I am particularly fond of slices of tomato and small onions on bread.

I remember Prague as a very lovely city, with its fine bridge, its ancient synagogue: a dream of a setting.

What were we to do? My mother was in Germany with my brother. Finally, one fine day in September, we succeeded in getting back to Berlin by train.

No sooner had we arrived, late at night, than my uncle came and told my father to leave at once, this minute, because that very morning all Jewish men of Polish origin had been rounded up to be taken back to Poland.

As nobody wanted them there, they were penned up in no man's land until the Germans invaded and shut them up in the Polish ghettoes and then killed them in extermination-camps.

It was the beginning of the end.

So my grandfather and my uncle immediately informed my father, who left that very night.

I don't know where he intended to go, where he was supposed to go. He just left: he stopped in Belgium. When he left, he can't have taken much with him. And we stayed behind in Germany, hoping to join him in the near future, but we had to find a way to do so! I suppose we didn't have any money, as one can't sell off one's business and dispose of one's furniture from one day to the next, especially since – as my sister remembers – the business was already in the hands of a neighbor who was an SS man and who got my father to work for him and pocketed all the cash. And as for the furniture, the neighbors told my mother: "Why do you want us to buy them from you, Mrs. Tieder, when tomorrow we can take them for nothing?"

It's not easy to get away with three small children either. So I don't know what happened; I know only that it was a very somber period, especially for my mother, burdened with three children and having to make decisions entirely on her own.

And then one fine day, coming home from school, we found the house empty. Mother wasn't there – she had been arrested by the Gestapo. I won't say it was the longest day of our lives, there were to be so many others... but, children though we were, we knew very well that when people were arrested there was a very good chance they would never come back.

Fortunately, our uncle and aunt, who lived nearby, were able to take us in. But however nice people are, however close to you, not to be in one's own bed, not to have one's mummy and daddy, to be out of one's own place, lost...

What was going to happen?

They finally released my mother. I learnt afterwards that they had arrested her for "illicit currency trading." What next!

Many days passed before we were able to join our father.

Finally, in December 1938, my mother succeeded in leaving after a thousand adventures.

We slipped away from Berlin and then got out of Germany, I don't know how. I only remember how frightened we were in the train. Some people escaped on foot across the frontier.

I don't know if my mother had a false passport or a visa. I only know that I shook with fear, and that a few days before leaving we were put up at our grandfather's. We weren't too happy there, although he was our grandfather and we liked him.

However, our defenses were working. The slightest thing made us laugh. When grandfather burped or made little noises as old people do, this gave rise to endless bursts of uncontrollable laughter.

How wonderful these defensive reflexes of children are, at least when there are several of them together! To have someone to wink at, someone who understands, who knows. A whole folklore, a common language, a complicity, thanks to which you're not a total stranger.

Then, one evening, my mother took us on a train. It was in the middle of winter; it was cold and the weather was foul. She didn't take much with her either from the house or from the shop. I don't know if the house hadn't in fact been looted, if the neighbors hadn't come to grab what they could.

Whatever the case, we had left, and my mother – I still take my hat off to her for this today – had found a way of bringing three children from another family along with us. I met one of them by chance in Tel Aviv in 1953, and he recognized me.

We got off at Antwerp, in Belgium, where my father had rented and prepared an apartment. Well, prepared in a manner of speaking. There were a few orange crates which were used for everything. That's why today this sort of camping doesn't frighten me. I can't say I like it, but give me a makeshift situation and I'll create you a home out of nothing.

Life continues. It's not that the latent connotations of these situations don't give me a lump in the throat, but I don't panic. It's not material things that frighten me most.

We found our poor father very thin after these few months all alone. He had managed as best he could, having no special profession. What was he able to do? He had run a business, but he didn't know the language – neither Flemish nor French. Although there was a reception committee, they weren't really equal to the task. If you begged them to do something, their answer was, invariably, "Have patience."

Finally, we succeeded in settling in after a fashion, and we gradually began once again to have a more-or-less normal family life. It must be said that Belgium was a country where it was possible to live. The Jews lived there as in Poland.

In Antwerp, there was a whole Jewish quarter where you could see people dressed in *caftans* and where you could procure kosher food. There was an abundance, so much that our eyes popped out of our heads! There were sausages... meat, things beyond imagination. The seller of herrings, "Youkelherring," was a bit of a simpleton. We laughed at him.

On Shabbat, we would go to synagogue. Here you could live as a Jew openly, without fear, without restriction. My parents must have known this kind of life in Poland, but for us it was a discovery. In Berlin, we always had to live in a low-key fashion.

In Antwerp, we were sent to school. My brother was enrolled in Yesodei Hatorah, a Jewish school, and my sister and I were sent to a Flemish school with the local children. We felt completely lost in the midst of the little Flemings who spoke "*beukele meukele*" – a language that seemed to us a sort of German *patois*, which made us laugh. There were scraps of phrases we understood, and others whose meaning we guessed at, often misled by "false friends."[1] This whole jargon seemed ugly to us, and we wanted to learn French. We had no wish to learn Flemish. But the French schools were open only to wealthy Walloons, to the nobility, to the aristocracy, whereas the local city school – the only one we had access to – was Flemish-speaking.

Thus, coming out of a Jewish school, we were thrown into a cold and alien universe and were totally anonymous, not understanding a word, in the midst of children who made fun of us.

Certain phrases come back to me: "*Die enten die haben alle tinten*," which we understood to mean "ducks have all inks," because *Tinte* in German means ink, instead of "are of all colors." And so on and so forth.

We amused ourselves by making blots in the margins of the pages, making birds out of folded paper, inventing all sorts of things to pass the time.

Yet, nevertheless, at the end of three months we spoke Flemish like everyone else and we were given first prize in class, or rather my sister got the first prize and me the second.

The mayor of the city came to give us the book *Tom Sawyer*. For us, it was only the natural result of our work. It only followed! You can't be present without taking part.

In addition, we learnt Hebrew at the *Tahkemo'ini*.[2]

We went to shul on Saturday mornings and in the afternoons we participated in a youth movement. There was thus a connection with our previous existence.

As for my father, I don't know what he was doing. Did he go from door to door selling ties, an occupation we thought degrading? Were we given a minimal allowance by the community?

My brother, the youngest amongst us, was invited to lunch regularly by a Jewish family that lived near his school, which was too far from home for him to be able to come back at midday.

The fact that he went there to eat, in one of the better neighborhoods of the city, in a well-appointed flat with radiators, central heating and every comfort, made a great impression on me. But the two of us, my

---

1. "*Faux amis*" (false friends), a French term for similar words that have different meanings in different languages.
2. Jewish school.

sister and me, were very unhappy that our brother was taken away from us, and it was very humiliating.

My mother, for her part, had learnt to sew in Germany. She could always foresee everything. While bringing us up, she had learnt to stitch corsets and brassières, which in those days were made to measure. And as she was very clever with her hands, she worked at home unceasingly for a pittance.

Our neighbors, Hungarian Jews, were very nice people. They lived just above us and had a funny little boy. Little by little we got used to our new life. I remember that we used to go and play in the *Buite*, the ancient fortifications around Antwerp. There was grass there where children could run about.

What struck me most about the Belgians was their bicycles and their food. But on the whole it wasn't especially attractive or particularly welcoming for Jews.

The atmosphere wasn't too good, a bit anti-Semitic around the edges, and in the evening, removed from my familiar surroundings, I couldn't sleep. I heard strange noises, unfamiliar sounds. Was it a radio? We didn't have a radio. Perhaps it was our neighbor's radio, which spewed forth these weird, *unheimlisch*, unfamiliar, noises.

Below us, there was a florist's shop. In this part of the city, the houses were only two or three stories high, and they were invaded by pigeons which went *brou, rrou, rrou, rrou* from daybreak onwards in the little courtyard behind our place.

In Germany we had lived in a very fine apartment near a large park, with a very large courtyard and beautiful chestnut-trees. What a contrast!

I can't say we knew desperate poverty in Antwerp. To tell the truth, I really don't know. And even if we did, my parents – or at any rate my mother – always contrived to arrange things so that they were royal, princely. We celebrated Shabbat and the Jewish holidays.

Our social existence had regained a certain rhythm, and life went on, until one fine day, on May 10, 1940, all of a sudden, everyone woke up with a start. The sirens were wailing: the Boches (Germans) were invading the country!

I don't know how my parents did it, but in a minute we were all squeezed into a lorry. For my part, my sole reaction on that day (you know what children are!) was to say to myself, "Hurrah, we're not going to school today!"

Our playing truant on that day was to take us far afield. One must suppose I wasn't too happy in school over there, and yet I liked school, probably thanks to Herr Neumann and my father.

Exodus

We left the luggage at the station at Mons.
Mounts and marvels,
o'er mounts and o'er dales,
the "*Shabbesleuchter*," the "*Bettgewand*"
and the photos,
the last vestiges of the old shtetl
that survived the four winds
of removals
through the cities
of the exiles,
our luggage lying in the left-luggage room.
We lay down flat
between two railway-lines
trying to escape
the hell
of the surrounding bombardments,
pursued by the Germans,
jumping on the first train
with nothing
on our backs
but skin and bones,
tallit and tefillin,
mistaken for
radio communication
with the enemy.
Poor idiots,
taking for a spy
a chasid turned towards Zion
in this train of desolation
that never stopped going
round and round.

May 6, 1982

THE EXODUS AND THE CAMP

We left Antwerp on May 10, 1940 in a lorry traveling in the direction of Dunkirk.

Here we were in this lorry with several other families, also refugees, who had grabbed hold of their children and their *Bettgewand* (eiderdown). What do you take with you in these circumstances? You take the Bettgewand, the Sabbath candlesticks, some family photos and some other objects within easy reach, and you leave.

It was an adventure. I remember an enormous tunnel under the Schelde, which seemed interminable. We began to travel – on and on and on – shaken backwards and forwards in the lorry until the evening. In the evening, when the lorry stopped at Ghent, we got out.

An incredible spectacle! The road was black with people who were fleeing. The lorry had stopped near a railway-line, not far from the station, and the parents looked for somewhere to spend the night.

Not having found anything except a night-shelter, we nearly slept in the lorry. In the end, we nevertheless decided in favor of the shelter, a dismal hovel with a few planks, which served as beds.

The place was disgusting – the haunt of all the tramps of the city. It was a real nightmare for us, who had never really been outside the protective family circle, apart from a few slightly difficult episodes like our panic at the station at Marienbad.

So we slept in that shelter, and just as well! For in the morning there was no longer any lorry to be seen. At the place where we had left it, there was only a half burnt-out shell. There had been an air raid at the very place where we had thought of spending the night.

We therefore had to take a train. I don't know exactly what happened or why things turned out as they did. I only know that we left all our luggage at the station at Mons. Everything we had, except for my father's famous briefcase.

When we got to the station at Mons, we left our luggage at the left-luggage room, and then a new air-raid forced us to lie down between the railway lines and then jump without luggage into the first train said to be going to Dunkirk in the hope of getting a boat for England. But Dunkirk we never reached!

So everything was left behind in Mons: the candlesticks, the eiderdowns, the photos. And after that we traveled round and round, all over France, in one of those ghost-trains for more than a week, seeing stations with names unknown to us pass by us and being fed from time to time by the Red Cross at certain stops. We were unable to get out, and our legs were swollen.

All my father had been able to salvage were his tallit and tefillin, and every morning he stood up, put on his tefillin and said his prayers. They thought he had a radio transmitter and was within a hair's breadth of being shot as a member of the fifth column.

The air-raids came one after the other, and as I look back I see endless railway lines, railway lines and more railway lines, people lying on the ground under the lightning flashes and the deafening thunder of the bombs, and then nothing more.

We had rushed into the first available train in order to escape this inferno, and our things remained behind at the station. This train was one of those famous ghost-trains that just traveled on and on. How many days? Eight days, ten days, more? Nobody knew where we were any longer. We were unfamiliar with France and its geography. One day it was Calais, another Montauban. Impossible to say what route the train was taking.

After a period of days, perhaps weeks, we got off somewhere in the South of France, at Fronton, a little village near Toulouse.

I've never been back there. It's a principle with me: I don't go back

So there we were in the central square of the village – a vast square filled with columns of soldiers with great cauldrons-on-wheels, a kind of "mobile kitchen."

We were received there in a manner of speaking, and we were given bread and something to drink. We were put up in the hay-loft of the local château on a bed of straw, thrown together pell-mell with the Belgian refugees and squeezed side by side like sardines.

In a way it was the beginning of our survival experience, but it wasn't yet too tragic. As long as your parents are there, you feel yourself protected to some degree: you don't have to carry all your problems alone.

We walked around and around the village. There wasn't much there.

There were still a few things to eat, but we had no money, and everything was very expensive. A dozen eggs at that period must have cost about the sum a worker earned in a day – about a franc!

We did our best to go to the local farms every day to fetch a liter of milk. The others may have been fed more or less by the village, but for us it was more difficult owing to the requirements of kashrut.

Where laundry was concerned, my mother had to bend down on her knees and wash the clothes next to an old-fashioned wash-house by the side of a stream. I can still see her silhouette above the soapy water.

We were commandeered to help with the grape harvest. I've forgotten neither the lumbago nor the refusal to allow us to eat any grapes. Unbelievable!

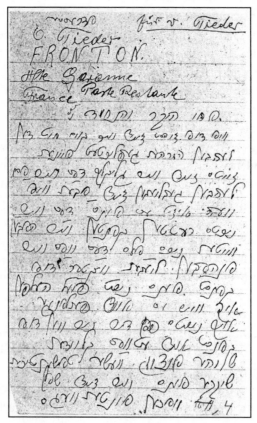

Photo of my father's letter from Fronton to his brother Victor.

Little by little, the troops went away. Only the refugees remained behind. Then the Belgians were allowed to return home, and all the non-Jews went away. Who was left in the hay-loft? The little foreign Jews. They had somehow succeeded in organizing themselves to procure oil or vegetable margarine, eggs and bread. I don't remember that I went hungry or that I was unhappy. They even managed to form a little *minyan*.[1]

O. Tieder,
FRONTON
Hte Garonne
Poste Restante
France
Summer 1940

Dear brother,

    As you can see, we've taken refuge here, having hardly been able to save our lives. On the one hand, we're glad to have remained alive, but how hard it is not to have been able to save anything! We now have nothing left except what we have on us. Dear Victor, you can't help us much, I know, so I don't ask you for anything, only, if you can, send us a few dresses, shoes, a suit, underwear, handkerchiefs. Four weeks traveling and nothing to wear. Here there are many thousands of refugees.

    We don't get any money either, not to speak of food. When one has nothing for one's body, it's very tough. I have written to our dear father but not received a reply. I don't know what to think. If you get anything from our acquaintances, or Redel (my mother's sister) or from anywhere else – whatever the case, you'll know how to manage – send it all to us. Let me have your answer soon, with news of everyone. More soon. May life be good to you. Many greetings and kisses to you and your dear wife.

Your brother

Translation of my father's letter to Victor.

---

1.   The quorum of ten Jews required for communal prayer; pl. *minyanim.*

For us it was an adventure, almost fun. Our parents were there, and as my mother wasn't someone to give way in the face of difficulties of this kind, we held firm. Until the day they came and said to us:

"Listen, you really can't continue to live in these conditions."

All of a sudden, it seemed that someone had actually been so kind as to begin to deal with our case. What a farce! Call-up next morning in the village square:

"We're going to take you to a place where you will get accommodation and work."

Like idiots, we went along. We were loaded onto cattle-cars, and next morning, surrounded by gendarmes, we walked towards the camp at Agde. I don't know if this was right away the camp at Agde or a different camp first, I only remember that we went through the town at the crack of dawn.

We found ourselves in a camp surrounded by barbed-wire fences. The men were put on one side, the women on the other with the children. The world was coming apart.

But what was most difficult of all, what was quite unbearable, was to be separated from our father. We found ourselves, together with our mother, cooped up in a shack, on the ground, on straw, in degrading conditions, in the midst of all sorts of people jumbled together.

It was atrocious. And the most terrible thing of all was to find vulgarity and nastiness even among our own people.

There were all sorts. One of the women got up every night, crazed, in a total panic, and chased after rats with a stick in her hand. Another stayed there all day long calling for her husband.

Until that time, my immediate surroundings had given me a certain image – an image imbued with human dignity, with nobility and beauty, with respect for oneself and others, and which owed nothing to money or titles or honors.

How could I conceive that many of the Jews who surrounded me would not correspond to that image?

We were closed together in sordid hovels, sleeping on the ground on straw in dirt, dampness and promiscuity. It was cold in the snow in that winter of 1940!

And we were still wearing our little summer dresses, the same ones we had worn since the month of May. I remained in a little summer dress for more than one winter. It was freezing cold.

(Many years later – forty-five, to be exact – when I began to concern myself with making bureaucratic preparations for my retirement, I asked for documentary proof of my internment and that of my family in the camps in the South of France. Strangely enough, none of the authorities concerned could find in their archives any trace of our stay there. Similarly, although I was a war orphan and had received a scholarship on the strength of that, no trace of that decision was found by the authorities).

In the camp, we didn't eat, we were dying of cold... The wicked guards hit us, the French gendarmes or security police struck pregnant women and beat us up, as on the occasion when we succeeded in sneaking through newly laid sewer pipes and barbed-wire fences in our summer dresses in the depths of winter.

Every morning, there was a roll call. A woman pushed the door open abruptly and yelled, "Head of the hut!" She called out the names and then doled out a dreadful liquid supposed to be coffee.

It was impossible to see our father; we knew only that he couldn't be far away. Then we managed to trace him. He too slept on planks, but among the men, conditions were even worse.

From time to time, we managed to sneak through to them. We went through the thick sewer-pipes, then through the barbed-wire fences. We children succeeded in slipping through to see our father. We sometimes even managed to get out of the camp in search of a bit of bread, a little oil, what have you... a clove of garlic, just enough to make what was called "*penitzlech*."[2]

One day, my sister and I brought back to the camp a piece of bread and an onion. On our way back, the guards caught us. They stuffed the onion in our mouths and hit us on the head. They didn't have to! In the free zone, they didn't yet have the Boches behind them.

Despite the fact that we had been caught once, we continued to go out to see our father. The state of neglect in which he lived in the men's quarters pained me, because where my mother was it was always clean.

She was never involved in any of the affairs that poisoned the life of the camp. Her little corner was tidy. Our meal was a bit of bread, which we toasted by placing it against the side of the stove. My mother managed to make something to eat with the little there was. The circumstances

---

2.   Toasted bread rubbed with garlic and spread with a few drops of oil.

may have been what they were, but my mother, for her part, remained what she was, regardless.

My father was infected with lice all over his body and looked so miserable – sad and dejected! After the war, I found at my uncle's a letter my father had written from this camp asking for help. I wonder how it reached him.

The children had to take compulsory walks on the jetty, a sinister pier buffeted by a stormy sea, cold wind, snow and in shoes that were no good whatsoever. In a camp adjoining ours there were Vietnamese, so short in stature that we thought they were all children with their little black teeth and their peculiar dress, resembling Mao jackets. They had wanted to fight for France and had not been able to be repatriated, so they were dumped there like animals.

There were also disabled Spanish republicans – a whole nightmarish universe.

For latrines, holes had been dug at the edge of the camp. It was beyond description. A peasant would never provide his animals with such unhygienic and unlivable conditions.

And we knew we were in the antechamber of death. Everything was there except for the cremation ovens, and those wouldn't be long in coming. We kept saying that we had to get out at all costs. But how? You don't know anyone, you don't know the language, you are penniless, you have no identification papers. What can you do?

One day, the Red Cross came to look at the place. Then a miracle happened. Among the inspectors was Rabbi Schilli, who I suspect was behind this inspection. The visitors were taken around the camp by its commandant.

My sister and I immediately recognized Rabbi Schilli as a Jew. He had a beard and a hat. We went up to him because the adults wouldn't have dared to, and we spoke to him in German. We told him not to believe a single word the commandant had said and to visit the camp with us.

By an extraordinary stroke of luck, he came from Alsace and understood German. We organized a parallel visit for him, following which he set in train a whole plan of rescue with, above all, the children in mind.

He succeeded in bringing into the camp a Jewish doctor from the O.S.E.[3] – Dr. Malkin, a marvelous man with beautiful eyes. From that

---

3.   *Oeuvres de Secours aux Enfants*, Organization for Aid to Children

moment, all the children for whom a medical pretext could be found were taken out of the camp.

Thus, my sister and brother left for Moissac in January 1941 thanks to a primary tubercular infection in the case of the former and a persistent impetigo in the case of the latter. But as I had neither an impetigo nor anything else of the kind, I remained in the camp with my parents, envied by my brother and sister.

Then, one morning in April, my father put on a Red Cross armband, which he had the right to wear owing to his service as a medical orderly in the First World War. He put on his armband, declared my mother sick, and took her to a hospital in Montpellier, the town where Rabbi Schilli served as a chaplain. We finally had someone to speak to!

We went through the gates of the camp at daybreak, passing the sentry who was half asleep, without any official authorization, under the protection of my father's armband and my mother's gallstone problem.

At Montpellier, my mother found herself in the hospital surrounded by good sisters and crucifixes, while my father stubbornly sat with me in Rabbi Schilli's waiting room. We were supposed to return to the camp.

I don't know how Rabbi Schilli found an alternative solution in keeping with the laws of Vichy, but, however it was, he obtained for us a work contract in a village where a house had been requisitioned for refugees.

Nineteen Forty-two

That non-kosher
lamb cutlet
authorized by father
in the midst
of the occupation,
how good it was,
that permission for life
granted
when all seemed over,
cooked on the fire
in a neighbor's home,
while they knew famine
in that "dump" where
we were prisoners,
except for a few vegetables
raised on a tiny patch of earth
lent by a kind-hearted
Italian farmer,
and except
for that liter
of milk a day
sent by my teacher
the extraordinary
Madame Bonfils
whose farmer-husband
was the sole resister
in that village
of collaborators
– from the doctor
down to the postman

and the gendarmes.
What pluck that must have taken!

My parents
must have had it too
in order to continue
to keep kashrut and Shabbat
for themselves
without cheating
in conditions
so extreme!

May 13, 1982

LE SABLET

So there we were, in our famous village of Sablet-près-l'Ouvèze, in the heart of the Comtat Venaissin, between Vaison-la-Romaine and Carpentras, which we knew as well as the planet Mars!

Le Sablet was one of those typical Provençal villages perched on a hill, with little streets winding up to the church at the top, cats slinking around everywhere and gutters running down the middle of the unpaved and unevenly cobbled streets.

Having been assigned to this place of residence, which was the only way to avoid returning to the camp, we had moreover to pretend to be comfortably off, because we had presumably been given the right to reside there only on condition of never asking anyone for anything. In reality, we survived thanks to a small subsidy provided by a Jewish organization.

In addition, thanks to Rabbi Schilli, my father had obtained a vague work contract signed by a certain Monsieur Bonfils, the husband of the schoolmistress, a large-scale agricultural landowner, the only decent man in the village and the only one to belong to the Resistance.

Later, he and his wife were denounced by the village.

In order to justify having this contract, my father had to go all the way down the Ouvèze, a tributary of the Durance, one of those half dried-up little rivers, very wide, with a bottom filled with pebbles. He was expected to go and look for wood there and drag it to the top of the hill.

So, dressed in his town suit, which was all he had, he went around with his faggots of wood, and I was distressed to see him sweating, bent double under these bundles, thin as he was from the camp and all he had been through.

We had nothing to put on our backs, nothing to put in our mouths and not a penny in our pockets. I believe my father was paid nothing, or hardly anything for this work. Already in giving him this contract-as-an-alibi, they had done him a favor.

And you know, even there, in Le Sablet, he didn't eat any meat. He didn't have much to put in his mouth, and my parents continued, despite everything, to eat kosher, thus depriving themselves of the little they might otherwise have obtained.

They provided us with a little house, which in fact had been requisitioned for refugees, not for Jews.

So all three of us were here in this old house, without water, without electricity, without any sort of comfort. In order to relieve ourselves, we had to go down in the darkness to the cockroach-infested cellar. We spread it over with ashes as best we could. I have nightmares about it even today.

Where could we have gone? But after the horrors of the camp, it was paradise. The house had belonged to some peasants who had built themselves a more comfortable farmhouse in the plain below, at the edge of the village. Their former home, now vacant, had been requisitioned.

I also imagine that Rabbi Schilli had done all that was required in order that the local representatives of the Jewish organizations would provide us with the tiny allowance given to refugees.

We were thus supposed to receive some vague amount from a Jewish organization which looked after refugees, a ridiculous sum, which they never sent and which never arrived. An assimilated Jew had been given this task.

I don't know if I ever saw him, but, as I remember, I remonstrated with him, telling him: "Don't think you are so high and mighty; what's happening to us is liable to happen to you too. When they're finished with us, they'll go for you." Once again, I was, unfortunately, a prophet. They didn't send the money and we went hungry, lost in the depths of the countryside.

Having picked up a few scraps of French at school, I became responsible for all relationships with the outside. I acted as interpreter, and I went off to literally beg one or two eggs from the peasants, deploying prodigious diplomacy in order to make them understand that I was willing to pay, yet at the same time arrange things so that they wouldn't ask me for money!

In order to do my homework, I went in the evening to the dressmaker, who didn't live far away: there I could at least see clearly in the light of the electric lamp. In exchange for the use of her light, I picked up her pins.

I collected pins, I went to people, I saw baskets full of eggs. They said, "*Ah! Ma pauvre, je rregrrette* (my poor girl, I'm sorry), I haven't got any!"

One day, I wanted to pick up an apple, a half-rotten apple lying under a tree. The owner saw me and let loose his dog on me, calling me all kinds of names. My legs shook and refused to go forward, and I ran and ran, saying to myself, "That's it! He'll hand me over to the gendarmes and we'll all get caught."

The schoolmistress has remained for me the image of the ideal France: generous, loyal and open. She had an incredible open-mindedness and humanity and a heartwarming way of receiving you. She could understand things without any explanation. She had had the opportunity of leaving her village in order to pursue her teaching studies, and so she didn't remain limited, xenophobic, anti-Semitic, racist – rejecting anything that doesn't resemble you. And me, an utterly lost little girl with two bewildered parents who couldn't speak French (not that I knew much myself)... I suddenly became the liaison with the outside world. Perhaps my vocation as an interpreter dates from that time. As a pediatrician or psychoanalyst, I have never done anything else than to serve as an interpreter for people who lack the words to describe their problem.

So the schoolmistress had a sympathetic attitude towards me, especially as she and her husband were the only non-Pétainists in the village. But she was obliged, poor woman, to get the children to sing "*Maréchal, nous voilà*" ("Marshal, here we are") and make them comply with all the official pretences and write essays about the exploits of this "great man."

The language I learnt in class. Since May 1940 when I arrived in France, it was the first time I had been back to school. Everyone made fun of my ignorance.

In the first dictation, I made more than forty mistakes in a single sentence, but at the end of two months I only made ten, and after three months none at all, whereas the others still made ten! Nobody forgave me for this, especially as the teacher was fond of me.

The day came for us to sit for the *certificat d'études* (an examination given at the end of the elementary course of studies). I couldn't go: it was Shabbat.

Much later, her son told me how one evening she had laughed heartily on correcting my essay on the *Maréchal*. I had made a very significant mistake in my French: instead of speaking of his "action," I spoke of his "agitation." He added that she and her husband often burst out laughing when reading my essays.

This extraordinary woman gave me a liter of milk every day, which I carefully took home.

Much later, I learnt from her son that she died of cancer. It was her husband who had given us the work contract which had enabled us to be accepted in the village.

Apart from them, people were nauseating, beyond imagination. They were all collaborators, down to the postman.

I forgive them all, except for one: the doctor. This is perhaps not unrelated to the fact that I have practiced medicine in the way I have.

He lived opposite us, in a magnificent, large, bourgeois residence. I can still see the door closing, I can still hear the piano playing, while we were there dying of fear, hunger, cold, isolation and loneliness.

One day, I don't know exactly why, my mother began to worry. I think I had a touch of goiter and she took me to this doctor.

The way he received us, the coldness, the indifference! All he could have done that day and didn't do!

I don't forgive him his attitude. I have never been back to this village: perhaps I shall never go back. The schoolmistress's son invited us, however. Recently, when we were on holiday at Ramatuelle, as soon as he knew we were there, he set out on his way and came to see us.

Apart from this schoolteacher, her family and two others, all the other people in the village were bastards. I can excuse them; I can understand them. For these "worthy" folk who lived in the countryside, we were strangers, intruders.

So at Le Sablet, my parents continued to eat kosher, but as I was a growing child they allowed me to eat non-kosher meat and even peas with worms (forbidden according to Jewish dietary law).

I had a little saucepan, and I went to our neighbor, an old lady of ninety, to cook my meal on her hearth and to eat it on the spot. Still today, I must admit that I like lamb cutlets, probably because it was "the forbidden permitted," a means of survival normally refused but granted by my parents.

I'll never forget one detail. The old lady would pass water in the middle of the street, standing upright with her legs apart, above the gutter, without even lifting her long dress.

As for the doctor living opposite, why did his behavior make such an impression on me? I forget how he answered us or what happened, but I have the memory of a man of stone. Afterwards, I said to myself:

71

"Well, one may understand, at a pinch, that peasants who have never left their soil, who have had the traditional Catholic teaching of contempt drummed into them for two thousand years, who imagine that Jews have horns and tails, would be frightened of strangers and suspect that they come to steal or commit rape. But that a doctor, after at least seven years in the city where he has studied and where he has seen white people, black people, men and women stark naked, in their most wretched condition, from birth to death, should still be so inhuman, is beyond my comprehension!"

Ki ger ha'yita be'eretz mitzrayim – "because you were a stranger in the land of Egypt."

All my life, I have tried to return good to those who have done good to me and to return good even to those who have done me harm. That's how I was brought up.

What exactly happened during this consultation? It hardly matters. Everything is in what is *not* said, in the gestures, in the presence, and in this case in the non-presence, and a child perceives everything.

This man could have played an extraordinary role! What would it have cost him to give the ghost of a smile? To try and reassure us: "Yes, madame, I quite understand. Your situation is terrible, but don't you worry about your daughter." The whole world was against us, and so was he.

Indifference, silence, complicity in rejection. He was supposed to take care of people, but I know he didn't take care of me. My sickness was somewhere else other than in his cold diagnosis. Someone who takes care of a patient first of all takes care of human problems.

It's no accident that I have belonged to a "Balint" group.[1] In my first year of medical studies, on the day I started my hospital training, I was in the department of Professor X at the Salpêtrière. His assistant, whom I called "Hitler," made his visits at a brisk, soldierly pace, followed by his retinue, I might almost call his court. I don't know what they represented for him – his courtiers or his bootlickers.

He lifted up the sheets with a rough gesture, mumbling a few words, didn't say "Good day," "How are you, madame?" or anything whatsoever, left with the patient still uncovered, and knowingly told the head nurse: "Number so-and-so, blah, blah, blah, blah... "

---

1. A method of training doctors to listen to the patient, named after its inventor, a Hungarian Jewish doctor.

So I let them continue. I covered the patient, took her hand and said a few kind words.

When I had opened my pediatric clinic, as soon as a mother crossed the threshold of my consulting-room, I knew exactly how things stood: why the child wasn't sleeping or had a stomachache or vomited or did badly at school.

As soon as we set eyes on each other, I tried to understand what was going on around the child, and tried to make each one feel I was present there with them and to give each one some human warmth, a little understanding, something that would give them the strength to overcome the worry of the moment.

Only, it isn't simple or easy to operate in this way, and that's why doctors protect themselves against this approach, erecting an invisible barrier, and are content to write out a nice prescription: "Let's stick to medicines, and then I can sleep peacefully."

I was made into a "thing," despised, disregarded, deprived, wiped off the map – a "stranger in Egypt" – and when now I sometimes find myself in a position of power, I don't use it for my own benefit but in order to help the other person also find his place.

I don't say this in order to boast. I simply can't do anything else, and I think everyone should act in this way. As soon as I see someone who wants to use his power at the expense of others, I protest vehemently or I leave.

In this God-forsaken village of Le Sablet, what I found very distressing was to see my parents reduced to a state of impotence. And I understood, long before becoming a doctor, that in order to care for children one must also know how to listen to their parents.

Later, in the institution for children where I was the pediatrician, children would come and say to me, "Don't you want to see my mother? Call my mother. Don't you want to see my father?" It was a way of telling me, "If I'm sick, it's because I have to carry my mother's problems which are too heavy for me, so please deal with them, and I can go off and play."

For my part, I never played at Le Sablet, or hardly at all. My sole pleasure was the bicycle; I don't know who lent me one. So when my parents went for a walk, I got on "my" bicycle. It was freedom, wind in my face...

We were in this village of Le Sablet from April 1941 until the round-up of August 1942. My father, on arriving there, had a reaction one would not have imagined. At first he walked around everywhere as though in a trance. He was there, in this village, quoting passages from the Talmud, saying, "Look, look! See – it's exactly like Eretz Yisrael. Look at the figs, look at the grapes!"

This is where you realize the power of study which kept alive through time and space, solely by means of the Book, a reality from which we were completely cut off, deprived for centuries, so that the day you meet this reality you recognize it instantly.

As he walked around, my father said to me: "Avignon, Cavaillon, Carpentras and Lisle-sur-Sorgue were four flourishing ancient Jewish communities where great scholars lived." He knew about them from literature. A whole chapter of Jewish history opened up before his eyes.

Believe it or not, we celebrated Shabbat! We celebrated the holidays! All work came to a stop and we would go off for a walk. We must have looked as if we had fallen from the moon with our city hats, our threadbare suits, our pale complexions, our thin, wasted bodies, not speaking the language...

On Shabbat, my father would sit with me and study the *Pirkei Avot* (Sayings of the Fathers) and the weekly *parasha* (reading of the Law). We prayed together, we sang, he told me stories as he had always done and endowed me with a treasure that I have since carried with me everywhere.

When I was left all alone and had to hide, I heard it all repeated in my head and I was able to hold out.

I never heard my parents complain. My mother, an extraordinary woman, succeeded in dressing us impeccably even when we had only one piece of clothing. Even in the concentration camp, we looked like Rothschild's children. From a handkerchief she cut out a little white collar, from a piece of blanket she made us a dress.

In Le Sablet, we went gleaning in the fields like Ruth; we gathered up the barley that was left, from which my mother made erzatz coffee, imitation fisch and imitation *fleisch*,[2] turning an old coffee-mill for hours.

For days on end, we ground the stuff, we roasted it, we put it through an old sieve. I don't know how my mother managed, but in the end we always had something.

Here in this village, cut off from the whole world, we turned in circles. Our sole umbilical link with the outside world was a Swiss journal, *Die Weltwoche*.

---

2.   Meat in Yiddish and German.

As early as 1941 and 1942 we knew that Jews were being deported and killed in camps, and we knew that this would be our destination too. We knew for a fact that we were only on reprieve, a reprieve that could be terminated from one day to the next as decided by the all-powerful invaders with the complicity of the French.

For us, Le Sablet was an absolute desert. During this period, in 1942, my brother and sister were already in a children's home, and I was left with my parents. The three of us were lost in this village.

We also received a few letters from my brother and sister, and once they even came to see us during their holidays. It was extraordinary to have all five of us together.

It was only thirty years later that my brother, my sister and I were able to exchange reminiscences. Soon after their arrival at Moissac, my sister was sent to another children's home where there were only girls, regretfully leaving my young brother alone and in total distress.

In this home, a subsidiary to Moissac, at Beaulieu in the Dordogne, my sister, instead of eating, would save her meals to make food parcels for my parents.

Madame Gordin, the director of this home, a fine pedagogue, called her in and said to her: "Listen, you're going to eat. Don't worry, come to my office and we'll make a parcel for your parents." How could my sister eat if she thought that my parents had nothing?

My brother told us on that day when we were finally able to talk and cry together, how during an outing with the Moissac *Éclaireurs Israélites* (Jewish Scouts), he had brought with him a bottle, which he had filled with blackberries to send to us. Within a few days, the blackberries fermented and the cork popped.

An Italian living in the village lent us a tiny plot of land where we sowed some haricot beans and some potatoes. We went to the garden, watered it, weeded it and dug the soil, and it began to grow. The first crop from the garden appeased our hunger a little. The second crop, we never saw. The round-up had already taken us away.

Before the round-up, we were always getting new forms to fill in, and I saw my mother's expression cloud over because she knew the diabolical intention of these repeated census-takings.

She wrote heartrending letters, sometimes in German, sometimes in French (I did the translation) to the woman who directed the home in Moissac, begging her to let my brother and sister come to Le Sablet during their school holidays. These letters were masterpieces of diplomacy and distress.

The directress got my sister to do dressmaking, and my mother wrote to her, "Do you really think dressmaking is suitable for my daughter?"

Photo of the letter from Sarah Tieder (Ida's older sister) to Mme Simon (Shatta).

Beaulieu 28.7.41

Dear Madame,

I have just learnt from Madame Gordin that I'll be leaving for Moissac, as the O.S.E. wishes, after I have taken some steps, to take me in, as when I left for Beaulieu I asked the O.S.E. to be so kind as to keep me at Moissac. But now the whole situation has changed. My brother, who missed my parents very much, needed me, but now he has calmed down and adapted. He has made a lot of progress and is even in charge of six younger scouts, which shows that he feels good there. As for me, before coming to Beaulieu, I was told that it wasn't good here, but when I arrived I saw it was all right, and I like it very much. My parents, who are reassured that I am all right and that my brother has calmed down, have no desire for me to go back to Moissac. I have already made progress in cutting and in dressmaking.

I am sure that I would also like it at Moissac, but it would disturb me a great deal to stop in the midst of the work and to start again. That way, I would also lose a great deal of time. Moreover, I have begun English and commercial correspondence… and to leave all this in the middle!

I beg you, dear Madame, to be so good as to leave me here, and I apologize for having put you out so much. I am very sorry. I thank you for having had such good intentions towards me.

I hope you will grant me this, and I send you all my thanks in advance together with my heartfelt greetings.

Sarah Tieder

Be assured above all that I know that what you have done was for my own good. Thanks again!

Translation of the letter from Sarah.

My sister, a super-intelligent, brilliant girl, highly motivated for studies, later studied for her exams in medicine in very difficult conditions and passed all of them with flying colors!

So my mother asked whether my sister would really like dressmaking, and if it was truly her vocation. Knowing her daughter, she guessed how miserable she must have been sewing for hours on end.

At the same time, my parents also sought an occupation for me, because they saw that things were going from bad to worse. There was no question of studying: one had to earn a living, and quickly, so they thought of getting *me* to do dressmaking as well. But I already couldn't stand the sight of pins. They also thought of hairdressing. A hairdresser – me, who has never to this day been able to use a hair-curler (something which probably dates from that time)!

The general impression I retain of Le Sablet is one of immobility and solitude, isolation and estrangement. We were totally cut off from everything. All this in a wonderful landscape to which tourists flock nowadays. For me it was life and death that hung in the balance.

Once – just once – I went out with *Âmes Vaillantes*, a sort of Catholic girl guides. We went as far as Buis-les-Baronnies, a lovely excursion in the mountains near Mont Ventoux in the heart of a gorgeous landscape, where we devised all sorts of games in a thyme-scented *garrigue* (area of scrub).

Photo of the letter from Mrs. Tieder (Ida's mother) to Mme Simon (Shatta).

Sablet 9.7.42

Dear Mme Simon!

I have just this moment heard from my daughter Sarah that she has been very successful in her primary school examination. I am most satisfied, for this poor child has wanted this for some years, but, because of the troubles of the period, this was not possible for her. Now the thing has been done. You, Madame Simon, who have helped her in this, I thank with all my heart, the heart of a mother for her child. I also thank you for all the education, kindness and everything else you have given my children throughout the year.

Now the long vacation is coming up, I beg you from the bottom of my heart to give my daughter Sarah the possibility of spending it with us so that during that time our longings may be assuaged on either side and our love will give her, in the coming year, courage and renewed strength for her work. As a mother, I am sure you cannot refuse me this request, for which I thank you very much. I also beg you to give me your opinion on the following matter:

Is my daughter Sarah gifted at dressmaking, and is she capable of one day becoming a good dressmaker and of earning a living independently in this way? After two years of apprenticeship, one ought already to be able to see whether she has any aptitude and taste for this profession or whether she sews only in order to pass the time and in order to use the knowledge she has gained when she founds a family. I am very concerned about her future. From Martin we have some very pleasant news. It seems that he feels good over there.

We hope that he will return from there in good health. Thanking you once more for everything, I beg you to accept my best sentiments and best wishes.

Berty Tieder

Translation of the letter from Mrs. Tieder.

But, as for me, I had long before lost the habit of playing with other children. We sang "*Les Âmes Vaillantes, pures et conquérantes*" ("Valiant souls, pure and victorious"), but, you understand, they were Catholic, and as I heard myself sing I felt myself to be completely alien to the sounds which came out of my mouth. I didn't know any of these girls. I was about their age, and I was a thousand years older than all of them put together.

It was then – as I'm aware today – that I acquired the "faculty" of doing something and observing myself at the same time. I suddenly became a split personality. There were games I had to play for the sake of the outside world, in order to obtain what was needed for the family to survive, and on the other hand there was what one was really thinking inside.

When I turned up and had to say, "Good day, Madame, blah, blah, blah, please excuse me," in order to try and extract an egg from someone – say what you like, this was no work for a child.

Normally, one would say, "You know, my parents, they are hungry. You know, you ought to give us something. We don't have any money." But I learnt how to keep silent, not to say what couldn't be said because certain words would put us in danger. It was a whole apprenticeship.

This went on until the horrible round-up of August 26, 1942. I was visiting the Sokolowskis in Avignon, and in this way I was saved by a miracle.

The Train

It's always at the crack of dawn
that one takes the train
to escape,
and that in your last bed
they come to get you.
It's always at the crack of dawn
that they take you
half dead
out of your goods-train
or cattle-car.
No, there's no one on the platform
waiting to embrace you.
This is where your fate
is shattered,
your road comes to an end.
Here, there's no tomorrow:
couples are separated,
children carried away.
Here, they take away your clothes
and whatever remains of your life
is gone,
while over there
they carry on as if they didn't know,
as if life could still continue
while so many human children
go up in smoke.

November 8, 1981

THE ROUND-UP

In the midst of our wretchedness, one day, a miracle happened. On a visit to the local market to find some food, my father saw someone who looked like a Jew. He said to himself, "Now, this one, surely..."

He went up to him and whispered "*Shalom aleichem a Yid*,"[1] and the other replied "*Aleichem hashalom a Yid.*"

It was Monsieur Sokolowski of Avignon, a worthy Jew who had come to France from Poland or Lithuania in the nineteen-twenties and had settled in Avignon with his family.

To earn his living, he went from one market to another selling all sorts of odds and ends: small combs, threads, needles, ribbons.

Just imagine what it was to meet someone to whom you could speak in Yiddish! We soon got to know this very nice family.

My parents were not fools: they'd lived through the First World War, they knew what it was. They were familiar with persecution. Every day, we received more and more forms to fill in. We felt the danger coming, although we didn't know where it would come from or how it would come.

My mother had premonitory dreams. One night she had a horrible dream of a river of mud with lots of sacks along its banks. The river carried away all the sacks. Next day, she said to me, "There's something bad brewing; we must leave. But we can't get away from this dump, we can't do anything. You go to Avignon."

As I was under fifteen years old, I still had the right to take the bus without a special pass.

"Go and see the Sokolowskis. Ask them to find out if whole families are being taken, or only the men."

Nobody knew anything.

"If they're only taking the men, we'll stay here; we'll hide father. It's easier to look after one person, to bring him food... In any case," she added, "one

---

1. "Peace be unto you, Jew.

can manage better in large towns. In this isolated village, we are lost. Go and see them, and ask them what it is possible to do. We *have* to do something."

Everything began to fall apart. Everything had fallen apart so many times, and each time in a different way.

One day, things really did fall apart. It was August 25, 1942. I set off in my little summer dress and my light canvas shoes, and I went to the Sokolowskis. They received me very warmly, with great kindness, in a real home with real beds and things to eat.

"Stay here, stay with us. You can eat, you can sleep. We'll go and get some information."

They knew someone vaguely at the Préfecture (administrative center of the region), but when he came back that evening, Monsieur Sokolowski said to me:

"I don't know anything. Stay here tomorrow as well. Stay, we'll try and find out."

But next day, they still didn't have any information, so I went back the next day nevertheless. I took the bus and I calmly returned home.

When I got off the bus, there was no one there. My father should have been there. There was no one at the bus stop? My heart missed a beat. I said to myself, "What's up? There's something wrong." I tried to reassure myself as I walked up the hill.

Provençal villages are all perched on a hilltop, and we lived right at the top in one of the alleys not far from the tower of the church. I arrived home; I saw the shutters closed, the door sealed up. Not a soul! I stood petrified in front of that door; I stood there like an idiot...

Everything stopped. To describe what it was like, I always say (I can only say it in Yiddish): "*Der Himmel ist mit schmattes verstipt geworden.*"[2]

There was no more life: nothing, nothing at all. I began to cry, rooted to the spot in front of the door.

Then the little old lady who lived near to us came out and began to say to me: "Don't worry, my child, they're not far away – they'll come back."

Don't worry!

But I, who was only a youngster, I knew. I knew perfectly well: either they had already been shot and had fallen into a nearby ditch, or else they were on their way to a death camp and the game was up. I knew how things stood; you could say what you liked: "Don't worry, my child: they're not far away, they'll come back"!

---

2. "Heaven is stuffed with rags."

These peasants didn't know what was going on, but me, with all I had lived through, I knew: I had come from Germany, I had come out of the concentration camp; I knew. You couldn't fob me off with any stories. So I asked just about everyone, and they told me what had happened.

They came, there was a round-up.[3] Who came? French gendarmes.

Couldn't they have warned my parents in this little village where everyone knew them? I was just a tiny little thing, but I was older than all these adults. I said: "I have to find out where they are."

As always – it's the same today – when I see that nobody has any imagination or initiative or courage or strength when it comes to moving a glass of water a few inches because they see no reason to do so, I refuse to give in just like that.

---

3.   More than fifty-five years after these events, the book *Un Hiver en Provence* (A Winter In Provence) by Isaac Lewendel (Editions De l'Aube, 1996) came into my hands. The book deals with the persecution of the Jews in Provence during the war. It describes the military precision with which the French police prepared these round-ups of a few Jews. The author cites a document, a report of August 26, 1942 of the Gendarmerie Nationale in the town of Orange, a letter classified as secret, No. 7714. The subject was the rounding-up of foreign Jews. It describes the "operation" in five villages in the region. In the account of the arrests there is a passage dealing with the arrest of my parents:

> In Baumes: The gendarmes presented themselves at 4.15 a.m. at the home of the family of Osias Tieder at Sablet. They received no answer to their summons. At 5.45, the mayor of the village was called, and he had to find a locksmith to break open the door. The rooms and attic were searched without success. They finally found the husband hiding behind a door in the cellar, and the woman Bracha Tieder was found lying in a corner of the room completely covered with refuse.
>
> The daughters: Sarah Tieder is in a scout camp at Bussière-Vieille (Creuse), and Ida Tieder, who had traveled to Avignon the previous day, was to have returned to Sablet on the evening of the 26th.
>
> The son Martin Tieder is in a preventorium at Marvejols (Lozère).

It is shocking to see how a French official (the mayor) enthusiastically co-operated with the Nazi extermination machine and how the police described in dry language and with evident contempt the terrible tragedy of two innocent Jews trying to save their lives. Unfortunately, this attitude was by no means exceptional but was characteristic of almost all the French governmental hierarchy, who abandoned and even willingly delivered up the Jews who lived within their borders in this fateful and disastrous period of the Second World War.

I said: "I want to know where they are: you absolutely have to find them for me." I wanted to know at all costs in order to join them. Wherever they were, I'd go there, and if they were going to die, I'd die with them.

There can be no such thing as living entirely alone. Especially as I thought, "If they've been taken, then everyone has been taken. It's all over; all the Jews have been taken, including the Sokolowskis, my brother, my

Photo of the postcard sent by Ida's mother from the camp of Les Milles.

85

28.8.42

Dear Ida,

    We have reached the camp of Les Milles all right and we have already settled down. Please arrange things so that you are brought here, and bring with you the blankets, the plates and dishes, and also some potatoes, the spoons, some wheat and the coffee mill, and also a sheet.

    The main thing is the little round [grains] for eating. You're Hungarian, that's fine. Papa has a birth certificate. I kiss you.

Your mother.

Give the bag personally to the mayor.

Translation of the postcard sent by Ida's mother.

sister, everyone. What am I going to do? Am I going to wander around on earth all alone?"

My brother and sister were at Moissac in the children's home. They had just been to Le Sablet for a short holiday. And if I'm here today, it's not because I'm a hero but because it was "written somewhere" that I had to be here. It had been decided in some other place. Those who imagine they're great heroes because they've stayed alive forget that stronger people than them have disappeared.

So I pestered everyone, beginning with the mayor, Monsieur A. They succeeded in tracing them. They were already in the camp at Les Milles near Marseilles. He arranged for me to sleep at Le Sablet in the village convent that night: a horrible, horrible night, with a crucifix over my head.

You know, on these occasions there is never anyone to hold your hand or even to give you a smile.

So they had found them at the camp at Les Milles near Marseilles, and I insisted once again: "I want to join them."

"But you can't, my child."

I didn't have a *sou*; I had nothing. There I was, *na va'nad*,[4] naked.

---

4.   "A fugitive and a vagabond" in Hebrew, used in Yiddish.

I was fourteen years old. I nagged and implored them so much that the mayor set about making further enquiries. Where there's a will there's a way! The Préfecture finally gave me a safe-conduct certificate, permitting me to take the bus and then the train free of charge.

I don't know what seized me when I reached Avignon. In Avignon the train goes over a kind of little bridge, which spans a number of little streets running transversally to the railway-line.

It was in one of these little streets, the Chemin des Sources, that the Sokolowskis lived. When passing over this little bridge, I said to myself, "Alright, I'll get off, I'll go to them. One never knows: perhaps they haven't been taken. I'll tell them what has happened."

Without a second thought, I got off the train at Avignon and went to the Sokolowskis. They were all there.

From that moment, I wondered if I was dreaming. I asked myself: "Is it possible that somewhere in the world there are still people who live normally and carry on as if nothing had occurred?"

Was this possible?

I tore my hair out. Already when we were in the camp, when we were refugees, when we arrived in Belgium, I had had this experience.

The Sokolowskis were very kind, but you can't imagine the state I was in! I sobbed and sobbed. I told them everything, and they said to me: "Listen, you're not going."

"Yes, I *am* going; there's no question about that – I'm going"

They insisted that I eat, that I sleep, hoping in this way to hold me there a little while until I calmed down.

Seeing that there was nothing to be done, they finally came up with an argument. They said they would do all they could to get my parents out, but that it would be easier if I wasn't there as well.

I gave in. I sent a letter to my parents, telling them where I was. My parents, for their part, had already written to me. One couldn't send letters by post. One had to seize every opportunity and ask those who were traveling to deliver one's correspondence, which was very dangerous.

From my parents, who were sent to the camp at Les Milles, to Rivesaltes and then to Drancy before being deported, I received perhaps one or two letters in which my mother was preoccupied with my welfare from a distance. She gave no thought whatsoever to her own fate; the letter was full of practical advice. I was told to get my shoes back, to try and take a sack of potatoes out of the house (as it was sealed up, I could no longer get in), to sell the crop of haricot beans and to ask the schoolmistress's husband for a little money, just enough to provide some food and permit me to survive. She imagined her daughter to be completely alone – alone in the world.

I got a letter from Rivesaltes. And you will understand what outrage I feel when I hear people say that they let themselves be led like sheep to the slaughter. They struggled as best they could: my mother told me in a coded jargon in Yiddish that she gave them to understand she was pregnant because pregnant women were not being deported, that they tried to exploit their nationality as Czechs of Hungarian origin because Hungarians were not yet being deported. They were groping in all directions. They told me: "Above all, don't come here. Stay with the Sokolowskis."

One day, a card thrown from a train reached us. I didn't receive it; it was my sister at Moissac. She got it as they no longer knew where I was. My father wrote to my sister: "I'm separated from mother: I'm being taken in an unknown destination. God alone can help us. Search for mother, and search for Ida at the Sokolowskis."

I think they were at Auschwitz. I learnt this much later. After the war, they were not among the deportees who returned; nobody had heard anything about them. It was known that they were taken to Drancy very quickly. That was all.

For me it's a nightmare, and for years I had horrible phantasms. Every time I saw a tramp in the street I wondered whether it was my father who was there, unrecognizable, and I heard my mother shrieking in the

gas chambers under torture, enduring unspeakable sufferings. They put rats between her legs.

Our cousins from Belgium were at Rivesaltes with them. They succeeded in getting out thanks to their aged mother, and they were all

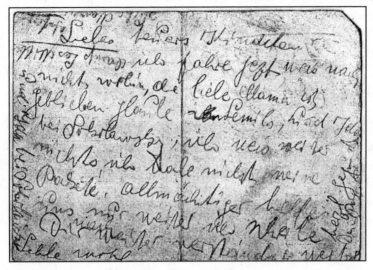

Photo of the postcard from Ida's father to his daughter Sarah while being transferred from one camp to another.

2.9.42

18 Quai du Port, Moissac

Dear beloved child,

I am now on my way, I don't yet know where to. I think dear Mother has remained at Les Milles and Ida is at the Sokolowskis. Apart from that, I don't know anything.

I haven't got my things. May the Almighty continue to help us. I shall write to you again; be well. I give you a big kiss.

[In the margin], Look for Mother, and look for Ida at the Sokolowskis.

Translation of the postcard sent by Ida's father to Sarah.

put in a special camp for the elderly in France. From Drancy onwards, nothing more is known about my parents.

After the war, my sister went from bureau to bureau in search of information. We were able to discover the date on which they were deported from Drancy. They had already left in September 1942.

It all happened very quickly, and, there again, I am haunted by one other phantasm. I wonder if they even reached their destination alive. I think they were in Auschwitz. I received the confirmation long afterwards through Serge Klarsfeld's registration book. My father left in convoy number 30 on September 9, 1942, and my mother left in convoy number 33 on September 16, 1942.

To touch this reality, to open Klarsfeld's book, was no easy matter. All I know is that I refused to know. I always hoped they'd come back.

May 8, 1945, V.E. Day, the day of the Allies' victory over the Nazis, was a time of great celebration throughout the country. The crowds were ecstatic. For me it was the hardest day of my life.

Suddenly, I had to face reality. The war was over; but for me it would never be over. It was the interminable beginning of the end. Until that time one had clung to a hope: now there was nothing.

For years, I hadn't complained of my fate. Whatever befell me I accepted, and I thought of my parents all the time. I remained in the intolerable situation of holding myself responsible, of feeling guilty for having survived, telling myself it was all my fault. I thought that if I'd gone back a day earlier, I might perhaps have saved their lives.

The day I realized this was madness was much later when I came together with my sister and brother, and they told me the same thing. On hearing them, I said to myself, "It's crazy what they are saying! It doesn't make sense." At that moment, I realized I had been thinking in exactly the same way as they had.

The only objects we got back after the war were a few jewels that my mother had probably entrusted to the O.S.E. in the camp. They were in a little bag made of jute, which we received one day long afterwards.

The bag had been rifled. All that was left was a pair of fragmented earrings, a watch-chain, two wedding rings and the little ring my father had bought my mother for their engagement. They had got rid of them in order to help us.

We divided these few keepsakes between us. The engagement ring went to my brother to give to his fiancée. For us penniless students nothing could be more natural, but one day my sister-in-law gave it back to me, saying there was no reason why she should keep it and that this ring was for me. I wear it every day, but tell myself there is no reason why this should be so.

After the roundup, the most somber period was the very beginning, when I hoped at first that they'd get out of the camp, when I hoped there was something I could do to bring them out. Then I realized there was nothing I could do, that I would have to drag myself around all alone, completely powerless.

Where was I to go? What was I to do? Why should I remain alive? To be rounded up at the next street corner? To be a sort of parcel which is carried here and there, to be an object of charity?

At that point, I began by staying at the Sokolowskis who, I must say, were quite extraordinary. They had a sense of hospitality, in the true meaning of the word.

It was a large house; it was open. It was a family with many children: one more or less didn't make much difference. You didn't feel you weighed on them. I was almost naked. I was given a dress, a coat and a pair of shoes belonging to one of their daughters who has remained a friend. It was a magnificent dress, a flowered dress with a little white ornamental frill and a white collar. It was so long since I had had a real dress! I shan't forget the only dress I wore during the war.

The coat was brick-red and had a fur collar. Between the fur and the lining I sewed a passport photo of my father and mother I had with me (I don't know how that came about), and my parents' last letter.

Throughout the war, I went around with this sewn in my collar, at great risk to myself when I went into hiding and carried a false name, and with the pair of shoes they had given me I thought I was pretty.

This was no dress made out of a blanket in the camp! And once again, it reflected the sharp contrast by which I was torn between a normal home with a normal life, and my situation of famine in my heart and my reality. It wasn't easy to reconcile.

What are my memories? The Sokolowskis got up early in the morning and I accompanied them to the markets. Everything seemed to me cold and dismal.

I've never forgotten my parents' letters, their concern, their advice, their desperate attempts to help me from far away, from behind barbed wire.

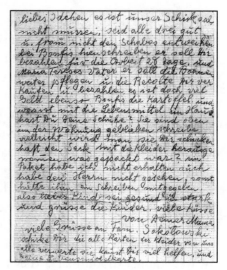

Photo of the last letter from Ida's parents sent at the end of August or the beginning of September 1942.

One day when we were still in Paris, I tried to write a letter to my son in Israel. He had written to me and spoken of his problems. I troubled my head as though I was crazy, and I asked myself: "What should one do? How can we help him? And yet he's big enough; he ought to be able to manage on his own a bit." But I couldn't bear to be so far away and unable to do anything.

Now that I have children of my own, I can understand how terrible it is when you can't do anything whatsoever for your own child.

As for me, if I had wanted to, I could immediately have taken an airplane and gone to see them, but that day, as long as I hadn't written that letter to my son, nothing went right. I was finally able to write it. I didn't know whether I would send the letter, but I had written it. I knew there was a solution, that I was able to do something, even if he didn't need it. I was *there*. Did I exaggerate in the opposite direction? I'll never know if my children are any the better for it or not.

I was thus for some time hidden at the Sokolowskis, but after the visit from the gendarmes they had to find me another hiding-place. It was once again an uprooting. I was all right at the Sokolowskis, except that when you are living with a family other than your own, the others have their family and you don't have anything.

Dearest Ida,

We're here, more or less; we don't know what awaits us. Stay where you are or leave for Moissac. May the Almighty continue to help us from now on. Keep well. I send you a kiss.

Your faithful father

Dear child,

How glad I am to know you are at the Sokolowskis. Stay there for the time being until the O.S.E. takes you to Surali or to another [children's] home. I am giving all my jewels to the O.S.E. so that they can pass them on to you. Sew them [into your clothes] somewhere so that they will not get lost. Perhaps we'll see each other soon. I am also sending you a parcel of clothes and also money, but I don't yet know how much. I will write to you again soon. All the people here are sent to the occupied zone. I don't know what will happen to us. Where you are concerned, the O.S.E. will take care of everything.

Dear Idchen, it's our fate... Don't be rebellious, all three of you be good and pious, and don't desecrate the Sabbath.

Write to Bonfils asking him to pay for the 28 days of work, and to Marie Térèse's father. He should continue to look after the haricot beans, sell the produce and pay. It's a lot of money. Bonfils should do the same with the potatoes, and what's happening with the food in the house? Do you have the shoes? They have remained in the house upstairs. Write: perhaps they'll be sent to you. Have you taken out of the house the bag with the clothes which were packed? I haven't received any parcel and I haven't seen the gentleman either, or I would have given him a letter. That's it, dear child, be well and strong and give greetings to the children. Many kisses from your mother.

Many greetings to the Sokolowski family. I am sending all our ration cards for clothes and your ration card for food. Use them; it can help you a lot.

Translation of Ida's parents' last letter.

The woman the Sokolowskis knew, with whom they hid me after the visit from the gendarmes, was expecting a child. She was an ill-natured woman who treated me as her little maid-of-all-work, got me to clean the lavatories and spoke to me in such a hurtful way! I was very unhappy there; it was total exile.

As the situation was getting worse from day to day, the Sokolowskis set about finding a solution. The man at the Préfecture with whom they were friendly said: "Look, there are organizations which look after children." They then got in touch with the O.S.E.

I was soon placed in hiding outside Montpellier with a non-Jewess. It was at the time of Yom Kippur, at the beginning of autumn. I was dying of hunger at her place, while she had big baskets of grapes that tempted me. I pinched some in passing and felt horribly guilty for "stealing," stupid as I am.

I remember that I fasted on Yom Kippur. She found nothing better to give me on the eve of Yom Kippur than pork pickled in salt or pig in some other form. How could she know?

But in these circumstances, when it's a matter of life and death, you have no choice. I tried to reassure myself with the thought that my parents had got me to eat non-kosher meat. So I ate and I was thirsty the whole day. I was dying of thirst.

The woman had a meadow with a goat that I had to look after. One day she gave me a newspaper to keep for her and the goat gobbled it up. I thought she was about to kill me!

I was alone, I didn't see anyone; I had practically nothing to do. Hidden away, cut off from the world, I couldn't stand it any longer, so I began to say that I wanted to go to school. I kept repeating that I wanted to go to school, not to this woman but to the people of the O.S.E. It was they who had put me in this place, after all. They had taken me there like someone who been blindfolded and just dumped...

I constantly said: "I want to go to school, I want to go to school, I want to go to school..." In my little head, something had "clicked." If everything comes to a stop, if there's no family, if you're alone, there's school, a place where life is still possible, where you are one individual among others, where courage, intelligence and effort can pay off.

Instinctively, I knew it was the only place where I could survive. I insisted so much, I pestered them so often that one fine day in September or October 1942, a certain Madame Mazour, a very nice lady with a smiling face, came to fetch me.

I suddenly saw someone who spoke to me in a human way. She respected children; there was something welcoming about her. Moreover, she was educated – a Doctor in Biology – and good-looking. One felt she was someone who wasn't helpless, someone with whom one could identify.

She had long been working with the O.S.E. She took me to an O.S.E. home called Le Couret near Limoges. The place seemed to me horrible. It was a home just for girls, but there was a school.

The home was directed by a couple. She, a super-intellectual, gave classes in Latin, which fascinated me. I was very pleased. In three weeks, I had reached the same level in Latin as the others. I was at the top of the class; I was jubilant.

I studied from morning until night. It was fantastic, apart from all these girls who walked around completely naked, sang, squabbled and exhibited all the meannesses of a little feminine society with which I was unfamiliar and which I can't stand even today.

A rather hard Polish Jewess woke us up as early as six o'clock in the morning. It was cold in winter in the Limoges area. We were taken outside: we had gymnastics in the freezing morning air and then cold showers. In short, it was a very maternal environment, very family-like, very warm, very pedagogic.

I was as wretched as could be. Without my studies and one or two nice girls, I would have died, or just about.

In addition, I still hadn't had any news of my brother or sister. I didn't know where they were; I didn't even know if they were alive. I didn't know a thing.

Until one day, miraculously, a letter arrived, I don't know by what means. They had written to me. They were at Moissac; they were alive. My brother wrote: "I'm having my Bar-Mitzvah on the fifth of December and I'm inviting you...!"

I stood with the letter in my hands, looking out at the landscape. How beautiful it was. We picked beechnuts and ate raw chestnuts. I liked to run in the meadows...

The Dream

How does one make
the dream become reality?
Believe, and work
for it to come about!

December 19, 1982

SURVIVAL

One day my son Olivier, when he was still small, said to me, "But mummy, if the Germans were after you, you must have had to run awfully fast in order not to get caught!"

When I read my parents' last letters now with the eyes of an adult, I am each time more conscious of their pain. Their whole concern was to find a way to do something for us, to help us materially, to help us spiritually, to find a way to give us strength.

So I succeeded in keeping in touch with my parents until nothing more was known of them. Only the card thrown from the train by my father showed us that he was all alone, deprived of everything and traveling in an unknown direction.

And then there were other miracles thanks to which I remained alive. Because this wasn't all: believe it or not, French gendarmes came once more to arrest me, this time at the Sokolowskis as I hadn't turned up at the camp of Les Milles. They really needed me!

They searched the whole house from top to bottom, the entire length and breadth of it. I was in the toilet and there they didn't look, and yet it was just opposite the entrance.

One night not long ago I dreamed of a cake. I work a great deal on my dreams: it's my way of tracking down my true hidden self. I dreamed I was making cakes on black baking-sheets as my mother did in Germany. One took them to the baker's or we put them in the oven ourselves.

In the dream, there were slabs and I made something like pizzas and *hallot* (braided bread made for the Sabbath), but the two resembled one another. I suppose it is my way of placing myself between the Jewish world and the outside world.

I also dreamed of eiderdowns. Eiderdowns and baking-sheets are key instruments for living, connected with my parents' home. We wouldn't leave without our eiderdowns, and we took them with us when we left Antwerp.

If you have an eiderdown, you won't die of cold even if you no longer have a roof over your head. And what about the baking-sheets? With them, you continue to feed the family. Even if you have only a tiny quantity of flour and a little water, you make challah and pizza. It's survival!

But this is not enough: you also have to know how to survive!

Why the baking-sheets and eiderdowns of my dream? It was because it was as though life had come to a stop at that point, as if something had been blocked forever which I tried to recreate by literally reinventing it, as it was impossible to reproduce in a stereotyped manner.

I couldn't recreate a framework similar to the one that formerly existed. It was thirty years before I was able to open a prayer book and pray. Until my return to Israel, I couldn't say a prayer aloud.

To return to the family mould, to conform to the model of one's parents was no longer possible; it was death. I'm far from being the only person to react in this way: three generations have been affected in the same way as I was: the grandparents, the parents and the children.

And I tremble to think that this could be passed on to the children's children. But in order that this should not happen, it is necessary that the children should see clearly where they are concerned.

For many people, it was only possible to live afterwards if one escaped from Judaism, or rather its forms – anything that even remotely resembled certain images from one's previous life, anything that was perceived as something dangerous, something doomed to death, something fatally associated with death.

If you stick your finger in it, you're caught, you're dead. And after the war, many people said, "Anything, but not that for my children! Anything, but not *that*: we don't want any more of it!" They preferred to have them learn the catechism, to see them assimilate. They wanted to forget, not to have anything to do with it. And in this way, they themselves carried out the ultimate death-sentence.

They remained physically alive but no longer existed as what they were. In a way, it was hardly worth their having survived.

It's a hard thing to say: I wish them to be in good health, but can they ever enjoy good health? I doubt it, because nobody can live if he cuts himself off from his roots and stifles his inner nature.

It's as though you took a tree, and in order to give it life and allow the sap to rise, you made a hole and filled its roots with cement.

On the one hand, I felt I couldn't live without this heritage: Shabbat and the holidays were paradise, they were life, and on the other hand, every time I approached this world – and I know people who still feel this way – my sore point was touched and I couldn't bear it. I drew close to my world, but it was like a mirage: it wasn't *it*; it was never it. Never. I will never find it again.

We had been completely cut off from our roots because we were cut off from everyone in our background. We were the only ones in France, cut off from a huge family, which had disappeared or had been dispersed in other countries.

Alone in France, without any surviving relative, without anyone who could tell you your grandfather's name, without even a photo, with nothing, nothing, nothing – not even a single object.

After the flood, we were cast adrift stark naked, at least morally speaking, and physically we were left in total solitude.

What we had been through had transformed us to such a degree that supposing that suddenly – *abracadabra* – our home and our parents had been restored to life, that everything was once more as if nothing had happened, we would never have been able to reintegrate into our surroundings.

We were no longer the same: fate had left its mark. Impossible to go back.

In any case, not to advance is to retreat, and to retreat is to die. Go forward or perish! We would say this laughingly with my brother; we said it with regard to our studies; but it applied to everything. We couldn't allow ourselves any leeway.

Some people have "luck." They always remain in the same groove; they always repeat the same gestures mechanically. There is no break in their lives; they have no problems. Everything is taken for granted; everything is as natural as breathing, as comfortable as a piece of clothing made to measure passed on from mother to daughter, and so forth.

I'm always flabbergasted when I see families which haven't been touched. For me, it's unthinkable. To have a loft, family photos, objects handed down from one's grandfather or grandmother, or even from one's parents, is beyond my comprehension.

After the war, we found relatives in England, but it was too hard: we felt ourselves to be strangers, and this feeling of not being able to speak the same language was terrible.

We had become children from institutions; children abandoned to nature, children who had become old even before they had been young.

We had the good fortune to have been given a home at Moissac, but what institution, however remarkable, could ever replace one's own family?

Moissac, as we saw it at the time, was – despite all – exile and assimilation. I'll never forget my father's expression on the day a "little boy scout," one of the heads of the E.I. movement,[1] came to fetch my brother and sister to take them to Moissac.

He was very pleasant, very obliging. But when my father saw him with his short pants and his very French manner, he turned sadly towards my mother. He didn't say to her: "How horrible, my children are being taken away from me!"

And God knows his heart was bleeding at this forced separation. He said, "Look! They're going away with *shkutzim*."[2] It was true, although relatively so. They were very assimilated, very gallicized. He had seen that at once. That was his sole concern: that his children should not lose their identity.

---

1. E.I. is E.I.F., *Éclaireurs Israélites de France* (Jewish Scouts of France).
2. *Shkutzim*, non-classy gentiles.

Moissac

A place of life and light
amidst our misery,
Hakadosh Baruch Hu
sent us the E.I.,
Shatta and Bouli
to save our skins
and enable us to survive.
Children who had come out
of the camp
without their parents
had the good luck
to be taken in
by this children's home
like a permanent scout camp.

I see before me a clean, attractive house,
tablecloths, flowers...
no tears –
children who laugh and play,
play pranks, study and pray.
Life goes on...
Here they think of
providing us with food and clothes
while in the world outside
they hunt us down.
They teach us a trade
and to live in society;
we dance, we sing,
we go away
on holiday
to movable camps.

We talk, make friends.
The leaders are there
to protect us from the
murderous designs
of the Nazi fiends.

They hide us with the French
with false papers for each one
and then come and see us
so that the time
will not seem too long.

Then, after the war,
we return to this home
as to family,
united in a common sadness
though hidden
(for life must continue)
and in the satisfaction
of still being there.
Each of us went his way
with all he received;
our friends remained
our family,
Shatta and Bouli
our ultimate address.

We thank them for these years,
which gave us so much
in a time of distress:
Shabbat, holidays, birthdays,
our Jewish collectivity regained...
dignity maintained
however great
the difficulties were!
That's the greatness of the Jews,
amidst the horror,
solidarity;

but some equal to the task
there must always be!

Jerusalem, January 28, 1994

MOISSAC – MY STROKE OF LUCK

Compared with my parents' home, how wretched Moissac was! And yet, their way of doing things was one of the best possible in the situation.

At Moissac they saved your skin, but at the same time you couldn't be truly who you were.

In a sense, it was the most brilliantly conceived orphanage that anyone could have thought of. The circumstances were such that nobody could have done better, but all the goodwill in the world can never replace the presence of one's parents.

The home had been founded by some of the heads of the Éclaireurs Israélites de France, a youth-movement created by some remarkable personalities, including Castor (R. Gamzon) and Edmond Fleg, who in the 1920s became aware of the need for a Jewish scouting movement.

Previously, people went to the *Scouts de France*. It was very well-regarded. They went to the Catholics, or rather, to the Unionists, the Protestants. It was the great fashion, the "*ne plus ultra.*" One was very glad to have been accepted, that one wasn't treated as a verminous Jew! As soon as you were taken on by the Unionists, you were no longer a Jew from the other side of the Danube.

One had to show one's credentials and not be a seller of *shmattes*[1] at the Carreau du Temple... that "Temple Square" where you were at home and sold shmattes. You'd been thrown out of your true Temple, and all you could do to subsist was to sell shmattes. It was all you were allowed to do.

This integration had its value, but at what cost for the Jewish identity?

So a Jewish movement was set up, which was autonomous while maintaining brotherly relations with the other movements. Those in charge were highly respected persons: engineers from the *grandes écoles*

---

1. Rags in Yiddish

(the most prestigious professional colleges) or academics – a social status that saved many French Jews, at least those who had been in France for more than a generation, those who didn't live in ghettos, and sometimes, following after them, a few of their brethren who had arrived more recently.

But where their Judaism was concerned, they were at the point of death. It was only with the arrival of the foreign Jews that they were re-judaized.

Thus the achievement of the Éclaireurs Israélites de France was quite extraordinary.

Shatta, the woman-director of Moissac, was a "monument," a person overflowing with vitality, just like her family, which had immigrated from Rumania.

She had married Bouli, the son of an old French Jewish family. Having an excellent sense of survival, she had always known how to put herself on the side of the strong, trying to take hold of them in order to use them. Instead of being the alien, the victim, she went together with the powerful.

One day her mother, Madame Hirsch, told me the story of their family. It was a veritable saga. Her parents had died very early, and so, as a very young girl, she had five younger brothers and sisters on her hands. In order to marry her, a *shidduch*² was proposed, and the only condition she made was that the husband should take the five brothers and sisters into his household.

And that is how, already in the previous generation, it became normal for this family to look after other people's children, even a great many of them – a task which requires one to be resourceful, combative and very courageous.

One could in no way resemble the "degenerates" of the sixteenth *arrondissement* who expect the maid to bring them their croissant on a silver tray and are no longer capable of budging even when it is a matter of saving their skins.

It must be said that these eastern European Jews who were regarded as savages were really full of life, because being poor and unassimilated, with a very distinct identity, they always had to fend for themselves in adverse conditions of persecution or at any rate of rejection.

When nobody accepts you, you have to prove that you live somewhere, that you have the right to receive recognition.

---

2. An arranged match

So Shatta created in the Avenue de Ségur, at the headquarters of the Éclaireurs Israélites, as a prelude to the children's homes, a sort of center to which children could come, which was an innovation for the time.

In 1939, in view of the danger of war and of air raids, they evacuated all their scouts and succeeded in finding a building in the South of France to house them. It was 18 quai du Port at Moissac, a very pretty place, for Shatta by no means lacked a sense of the aesthetic.

There they created a kind of strategic retreat in the form of a permanent scout camp, having become masters of the art of organizing groups of children not by means of coercive measures but by inviting their participation in a cheerful and lively setting. In a scout uniform, everyone is equal. Clearly, all sorts of principles were involved, but at that period I didn't care about it.

Their pseudo-military trappings and all the rest of it seemed to me ridiculous. I was in no state for playing or pretending, but it was an excellent school for learning resourcefulness.

When scouts arrive in a place with their minimal equipment, they make do with what they find and life goes on. When you've passed through this school of having to invent out of nothing, you become capable of using your hands, you are able to size up a situation and recognize a path even when it isn't clearly marked; you're able to work in a team, take initiatives and assume responsibilities – a training quite different from that of school, mother, daddy and the maid.

There, people were given responsibilities at a very young age. And above all – and this was of primary importance – they weren't pariahs, as we were in Berlin, more or less penned up in a ghetto of Jewish aliens. They were fully fledged citizens.

There was no lack of visitors at Moissac. Officials of non-Jewish scout-movements and even senior representatives of the Vichy régime came to make inspections, and all these highly placed people greeted one another and were on familiar terms.

Moreover, relationships and even friendships were formed with the surrounding population.

You see, someone like Bouli, who had been educated in France, had school-friends who were deeply integrated into society.

If you were ever in trouble, you could give someone a ring; you knew on whom you could count, you knew on whom you couldn't. It wasn't as it was with us, Martians parachuted into the place, disconnected from everything, rejected everywhere, still under the shock of Berlin, where neighbors who previously had been nice to you from one day to the next no longer dared to greet you and, what is worse, already eyed your possessions.

So, in the house of the O.S.E., I'd received my brother's letter inviting me to Moissac for his Bar Mitzvah.

I borrowed five francs from the girls and I took the train at the risk of my life (it was in 1942).

One had first to go to Limoges and then take the train for Moissac near Montauban.

Trains were few and far between, and with my Jewish looks and the fear that grabbed my innards, which was probably visible to everyone for miles around, it was really dangerous.

I'll never forget the station at Limoges at two o'clock in the morning with the Germans on guard. These soldiers kept going endlessly to and fro along the platform.

Waiting for the train to arrive, I thought I was going to die twenty times over. Twenty times is an understatement! The train arrived; I got in. All my limbs were shaking.

German soldiers came in and sat down in the same compartment. I said to myself: "You're scared to death, my girl. Calm down, it can be noticed!"

I must have turned green, greener than their uniforms. I had pains in my stomach, I had pains everywhere. I was sick, sick, sick.

I got out in the early morning hours at the station at Moissac. Nobody knew I was coming. The way from the station – a little provincial station – to the children's home seemed interminably long. I had to pass along an endless canal, and everything seemed so sad and gray.

I got to the door. I saw children playing ball and I said to myself, "They're crazy! How can they play?"

At the time I arrived, they were clearing the decks for action. It was the day before the fifth of December, the anniversary of the founding of the home. This was the greatest of all days for the woman director of the place – "Her home, Our home."

They put on disguises – believe it or not – they put on disguises! It was a celebration in honor of all the bar mitzvahs together. It was a very healthy manifestation and really a very good thing.

But I had come from another world, I had returned from beyond the grave. So, did Shabbat, Bar Mitzvahs, football still exist? I thought they must have been out of their minds. The Boches would come and arrest everyone; they'd be there in five minutes! I ran backwards and forwards.

Every evening, when the staff members were playing cards after the children had gone to bed, I got up, went up to them and said, "For heaven's sake, do something. Can't you hear them? I hear their jackboots, I hear the sound of their lorries. They're going to take us, they'll take us all. Do something: wake up!"

Some of them still remember this. They were there every evening. They sat together, they smoked, they played cards. I couldn't understand what was going on.

I found my sister there and my brother, who celebrated his Bar Mitzvah the next morning. Well, celebrated is an exaggeration in view of what we would have liked.

There was an awful contrast between what should have been and what existed in fact, but at least he had his two sisters with him.

We had a terrific reunion. We spent whole days walking around arm-in-arm, telling our stories. I had been under a heavy weight, having held things in for three months already.

Three months? What am I saying? August, September, October, November – nearly four months in which I had not really spoken to anyone.

At least my brother had had his Bar Mitzvah and I was in Moissac. Moissac was a place where one could live, very different from the O.S.E. institution with its drab and constricting atmosphere.

Shatta had her faults, but she was very intelligent. At Moissac, you felt the palpitation of life. The system functioned on the model of the Éclaireurs Israélites: activities were organized for the children by the children, with a whole hierarchy of chiefs and deputies and a variety of inter-relationships between children and adults.

It was a healthy atmosphere and certainly a good one, but I felt myself to be terribly out of place and everything seemed to me a vain pretence: the scout salute, the totems,[3] the scout promise. I said to myself, "They're crazy. What do they think they're doing?" For me, all such performances were over; I only had time for serious things.

Often, sudden scenes would occur. Once, in the first days I was there, I was looking for my sister in this large house built around an internal

---

3. Nicknames given in special ceremonies

courtyard where the lavatories were situated on the ground floor. I came into this courtyard and I was told, "Your sister is here." At the moment she came out of the toilet, I heard Shatta beginning to scream as if my sister had committed a crime. She simply hadn't pulled the chain.

I think Shatta was not very fond of my sister, who always said what she thought. She wasn't one to accept automatically what she was told. At the age of six, she was already capable of getting up and saying to her teacher, *"Herr Neumann, Sie sind ungerecht"* – you're being unfair!

Seeing her scolded in this way was a double shock for me, first of all because my poor sister was being mistreated, and secondly because I discovered the sort of place I was in – a place where everyone had to line up in front of Shatta's door. She knew how to make people run after her: she was the head, the big boss.

So, once the Bar Mitzvah was over, she decided there was no room for me; I'd have to leave and go back where I came from.

There were reasons for this: they couldn't get me a ration-book.

I began to cry; I cried non-stop. I laid siege to her office. The secretary, a nice woman, was moved to pity. She thought a bit and said to me: "I've got an idea. You must be one or two years younger or one year older – I no longer remember – and that will do the trick."

As has often happened in my life, the situation was being reversed.

They had to find me an occupation. Everyone went to the school or to the workshop, but I was here today and gone tomorrow; I was on a visit, difficult to fit in. So they sent me to the younger children's house to make the beds.

As I was meticulous, a *"yekke,"* I made the beds in the way my mother did, and as with everything I do, I tried to do it well. They had never seen beds made in this way before: the woman in charge of the children was amazed. She ran to Shatta, saying, "Come and see how she makes the beds. This girl's okay."

That's how it was at Moissac. There were the girls who were okay and the girls who were not. There were the pretty girls and the girls who weren't. She said that I made the beds in a certain way and I ought to be kept. It was almost as if you had to ask forgiveness for being there.

I don't know what else happened. I think that at that time they must have sent my brother to the Alps, to a rest home created by Shatta because he had been in a preventorium.

As for my sister, I think they had already placed her in hiding near Grenoble, and so I remained alone in Moissac and I fell ill. I began to cough: I coughed and coughed. I'm sure I hadn't caught anything, but I was in the grip of a sort of irrepressible cough, which frightened people, so they sent me to the sick-room.

I was sick and in a very bad state. I was given honey; I had my personal ration in a bowl in the sick room. One evening, two young "patrol leaders," lovebirds who had been lingering outside, came in quietly. They were hungry. They went to the sick room, found my honey and ate it up. I couldn't believe my eyes!

How could people take something that belonged to someone else, and a sick person at that?

For them, it was quite harmless, but for me it was a sign that you don't count for anything, that you are *hefker* – abandoned, left hanging in the air. Nobody respects you or what you have. You have no corner of your own: you have nothing, you *are* nothing.

Shatta had no notion of this principle of having a corner of your own. On the slightest pretext she would take you out of your room. On the slightest pretext she would put you somewhere else. She would say to you: "If you don't like it, my dear, you can take the train tomorrow... "

Where would you take the train to, I ask you!

She wasn't fully aware and was ignorant of the most elementary psychological principles. She acted with the means at her disposal. She had the gift of preserving life in the most difficult circumstances, and this she succeeded in doing. She kept the home going with Bouli; she knew how to *shnorr*[4] money and arrange everything nicely. It worked, things continued and life went on.

Stronger than anything or anyone, believe it or not, she even stopped the trains! The stationmaster stopped the Bordeaux-Marseilles express for her: "Madame Simon wants to get on." And Madame Simon got on the train dressed in her grand uniform. If she was late, the train waited. She always achieved what she wanted. That was her good side.

But every coin has its reverse side. Some former members of Moissac to this day have difficulty in getting over her authoritarian ways.

As for me, I was a good little girl. I didn't want to give anyone any trouble. I only wanted to please, to do good, and I had a good sense of how to avoid situations where I'd receive blows.

---

4. To beg

I knew that I was naked in body and soul, that I couldn't do anything and I had no control over anything.

My only resource was my head, my diplomacy. I tried to get around obstacles, to attain my objectives in this world of all-powerful adults, to succeed despite everything in not being "slaughtered," to build my own little place in the sun, and to do this without destroying anything, without saying anything bad about anyone. That's how I had been brought up.

I remember that my first reaction when I was put in a room was, "There are some here who are smaller than I am."

Children would gather around me, would tell me their stories, their troubles.

I listened and consoled them as well as I could. I must have been fourteen years old. One thing I knew, and that's that I wouldn't open my mouth to speak ill of anyone at all, nor say anything about myself to anyone except my brother and sister, and even then... Except for them, I erected a barrier in order to survive. There was no substitute for the affection I had known, and I think that if anyone had wanted to show me affection, I wouldn't have been able to bear it. I remember that one of the girl chiefs once took me by the shoulder. It made me tremble; it was unbearable. I didn't feel it could be genuine. If one responded, one would inevitably be disappointed once again. I preferred not to respond and to remain outside.

I think psychotics react in this way. Having been abandoned again and again, they build a wall, and – that's it! – they never again want any contact with anyone and will never again be able to enter into a real relationship.

At Moissac during the war, the comfort was very relative. In the morning, we washed in cold water. We all lined up in front of a row of wash basins, each one in front of his tiny jet of water. The water was carried by a long pipe in which there were holes.

For me, material comforts are secondary, but the human milieu is of primary importance. These Jewish scouts were very assimilated, very gallicized, and I was a little Jewess who had landed amongst Jews who were no longer so Jewish in the way that I understood it.

They spoke Yiddish but were somewhat vulgar, lacking Jewish values and knowledge. Nobody, or hardly anyone, any longer knew what the Jewish holidays were. Nobody knew how to keep Shabbat. Hardly anyone really knew how to say prayers in Hebrew. Kosher eating was not given much importance.

It was I who, on arriving there, taught them to sing "*Ve'hi she'amda*."[5]

However, Leo Kohn, a German Jew who had emigrated to France, had already taught them a few Hebrew songs. He had contributed a few things and very gradually begun to undertake the process of a return to tradition.

At the beginning, prayer was confined to *Adon Olam* and *Aleinu Le'shabe'ah*, and it made me laugh to hear them.

I remembered my father's *bon mot* about this. He would say laughingly, "If you only say *Adon Olam* and *Alenu*, you'll only have the *kopf* and the *schwanz* of the *herring*" – you'll only have the head and the tail of the herring.

Of course, what I'm saying here is very subjective, and is relative to what I had known previously. The milieu was what it was, but I had a defensive reaction, a protective shell.

I saw them playing ball, flirting, daydreaming, but I had my own agenda: I devoted myself solely to working and study and more study. I was there; I had managed to remain there because I was good at making beds and I had touched the heart of the secretary who must have put in a good word for me to Shatta, or was it me who eventually touched Shatta's heart? I no longer know. I stayed on.

At Moissac in December 1942, the Germans already came with lists of people to arrest. Many children had to be dispersed and hidden. Héron, Fanny Alter's husband, who was later executed by the Germans, was still there.

I wanted to prepare for my *certificat d'études* (the elementary school final examination), and Héron helped me. When the day of the examination arrived, it was once again Shabbat as it had been in Le Sablet. So I said no and didn't appear. I was the only one who didn't except for a boy, Charles Landau, who is now on a kibbutz in Israel.

They managed to arrange things so that we sat for the exam on another day some months later in a different village, Beaumont-de-Lomagne.

I'll always remember a mistake I made in the dictation. The examiner spoke with the local accent. She said, "*Les vaches broutent des ronces*" (the cows graze on thorns), and I wrote "*rances*" with an "a," which means stale butter, and this spelling-mistake was a terrible crime. I didn't know

---

5. "It was this (Providence) which helped our ancestors and us"... a passage from the Passover Hagaddah.

the word "*rances*"; I'd merely written down what I'd heard. My French still wasn't too good.

I wasn't strong in sewing and drawing. A very nice girl sitting next to me gave me some help, and after the exam we started up a conversation. She was from a Jewish family living at Beaumont-de-Lomagne. The father had just been arrested and the mother was there with several children.

"So where do you come from?"

"I come from Moissac, a Jewish children's home."

"Then, why didn't you sit for your examination there?"

"Because it was on Shabbat."

Then I had an idea: I put them in touch with the person accompanying us. Eventually, the people at Moissac managed to hide the entire family.

One of the little girls in this family, the smallest, was later hidden with me. When she came on a visit this year from Canada, she searched for three weeks all over the place until she found my address in Paris.

One day, I received a telephone call: "It's Edith. I absolutely have to see you." She wanted to remind me of this episode.

I only remembered that she had been hidden with me and I probably did whatever I could to ensure that she'd be as little unhappy as possible. But that was all.

When we were at the high school, every Friday evening at a certain moment she would close her desk during evening prep, step over all the benches, come up to me, hug me, kiss me and whisper in my ear "Shabbat shalom, Shabbat shalom" very softly so that nobody would hear. I was her little mother or big sister.

So she had come to Paris to pay me a visit and to tell me that she had four huge, strapping young sons and a husband who had also been at Moissac, and that they earned a good living in Canada.

At Moissac, Héron and his wife had interceded on my behalf, asking the people in charge not to force me to learn a manual occupation for which I was so ill-suited. Manual labor was fashionable at that period; the Vichy régime praised its benefits. For the scouts, it was an opportunity to give back to the Jews – who for too long had been up in the air immersed in study – the use of their hands. But above all, all these children would very soon have to make a living. In this way, my brother ended up in a workshop for wrought iron and my sister in a dressmaking class.

Influenced no less by the situation than by the prevailing ideology, the Jewish leaders embraced the ideas of their persecutors.

Saül, who learned electricity, is today an electronic engineer in Israel; my brother, who learned to make wrought iron, is a pediatrician; my sister, who did dressmaking, is a psychiatrist, and Daniel who learned electricity is an aeronautical engineer in Israel.

All those who had something in them, and who came from families – I won't say "good" families, but close families where there was a real Jewish atmosphere from which they drew the strength which sustained them and held them together, and where cultural values were a driving-force – all these pursued their studies alone, often working at the same time to earn a living.

After Beaumont-de-Lomagne, I was sent, together with some others, to Le Sappey, where my brother already was, and from there we were transferred to a large building, a former hotel, in La Grave in the Italian zone, where we were with Fanny and her husband Héron.

Héron had been won over to my cause, and did his best to enable me to continue studying. He gave us lessons, and his influence counted for something when very soon afterwards, in April 1944, the children had to be dispersed and hidden under assumed names.

We were placed in accordance with decisions concerning our future, which had already been made. There were a few privileged cases: someone whose mother looked after the laundry-room, someone who was already a "big chief," someone whose mother directed another children's home and someone whom one of the chiefs considered super-intelligent. These went to the *lycée* (high school), and all the others, the foot-sloggers, were sent to peasants or priests.

You see, my whole life has consisted of a series of lucky breaks, but breaks depending on what is known as *nosei hen*[6] – finding favor with somebody.

All of a sudden, you find someone on your path, a *malach*[7] – someone who does what he has to do in order to enable you to continue on your way. He is a messenger, an "angel," according to the Jewish concept. He has a mission, something he must do, some precise thing at exactly that time and place.

---

6. Literally, "bearing grace in someone's eyes."
7. Angel, messenger

So Héron believed I ought to be placed in hiding in a high school. His wife was of the same opinion (she was the Fanny who had thought I made beds well. She now felt that I ought to be supported in my wish to study).

Fanny was in charge of the younger children's house. Her husband was executed a short time afterwards and she never remarried. She looked after children all her life.

So they pleaded for me to be placed in a high school, and I was really very happy about it as I would have found it difficult to be with a family. It was better to keep one's anonymity and to be left in peace than to be looked after the wrong way. Better a railway station entrance hall than a strange family.

We spent several pleasant months at La Grave. My brother was there; there was snow. The scenery was magnificent. We stayed opposite the glacier of la Meije in a former hotel – I don't know how they got it – and the whole group was very congenial. I got on very well with my brother; he was someone who belonged to my world.

The mountains were splendid, and I loved running about. You know, what I particularly like is to run on the slopes over the moss, to feel the grass, to hear the little mountain streams, the torrents at their birth. I love the whole landscape of the upper valleys. There my health is at its best. To each his own temperament and his own landscape.

Our group naturally had its own little folklore. We didn't stay long at La Grave as we very soon had to be dispersed once more.

I remember the day I was given my "*bifteck*" (beefsteak), a false identity-card with an assumed name: Irène Turlin. My great fear was not to remember this new name.

I'll never forget that journey. We crossed the whole breadth of France and I was taken to Sainte-Foy-la-Grande, somewhere in the Gironde beyond Moissac near Bordeaux, and hidden in a girls' school with some other children from Moissac who had already been placed there and whom I found again.

I was again separated from my brother who was sent to a convent, to some "good" sisters. It was quite a business. The one good sister gave him a bed next to a seminarist instructed to convert him and who worked on him from morning to night. And she tapped him on the head to make him kneel down, saying, "Boy, do your duty," – that is, pray like the Catholics! But he obstinately refused to allow himself to be converted because he remembered the passage from the portion *Re'ei* in Deuteronomy 13, which he had studied with my father, and which says that if anyone tells you that all that is written in the Torah is false or no longer valid, you will know that he's a false prophet.

And that's how he held out, how he didn't let himself be persuaded. And when he left, the good sister – the same good sister who put the seminarist in the bed next to him – said to him, "Congratulations on your courage and determination. I only wish all our Christians were like you!"

As for me, I was at Sainte-Foy-la-Grande. I hadn't been in the first form in high school; I went directly into the second form, but it was almost the end of the school year.

After three or four months I spent in the second form, it was already the summer holidays. I had to write compositions: I was going crazy.

I was always frightened of not being up to the mark. I wasn't with it; I wasn't used to their way of doing things, their paraphernalia.

Every time I gave in some homework, I wept out of desperation: I thought it must be bad. But when the results came out, it was "Irène Turlin seventeen, Irène Turlin eighteen." All the others were resentful. They thought that I was putting on an act, but I wasn't.

I worked according to an ideal which was different from theirs. And still today, I don't work according to other people's criteria: I work in accordance with my own demands.

Then we had to be dispersed once again, and I didn't enter the third form at all. I have all sorts of memories connected with this boarding school whose headmistress took great risks in agreeing to shelter Jewish children.

Two of the teachers even took the initiative of coming to see me at the home of Monsieur Gros, an architect in the Sainte-Foy area with whom I was placed in the period before the liberation, when it became too dangerous to remain in the school.

I don't know how many kilometers these ladies traveled on bicycle or on foot to teach me math and French free of charge. I'd like to thank them in person.

In the boarding school, we, the six Jewesses, had to act a part. We had to say that if we didn't go to mass, it was because we were atheists. But everybody knew how things really stood.

The girls all had their food boxes and received from their farming parents all kinds of appetizing things that smelled good, while we were dying of hunger.

Do you think that any of them even once offered us something from her parcel, the tiniest morsel of anything whatsoever? No, never! Not one of them did, even once.

When they went home, we were glad. We got their eiderdowns and we were able to sleep without shivering all night long.

During the holidays, they went off, and we stayed in the school and turned around in circles. I swotted and swotted. All the girls played *belote* (a card game), and I studied. How can you play belote when you have the good fortune to be at school? I thought they were out of their minds.

I was always hungry. There was a great pile of rotten carrots. I took some and locked myself in the lavatories and munched them where I couldn't be seen.

In connection with the lavatories, I experienced a nightmare that troubled my sleep for years. The first night I was there, I had an urgent need to relieve myself, and I didn't know where the lavatories were. I went around and around in the darkness, bumping against the beds and the washbasins, not wanting to make a noise or to wake anyone up. I was a stranger, a complete stranger, totally at a loss, without anyone to guide me.

How long were we in this school? Perhaps from April to June 1944.

Then I was hidden with this architect. The air raids increased, and I suppose it became too dangerous for us to remain in a group: people began to become suspicious. It was fishy, this group of girls without parents hanging out there. Everyone realized why we were there, I'm quite sure.

At this architect's, they were very nice. They had two little girls. A Polish woman came to look after them. Her presence frightened me, because the Poles...

À propos of the Poles, did I tell you this story?

One day at Le Sappey, where my brother was, I was at a window shaking out a rug. A man passed by below. He raised his head, looked at me and said: "*Jidge, cholera!*"[8]

You know the Poles: they have a way of spotting a Jew at a glance. And I was dying of fear, that old fear which was awakening once again, and which I believe I have unfortunately handed on to my daughter.

---

8. "Jew... cholera!"

Ida Tieder, 1943.

Sarah, Martin and Ida Tieder, October 1945.

Ida Tieder, 1949.

Martin and Ida Tieder, Moissac 1945.

Ida Tieder with Régine Lehmann and two friends, Suzy and Lorette, at Moissac after the war.

18 quai du Port, Moissac; the first home in Moissac (photo taken 40 years later at a reunion of the former "children" of Moissac).

Moulin de Moissac, where the Moissac children's home was located after the war.

1950, Hospital, Broussais. Ida Tieder in her first year as a medical student (second from right).

The wedding of Ida and Fred. Sitting with Shatta and Bouli. Paris 1957.

Ida and Fred under the huppa. Rabbi Léon Ashkenazi (Manitou), spiritual leader of French-speaking Jewry after the war, conducts the ceremony. Paris 1957.

The marriage of Ida and Fred at the home of President Léon Meiss. Paris 1957.

A Rav

It's not only a paragraph
repeated by rote
as though through
a loudspeaker.
It's also a matter of the heart
from mouth to mouth,
of reanimation in Zion
and of daily comprehension.
A little glimmer of light
amidst our terror,
a pair of shoes in our hands
to walk with our own feet
on our common path,
a piece of bread
to assuage our hunger
and an immeasurable compass
finally
to reorientate us
to the East !

March 6, 1982

IDÉE FIXE: TO STUDY IS TO LIVE AGAIN

As soon as it was possible to circulate, at the time of the Liberation, I don't know how, all the children found their way back to Moissac. The home was no longer in the Quai du Port.

Shatta had succeeded in getting le Moulin, an enormous building used under the Vichy by *La Jeunesse et les Sports* (Youth and Sports). Préfet Rouanet, who was the chief administrator (*Préfet*) of the Tarn and Garonne area after the war, had gone out of his way to help Shatta as much as possible. The plight of these hundreds of children remaining there all alone, their parents having been massacred by the Germans, had touched some good-hearted people.

So Shatta had obtained for us le Moulin, beneath which flowed the River Tarn. It was a very large place with an immense diningroom, a fine kitchen, many rooms, and, at the top, a large terrace. Compared to le Moulin, the Quai du Port, over there, seemed small and uncomfortable.

In the former home, at night, we relieved ourselves in a bucket. In the morning we washed ourselves, all together, lined up in front of a row of washbasins, boys and girls in turn. You'd hear people yelling, "Close the door!"

Here, on the other hand, each room had its own washbasin, almost like a hotel. The upstairs rooms weren't heated, only the ground floor was, and everyone clung to the radiators, where places were precious and few and far between.

So the home had been reopened. Some people had left secretly for Israel, which was Palestine in those days.

Others prepared to leave for America, where they had found relatives who asked them to come.

Others had found their parents again and left us, and then there were... there were all the others who remained.

My favorite place at le Moulin was the large library crammed with books, called the "Maurice and Daniel Fleg Library." Both these people had died during the war, and Edmond Fleg and his wife had provided the funds in their memory.

This house soon became the nerve-center of the Éclaireurs Israélites, a rallying point with a vibrant cultural life.

Immediately after the war, the children who returned from deportation, from Poland and elsewhere, were taken to children's homes – Moissac among them. For us, it was terrific, and indeed, for me personally, because they spoke the same language as I did and they had the same sensibilities, the same references. Friendships were formed amongst us that have not grown weaker with time.

They arrived all swollen, with an expression you can never forget, and always with this fear of going without. You saw them taking a bag, going to the vineyards and bringing back mountains of grapes. What a to-do!

Some were really sick, sometimes with great problems. These two or three boys with whom we could laugh in Yiddish were like a breath of air from our own world, as though from beyond the grave, something irreplaceable, for even in this Jewish home we remained total strangers.

The others didn't belong to our world at all. Nearly all the children who were there came from more or less assimilated families. They had lost the Jewish essence we still possessed.

I told you how during my period in hiding I would go around reciting to myself prayers or phrases from the *Pirkei Avot*, the Ethics of the Fathers, and many other texts that I knew by heart simply because with us it had been our daily bread.

These survivors from Poland sang as we had done at home and could say my name in the same way as my parents had.

There were plenty of problems. The end of the concentration camps was not the end of the odyssey. One of them told us how, after he had been saved from a concentration camp, which was already his third, he was again dumped in a camp – this time for "displaced persons" – deep in the Russian zone, and was unable to leave it.

The high-ups at Moissac were not very appreciative of my sister's independent character, so she was sent to Agen to take her *baccalauréat* (matriculation) instead of staying at le Moulin. As if she hadn't done enough wandering around!

I remember I went to see her once or twice. She told me all her problems and asked me what I thought.

Well, what was I to say? She had passed her matriculation after preparing for it all by herself, and I turned out my pockets, took out the little money we'd been given for soap and shoelaces, and she left on her own. She was the first of us to settle in Paris, in 1946.

And my brother? I have no memory whatsoever of his being at Moissac after the war. I think he was sent to the Maimonides school in Paris.

As for me, perhaps because of my position in the family, I knew how to keep quiet, to remain in my place, to carry on with what I had to do, blind and deaf to anything else. It didn't seem to me very glorious, but in adversity one protects oneself as best one can...

Once again it was a struggle for who would have the right to continue their studies and who would not. There were those who had been hidden in high schools, the "pets" of those in charge – those who were geniuses in the opinion of such-and-such a leader. And then there were the pretty girls. The geniuses had the right to study and the beauties had the right to nice dresses – especially those whom the leaders had their eyes on!

This brief account may seem to you a bit mean, but many people had a feeling of injustice. There are injustices even in families, and everywhere you are dependent on the label that is stuck on you, which determines your present and your future.

Each collective carries the potential of a system whose inevitable outcome is the concentration camp unless there's a human consciousness determined to prevent it.

"Moissac," said Shatta, "is our home."

And, for my part, if I struggle, it is perhaps because of my messianic vision of the world, because of my demands, which perhaps exceed the limits of human possibilities. But if I have these demands, it is perhaps because of what I have passed through: "*Ki ger ha'yita be'eretz mitzrayim*"[1] And it's with this experience that I work.

When I set foot in a school, before I even open my mouth, the children know. They immediately feel that I'm not on the side of the "grown-ups," that I'm not there to benefit from the situation at their expense, that I'm not there in order to betray them. There's no need to say anything: they know.

Because basically they suffer from the same evil. Even if I don't do anything, they feel that I've experienced what they're going through, that

---

1. "Because you were a stranger in the land of Egypt."

I've come out of it, and that although I've been liberated from it, I haven't forgotten. Doctor though I may be, I'm not on the side of the "grown-ups."

Clearly, what the children perceive, the staff, those who pull the strings, also perceive, and you become totally insufferable to them.

At le Moulin, I had to keep a tight lid on myself. There was a great staircase; the whole group of chiefs was at the bottom near the radiator, and every time you went down the stairs, they looked at you coming down, and each one passed a comment. There you were, classified once and for all, labeled, put in a drawer.

So I assured my liberty through silence and a constant concealment of my inner self. This having been said, everyone liked me very much. I was the girl who was "okay" and who got the first prize for team spirit.

One had to study, so I studied. But on top of that, when one came back from school, one had to help with the chores, wash the stairs, sweep up, peel vegetables. Otherwise, one was called an "intellectual," as if one somehow had to pay for the privilege of studying.

Out of the blue, I was made a "troop leader." Why not lead a troop, look after others? But I didn't feel I had the vocation of someone gifted with authority. So I said to anyone willing to listen that it wasn't for me, that I couldn't start giving orders to a flock. It wasn't something I was able to do.

I was quite willing to do what I *was* able to do: speak with the girls and perhaps read them stories, texts, prayers, make commentaries. There I was already in my element, which was the human element, whether in direct contact with people or via some cultural or spiritual medium. And that's what I did.

I became a troop leader nevertheless, as those previously in charge had left. But when one had to set up a camp, I said, "I'm not going alone; you must give me some men. Practical organization isn't my strong point, and anyway I'm frightened in the dark... I can't keep all these girls under control; a person can only give what he's got."

I'm not a "leader of men," whatever people sometimes think on seeing me in certain tasks. I'm able to give something to the degree that I'm receptive to others, and that's it.

A great deal of water had to flow under the bridge before I could gain the slightest confidence in myself, and even then, everything collapses over the merest trifle.

So I went to school, where one had to succeed. One had to deserve the right to pursue one's studies; one absolutely had to be first in class because that was the condition. Without top marks, you no longer had the right to continue.

So I studied. I got up at dawn, at five or six in the morning. In a few minutes, I was on the banks of the Tarn. It was splendid; I like the morning very much. At that hour, my mind is very fresh and clear and I work very fast. In the evening I don't work well, but I sat up nevertheless.

But in fact, we didn't have the right to sit up at night: one had to go to bed at ten o'clock. Bouli made the rounds and turned off all the lights. Me, I went to bed fully dressed, waited until he passed and then got up again.

As I couldn't work in the bedroom as there were other girls there, I slipped into the little bathroom where the light didn't show as there were no windows, and there I studied.

In the daytime, one often had to learn in the midst of a lot of noise, while everyone peeled vegetables, accompanied by singing, shouts and interjections. More than a hundred young people screaming in the dining hall, and you had to revise!

Later on, I sometimes studied in bistros, but today I can no longer concentrate amidst noise. I have to close all the doors. I can no longer stand it if someone talks, or if someone is listening to a radio or television. My husband can't understand this. He's happy when everything is on and everything's functioning.

It's as if I have exhausted my reserve of resistance to noise.

So I studied. I was crazy with anxiety when I had to face a monthly exam.

I hadn't been in the first form or the third form; I had only done the last term of the second form. I was now in the fourth form of the E.P.S., the *École Primaire Supérieure* (Upper Primary School) at Moissac, a girls' school run by spinsters, where an extraordinary atmosphere prevailed.

You had "*la Fialon,*" as we called her, the teacher of physics and chemistry, a real caricature of an old spinster. When she conducted experiments with sodium chloride on the counter, it was like being at the cinema. She thrust herself forwards, grew agitated, stepped backwards, wriggled and cried, "Watch out, it's about to explode!"

One day, she turned to us: "You from over there, you from the *colo*!"[2] "You" was us, the "others." I don't know what else she said, but I got up suddenly and said to her: "Yes, if I understand correctly, Hitler didn't finish the job, and you're carrying on with it."

Deathly silence in the class.

Me, the good pupil, who always listened when the others played at noughts and crosses or knitted behind their raised desks; me, who always sat in the front row in order to hear – I gathered my things and went to sit at the back of the class.

The teacher was in such a state! She stopped everything, ceased paying attention to anyone, began to go in circles around the class, passing in front of me, sticking her nose in my copybook. I went on strike as a form of protest.

There was also a teacher of Spanish who gave us so-called French lessons. In reality, as he was studying for a B.A. at Toulouse, he spent the lesson time reading the texts he had to study, and from time to time read aloud to us a passage that particularly caught his fancy.

The girls spoke louder and louder. When the noise reached a certain level, he said, "They're going to drown my voice!" When he tested them, they slipped answers to each other. "At least do it discreetly!" he said. I can still hear the sound of his voice and his peculiar accent.

There was a lady I liked very much: Madame Arpaillange, the English teacher. Languages were my domain: I felt comfortable with all that was foreign! Quite apart from the fact that I had done some English in Germany, and that German and English are close, I liked languages and was eager to learn. This lady was a fine person, very kind; there was something engaging about her.

After the fourth form, they changed our school. Once again, there was a discussion: would they let us continue to study or not? Because, in the E. I. they had certain ideas: the necessity of regenerating the Jews, giving them manual occupations, encouraging the return to the soil. The very ideas promoted by Pétain.

But who could have succeeded in turning me into a manual worker? I had *zwei linke Hänte* – two left hands. I was a perfect *shlemazel*.

When I have to so something with my hands, I give all my mind to it. I concoct things with my hands, but at what a price!

---

2. Abbreviation of *colonie* (colony), equivalent to a summer camp. This was the name people gave to le Moulin.

I'm not one of those who can function easily in the world of concrete reality. It's really not my strong point, and with good reason. A reality like the one assigned to us, you run away from!

So it came up for discussion once more: were they going to let me continue my studies?

Academically speaking, I was behind schedule. I was already nearly twenty years old and I hadn't got my matriculation yet! Was age really a disadvantage?

I was with kids much younger than myself who had no understanding whatsoever of the wonderful texts that delighted me.

In English, Shakespeare – it was life. Writers were people who thought, who considered human problems; people with whom I had a direct communication, with whom I could reflect. It was the same in French and in philosophy.

In math, I stubbornly did my best; in physics, I didn't understand a thing but I persevered.

My frame of mind is more suited to things that are intuitive and human, but when it comes to logic, it has to be absolutely strict.

In those days, math, up to matriculation level, was still accessible to those who could more or less reason correctly and who took the trouble to memorize. Without being a genius in this area, I more or less managed. I tried very hard, as with everything.

I had the impression of not being gifted at anything and that everything was difficult for me. Everyone made fun of me, because every time I gave in a paper or had a surprise test, I was sick. I saw everything from the outside with the feeling that things were inaccessible.

And I struggled alone in my corner. When they gave us our work back, I always got 18, 16, 17, excellent marks, as when I was in hiding.

How they all looked at me at that moment! But the day before, nobody would have thought of giving me a word of encouragement.

In the same class as me, there was Suzy, who was also at le Moulin, and we walked to school together. We had no contact with the pupils who were not from le Moulin. I can even say that I didn't go into any of the shops at Moissac even once, not even to buy a cake.

With empty stomachs, we pressed our faces against the shop window and saw the "chiefs" treating themselves to delicious cakes! Only those who were in their good books were invited to try some. I didn't belong to any "court" although I wasn't on bad terms with anyone. I didn't have any enemies. I must say I made a heroic effort not to have any. My real self was set aside, placed under cover. I was "a good little girl," *ein gutes Kind*, a little machine to give all-round satisfaction.

On the surface, we weren't unfortunate. We had good chums, both boys and girls; we sometimes laughed like mad; we had some good times; we camped in nature.

We were decently dressed. Our uniform – a scout uniform – kept us warm. And quite exceptionally, I once had a dress made for me, while generally you went to the linen-room where you were palmed off with old shmattes, outfits that ladies in America and elsewhere no longer wanted. The woman in charge, of a certain age, very dignified, who looked like de Gaulle, would say to you, "But it's very nice, it's very pretty."

Whatever you happened to put on your back, it was always "very nice, very pretty." And today, I can no longer look at a pile of old clothes.

The other day, someone said to me, "There's a sale on at such-and-such a store." I made an effort; I went there, I entered. But when I see a pile of garments thrown together all mixed up, I can't go near it. I run away.

Later, in England, when we had spent a holiday there, they made us gifts, masses of shmattes bundled together in parcels, which we would gladly have thrown into the sea or have left on the boat, but there was always some kind soul who ran after us: "Miss, you've forgotten something." *Alte shmattes*!

These things may not seem important, but they gave you the feeling that you somehow didn't have any hold on your life, that you were tossed around like these parcels.

The only thing that you did have some hold on was studying. So all my energies went into that and into maintaining good relations with those on whom my life depended. What don't little children do to please their parents, their teacher or their schoolmistress?

And when I hear certain grown-ups say of children that they're "bad," I blow up inside.

At le Moulin, we had no contact with the surrounding population. Our sole horizon was the walk to and from the school, along the road at the edge of the canal.

But Shatta did have contact with the people of the town, which earned us some festivities. On November 11 and July 14 we were commandeered for the parade.

In an impeccable scout uniform, you marched in step and stifled your irrepressible laughter. Salutes and the "last post" in front of the First World War monument, and the litany of the names of those who died on the field of honor and those who died on the field of honor and those who died on the field of honor ...

All those who had fallen in the Great War, what could that mean to us? Our dead didn't die on the field of honor, they weren't buried anywhere, nobody blew a trumpet for them and for them there was no march past. What were we doing there? We were like "extras."

We had no contact with the town and yet, in comparison with the others at le Moulin, who didn't attend school outside, we were truly privileged, not only because we were able to study, but because we were able to leave le Moulin. We had the opportunity of escaping from this closed-in world where everyone stewed together. Imagine children who spend their entire lives in the family circle, who do not have the good fortune to go to school or the possibility of competing with others or having any other roles except those assigned them by the family neurosis.

For le Moulin also had its particular "neurosis," with its laws, its favoritisms and its labels – a whole more-or-less distorted universe. We had the great luck to get out a bit, even if it was only a matter of leaving every morning and seeing other faces. You took your distance and all of a sudden you regained your dignity.

I didn't stay long at this school. By the fifth form I was already in high school. It was better. The mentality there was completely different. First of all, it was mixed. There were boys, and for my part, I have always felt very bad in a world made up solely of women. It's usually mean and petty.

And then, in the new place, the spirit of the primary school was left behind. The atmosphere was far more liberal. They did nothing whatsoever there, nothing at all! The boys used all their wits to find ways of working as little as possible.

The math teacher, Monsieur Cerise, was there in the classroom, and the boys climbed on the benches, danced and sang. Every five minutes, the teacher got up, made circles in the air with his pen, pointed it towards the pupils and said, "I give you two hours of detention! I give you zero as a mark!" This only made the temperature rise further.

And the comedy came to an end when the door suddenly opened and the principal appeared. In a split second, everyone was seated. When the door was closed, the circus began again.

In the philosophy class, the teacher brought into the classroom a game of lotto to draw lots for the number of the person to be tested. So two boys, numbers ten and eleven, worked in collusion: whatever number was chosen, whether ten or eleven, it was always the same one who replied. They operated as if in tandem. One was dim and the other very smart; one solved the problems and the other wrote down the answers for both of them.

At the beginning of the lesson, the class prompted our pal Isy to raise his hand: "Go ahead!" He would ask some question, no matter what. The teacher would answer, and that took half an hour. None of the pupils stirred, permitting the teacher to exhaust the subject. Then he said: "Ah, now let's get back to the point!"

Immediately, they whispered, "Isy, go ahead!" He asked another question and the hour had gone by.

For twenty-five years, this teacher fingered the same pile of yellowing pages, which were his lessons. Always the same ones...

Fortunately, at le Moulin there were nevertheless a few people who, intellectually speaking, had something to give. So we formed a little group: Georges Levitte taught us genuine philosophy, and above all there was Régine Lehmann with whom we could discuss things. And as we had access to the library, we devoured tons of books.

Régine came to Moissac after the war; she joined as a volunteer. At first, people made fun of her because of her physical deformity, but the mockery soon ceased. She was the only one capable of accepting the children as they were, the only one capable of listening to them, of receiving them. She was the only one, or almost.

When people made fun of her, our little group tried to surround her a bit, protectively. For me, who came from a tradition where each individual is sacred, and for all my close friends, most of whom had returned from deportation, it was necessary to help one another, to protect the other person at all costs, whether he happens to be handicapped or not.

The fit person must help the handicapped and not treat him with ridicule.

Régine, for her part, had come out of a completely assimilated milieu. On seeing what had happened, she returned to Judaism.

During the war, she was in hiding in the Upper Loire. After meeting Samy Klein, the chaplain of the Éclaireurs Israélites, an exceptional man later killed by the Germans, she gradually found her roots again. After the war, she said, "If we've stayed alive, it's in order to do something with our lives." And she did.

So I went to high school; I sat for my matriculation at Montauban. In order to take one's matriculation, one had to arrive the day before the examination and sleep in a sinister hotel. Without anyone to whom I could really speak, I felt anguished and lost.

At Moissac, we were out of reality, or rather we lived in another reality that distanced us from our tragedy somewhat. Parents were not in the picture, their memory was completely repressed; they were thrust aside, they no longer existed and no one tried to replace them.

This was one of the characteristics of the genius of Shatta and the E. I. milieu. They tackled the problems which seemed to them important in a very precarious situation.

I'm infinitely grateful to each of them for what they did and I appreciate the magnitude of their task.

꧁꧁꧁꧁꧁꧁꧁

PART II

꧁꧁꧁꧁꧁꧁꧁

Reconstruction

Seasons

Woman and man
is not to go "whim-wham"
but to reunite
life's flame
and in a nest
to nurture
a family's soul.

It's spring:
The weather's fine.
One loves,
marries,
enters into life.

Summer comes...
One builds one's house,
consolidates the situation
with the sweat of one's brow
and the joy of all these blessings.

Autumn's here:
One's already on the other bank
of time.
The children
have flown off,
the fruit is ripe,
the harvest's good.
We, thank God,
still riveted
to our nest.
Time flies,

taking us with it,
but blessed be the grain
that prolongs
the chain
of generations
and brings us back
to Zion.

So winter
with God's help
and this return to our place
merges with our children's spring
and we shall not be losers
but the beneficiaries
of time
moving forward.

February 6, 1986

THE DOOR OPENS

I met my future husband on the boat on my first voyage to Israel. For him it was also his first voyage, organized by *les Étudiants Juifs de France* (The Jewish Students of France).

Going to Israel in 1953, such a short time after the war, was quite an expedition. One traveled on boats which crawled along for a week in somewhat precarious conditions, and rubbed shoulders with hundreds of young people from all over the world. It was the time when people were beginning to go to Israel.

In 1948, none of us truly realized what the creation of the State of Israel meant. One wanted to go to what was then called Palestine; one wanted to live there.

I have found a few of the letters I sent to my brother at that period, in which I spoke of my plans, the questions I had.

Every year, we asked ourselves what we should do; we searched out the possibilities available to us.

In Israel, one couldn't reckon on a scholarship to pursue one's studies, and if we didn't study, what would become of us? Only just out of Moissac, we were on the street without anything or anyone behind us. We weren't even French.

But as children of deportees from France, we were considered "war orphans," which gave us the right to a small stipend.

In every letter, we said, "I'd like to go to Palestine" (it embarrasses me to say Palestine today) – "I'd like to go to Palestine, but... "

It was the year of my baccalauréat (matriculation), and questions arose about my future. And then the years passed: 1947, 1948, 1949... and we still dreamed of going to Israel, and the same dilemma always cropped up: if I go there, I won't be able to study. Here I can get a grant.

Studying – always this same idea. Everything came down to studying. Why was it so important to study? Having been relegated to the status of pariahs, the scum of the earth, for us, as for all those who had preceded us throughout Jewish history, studying was a defensive reflex.

The Jews have been reproached for being intelligent; the Jews have been reproached for having money. These two means were the only ones available to them to escape the all-powerfulness of their persecutors.

Through intelligence and hard work they succeeded in acquiring a profession. Those who became physicians of the caliph or the seigneur could in this way gain some power over the enemy they were facing and could try to intercede to improve the lot of their less fortunate brethren.

With money, they purchased their freedom. How many people still say to me, "With money we could have saved ourselves in the last war"! Perhaps in some cases.

Money has never been a fetish with me. In my family, they didn't live for money: money was a means to live. One needed whatever one needed.

As against this, spiritual matters, study, were the true values.

How did this affect my thinking? When I saw the *hurban*, the destruction, the catastrophe, I soon registered the situation: "You're done for, you're alone, without anyone to go to, without means, without any connections to help you climb the social ladder. You have nothing, nobody to carry you, to support you, to enable you to get out of this."

And as we were downgraded in every conceivable way, our only opportunity was school.

Our reaction had also been that of the old secular teachers of the nineteenth century who dreamed of promoting the interests of all the children of France by opening the schools to them, giving them access to culture, providing an equal opportunity to all.

And they devoted themselves body and soul to this ideal. I knew some of them.

The schoolmistress at Sablet was of this breed. She acted not in the spirit of class-warfare but simply in order to help those who were destitute and disadvantaged. As for me, I belonged to a sort of sub-proletariat: not an economic sub-proletariat but a historical sub-proletariat.

The Jews were the pariahs of the earth, and no human beings could have been more destitute after what happened between 1933 and 1945.

If we weren't burned in the crematoria, it's because the Master of the Universe, whether one believes in Him or not, hadn't included our names in His lists, that's all.

Wishing to rid myself of this state of being the pariah of the earth, of non-right to existence, of having no right to anything, I asked myself, "Israel? Studies? Which should it be?" I took up academic work.

Did I realize at the time that it was a way of asserting myself, of making myself independent so that I wouldn't be at the mercy of the first idiot who came along?

A thousand times, we had had the experience of what study could mean. It was a sort of conviction, an overwhelming force that impelled me: "I want to go to school, I want to study. I want to be allowed to study."

I was young, but I was already ninety years old and perhaps a great deal more.

Today I can only get younger.

In my experience, school was the only place where I felt myself to be fully a human being. I saw in the teacher's eyes that when I answered well he appreciated me, he liked me, I existed, if only for five seconds – the time he could savor the pleasure of having someone who responded to the effort he was putting in. Two minutes of presence.

Here I was in a territory where I could fight on equal terms with others and where I could snatch my right to exist through sheer hard work and my own resources, the only things I possessed: my faculties, my capacity for work, my willpower, my brain-cells, my intuition.

I no longer had anything. No universe, no parents. Nothing, nothing at all. I didn't even have the right to my memories. I didn't even have the right to my mourning; I didn't have the right to be sad; I didn't have the right to be an orphan, and I didn't even have the right to be unhappy. Above all, one was not allowed to look unhappy. It was like having the plague!

I loved studying; I loved it immensely. I was passionately devoted to it. I always had pleasure in studying and I still have pleasure in studying today. I pass my life in studying.

This morning, I didn't feel like getting up. I picked up a book; I wanted to reflect on a subject that interested me at the moment.

To go forward without stopping – that's what makes me feel alive and that's what nurtures my relationship with other people, one being dependent on the other.

So I threw myself into my studies.

It was study, study, study...

At Moissac, they didn't want to direct us towards studies because after the war no one had the means to support us.

It was, "My dear, get a manual skill quickly in order to earn your living."

But I succeeded in outwitting everyone with my child's cunning. And I've always met people who were able to help me to carry through my plans to the end.

I'm a believer; I've inherited the Chasidic confidence. I've always met on my path, at each difficult intersection, the people who could enable me to cover the piece of ground I had to cover, in the absence of which I would not have been able to continue.

You see, the directress of Moissac was not at all keen that I should go in for studying medicine: "Never! You can't take this course; it's far too long. And anyway, you're not French."

But before going to see her I had spoken about it to a social worker passing through Moissac who, as though by chance, knew some well-placed individual. She said to me:

"Oh, as for naturalization, leave that to me!"

So when Shatta said she was unwilling, I was able to answer:

"But I know someone who will help me..."

I've already said how much my brother and I wanted to go to Israel after the war. It was a kind of self-evident ideal.

After what we'd experienced in Europe, it was unthinkable that we should feel at home there. And that is still the case today.

Quite recently, I woke up screaming. Always the same type of nightmare. I identified Ramatuelle, the little Provençal village where we were spending our holidays, with the village where I lived during the war, and the vine grower who let the house to us became in my dream the man who had lent us the house at Sablet, our last refuge as refugees. His wife had just died (it was no doubt the death of my mother-in-law[1] that was on my mind). I screamed, "But listen, when you die at ninety in your own bed with your husband next to you, it's got nothing to do with it...!"

You see to what a degree the present is poisoned. When I go and spend my holidays at Argelès everyone is very happy, the weather is fine,

---

1. My husband's mother died in 1977 while the narrative was being recorded.

there's the sea... As for me, I walk around in Argelès and everywhere I see Rivesaltes.

Everywhere it's a nightmare! I see Vernet-les-Bains, I see Saint Cyprien, I see Agde,[2] and I say to myself, "Is it possible? Something's wrong. Everyone walks around, goes to the sea, bathes, eats, sleeps, enjoys himself. But, in that case, what about all that has happened here? What does it mean? What is real?"

It's as if this hell had never existed. If only somewhere in a corner there was a little road-sign indicating that my nightmare was a reality!

And suddenly, as if a trap door had opened beneath me, I fall onto the floor below. Suddenly everything stops, and I need three days in order to identify this trap door and all it conceals and come back to myself. After that, I slowly reemerge and tell everyone, laughing, "Okay, I've understood. Let's continue."

The disconnection only got worse after our "return" from Israel in 1972, when we attempted to realize our enduring dream of settling there.

Unfortunately, I didn't really feel at home anywhere at that time.

I nevertheless re-inserted myself in the Paris environment after a fashion, at least where my home and my work were concerned.

But every time I had to leave it, it made me sick. A fortnight before our vacation, I was ill. Why? Because leaving the house, for me, meant going back to the war on a final journey that ended at Auschwitz. It's always the same – always the same mountains to overcome.

You spend a fortnight preparing your suitcases in both a literal and a metaphorical sense, and that eats up all your energy, the little energy you still possess.

Then I begin to think of my children who are in Israel. I'm happy. I think, "I'll go to Jerusalem and lend a helping hand. I'll give them some help."

I arrive in Jerusalem but the house is not yet set up... Here we are again, I'm a refugee once more! Where does one buy bread, where does one find vegetables, meat? Here I'm disoriented, at a loss.

My husband, for his part, walks around. Jerusalem is beautiful; he's happy. Everyone's happy. The weather's fine; we're in Jerusalem! We rent a car, we see old friends, and I'm in a state of total distress because the memory of previous negative experiences once again invades the present.

---

2. These are all names of places where Jews were interned in concentration camps of evil memory before being delivered up to the Germans.

I come to a country where I'm supposed to be at home, but at the beginning I feel stranger here than elsewhere, where the landscape has become familiar to me in the course of time. And also because the country does not entirely correspond to what I had hoped of it and what I have within me.

But today, if I finally feel at home somewhere in the world, it's in Jerusalem.

People like my husband or my sister-in-law, to whom this ideal had not been handed down and who are better adjusted to reality, adapt to the country much more easily than I, who have this "crazy" age-old hereditary dream in my heart and in my head.

Then, every time I went back to Paris, I said to myself, "What am I doing here?"

My two sons are over there, my brother is over there, and lots of friends.

I often go to see them, and every separation tears me apart once more.

I once again take a fortnight to organize myself, to get used to things. I again begin to have my feet on the ground, to breathe. Then... we must be off.

And we leave. I leave my sons, I leave my brother and it's the war all over again.

So I'm both at once. I'm the mother who has just been rounded up and who is about to leave for Auschwitz, and at the same time I'm the abandoned child.

I'm sick as a dog for about a week, just long enough to gradually re-create my shell: my home, my work, my friends.

What a difference to 1953!

When I re-read the letters I wrote to my brother in 1953 and 1955 in which I told him about my first trips to Israel, I realize it was a fantastic period. Everything was lacking and yet it was terrific.

Apart from apples, tomatoes and cucumbers, nothing was available, and it was marvelous.

I had saved up money to go there, for with the grant provided to war orphans I couldn't get very far. I put together enough to pay for the journey. I bought myself a rucksack and just one dress, blue with a pattern of little squares and a large detachable collar which I washed and ironed every day like my mother, without any feeling of shame, although I rubbed shoulders with girls of good family who changed their clothes every morning and evening.

I was on my way to Israel!

143

Sunday, 19th July, 1953

On this boat, it's nevertheless remarkable how alive they all are. When they sing, everyone joins in, from the captain down to the lowest ship's boy. I found this again yesterday evening in Haifa. Everywhere they sing. And when you think of how hot it is and how sluggish that makes you, I admire them, I assure you, for having been able to set up a state from A to Z in such a short time. For there are houses, ships, etc... and they are well made.

Making this voyage is something incredible. Do you realize I am making the opposite journey from that of so many centuries of history in a single week, and am lucky enough to finally see in the distance the coast of Haifa, which so many people have dreamed of in vain?

Just imagine, everyone here is Jewish! It's so extraordinary, it doesn't seem real. The customs officials (who sprang to attention when we sang "Hatikva" when coming into the port), the police, the kids, the taxis, the collectors of old clothes...

Even the houses.

Haifa seems to me a pretty town. The houses are white with lots of terraces, trees everywhere, a brilliant light.

The blue sea can be seen from here. I woke up this morning at daybreak. There was a freshness and a terrible intensity. All the birds sang so loudly in this dawn which had hardly come to birth, but which was already brighter than entire days often are in France. It was altogether a sort of plenitude that I have never before felt anywhere else.

Translation of a letter of Ida to her brother Martin on her first voyage to Israel.

Monday, 20th July 1953

It's very strange: all the people one runs into in the street are Jews. The shops carry signs in Hebrew. Everyone knows everyone else and says "Shalom." Uncle Victor knows at least half the town: the man who sells "exprimos and gazoz" (an abominable drink but the national one), a police "big shot" who passes in his car, the head of the dermatology department at the hospital who lives up there on Mount Carmel not far from the sea, etc... It is said that this spirit of fraternity and comradeship, which disregards social position, is now dying out a bit with the recent immigrants who are in no way comparable to the former aliyot (people that came as idealists). I haven't been here long enough to be able to form an opinion.

One thing seems quite clear to me, however, and that is the feeling that everyone has of participating in everything that is done in the country. It's theirs. I went to an industrial exhibition. A nail represents terrific progress as it is manufactured in the country prac-tically from nothing, as industry is ten or twenty years old at the most... I think everything has to be seen here from an "internal" perspective, taking into account that it all began from nothing in a terribly hot climate. All work seems to me a heroic act. Except at night, when there's a marvelous coolness (the nights recall those of the south of France, with that warm scent of cypress, that clarity and intensity, but much stronger. It is something that is terribly close to me, but here one has the impression that these Provençal nights are "distilled," as it were, such purity and intensity do they have).

The fact of building houses, roads, factories, of cleaning, plant-ing, seems to me a succession of heroic acts and miracles. It's a country which is alive. People are extremely hospitable: everywhere I feel good and at home. You never have the impression (which I have never been able to shake off in London, for example) of being invited. No, you're there. One might say that people are happy at your presence. You don't feel any need to thank them; it's almost a formality. You come in, you sit down, you chat, you're offered something, you rest...

You chat with everyone (the bus driver, in flavorful German, all the way down Mount Carmel).

Translation of another letter from Ida to her brother Martin on her first voyage to Israel.

Over there, I found close relatives who were known to me. I found my uncle, my father's brother.

The others went to kibbutzim, but I'd had my fill of collectives. So, as my uncle who lived in Haifa had some room, I stayed at his place. I was with my family, something I hadn't experienced for more than ten or eleven years.

In the family circle, I could get up when I wanted. The time one gets up, though materially speaking an insignificant detail of no importance, represents anti-collectivity.

And then my uncle's presence, which I might describe as unconditional, was irreplaceable. It was no longer necessary to play a part or correspond to a criterion. You had the right to existence quite simply because you existed, because you were the daughter of your father who was his brother.

Even if he was sometimes a bit limited because he had chums who were somewhat Freemason, intellectuals who had come out of German universities and imagined that "the young lady from Paris must dance the tango and have plenty of clothes" – a picture which didn't exactly correspond to me.

All these fine gentlemen thought that they could place me in their universe owing to the fact that I was a student of medicine. Just imagine! Deep down, I knew that I studied medicine precisely in order to gain respect, but at the same time I greatly despised those who respected me solely on account of my qualifications. At last I had the impression that I had a home somewhere.

So I had found this uncle again.

I also found one of my father's sisters and two girl cousins as well as the woman who had helped my mother in Berlin, who told me about myself when I was little! As for me, I didn't even know my grandmother's name; I didn't know anything.

My entire universe having crumbled and finding myself completely cut off from everything and everyone, here I was, finding my roots again. And that was not all by any means. I could joke in Yiddish, I could talk in Hebrew, I could say what I had in my heart just the way I felt it, to anyone who sat next to me in the bus, and he would understand.

Everyone asked me where I came from: "From Paris." "Oh no, you don't come from Paris! Where did you come from before that?" And before that?

And I could tell them! I had a hooked nose and it was considered good-looking. I was a redhead, "gingy"; they knew that the Messiah would be a redhead. I was born in Berlin, yet I wasn't regarded as a hereditary enemy.

I could quote a verse from the Torah or the Pirkei Avot or the prayers, and they understood me! I was on the same wavelength. The birds in the sky and the people and the earth and the trees – they were all in harmony! It was unbelievable. I walked around and I didn't want to leave!

It would seem that at that period I knew a lot of people apart from my family. I had another aunt, a sister of my mother's, and many cousins whom I didn't know from Berlin and I hardly wanted to see, as all this had become so problematic after the war.

The family roots had been cut off. The world of Moissac was the only one that remained. How could one reintegrate the family? It wasn't possible. It was too painful.

And we, for our part, had evolved. We had lived through something. You had left behind your old slippers, your feet had grown larger and you could no longer get back into them. You had to change your shoes.

So, in the family we renewed contact with those with whom we felt at ease. There were the ones we were drawn to and the others. There were those we could be friends with, with whom we could establish a real human relationship, and who could reconcile us to the idea of "family," which had become strange to us.

At this period, I wanted to remain in Israel. Not only was my family there, but there were also people who had been at Moissac. And in every part of the country, in every kibbutz I came to, wherever I was, it was, "Hello, Ida, how are you?" There was always someone who knew me.

Israel in 1953 was the land of idealism. There wasn't that sort of capitalism that corroded everything afterwards. The pioneer spirit was still present, and those who were already there were happy to see us come.

They had rediscovered us, glad that we'd remained alive. We had any amount of things to say to each other and each one gave his own side of a long-awaited dialogue.

People in the bus whom I didn't know from Adam would speak to me. People I met when hitch-hiking would invite me to their home and offer me a shower, a cup of coffee, something to eat.

It's no longer quite like that today; the atmosphere has changed. I wanted to stay; I would so much have liked to have stayed. I don't know how many hospitals I visited or how many people I met.

I wanted to stay, but in that case I couldn't continue my studies. Who would have paid for them? My uncle had no money. In France I could get a grant, so I went back.

The dilemma of 1953 recurred in 1955 when I began to specialize.

Each stay in Israel lasted for about six to eight weeks, taking up virtually all my holidays. With friends whom I found again we toured the country with rucksacks on our backs and few needs, going from kibbutz to kibbutz.

I was the one who guided this little group I had met on the boat on my first voyage.

The meeting with my future husband took place as though by chance.

My brother who was away from Paris on that day asked a friend to accompany me to the station. I entered the carriage, looked for my reserved seat and found it taken. It was occupied by Guy Welles, one of a band of three friends, who, having the same reservation number as myself, had taken my seat.

Conversation started up, and on the boat Welles rejoined the two others, who had arrived there by hitch-hiking. One of them was Fred, my future husband. We began to talk, and discovered that we were both from Berlin, and that we had been to the same school and the same medical school.

When we got off the boat, someone came straight up to the three of them: "*Do you know a red-haired young girl called Ida Tieder?*" Do you believe in coincidence? What a journey! It was my uncle who, among hundreds of students, had picked out precisely those who knew me.

So I found people who belonged to my world. Perhaps if I hadn't been at my uncle's, I would never have been able to marry. In order to get married, one has to exist.

I saw photos. Those who had known me as a child spoke to me about my family. They spoke to me about my parents, my grandparents. They spoke to me about myself when I was little.

The students on the boat were Jews from England, Jews from Sweden, Jews from Denmark, Jews from Holland – from all over Europe, one could say. They all sang, danced, enjoyed themselves, rebuilt the world.

All of them were "more." The English were more English than the English, the French were more French than the French. In their demeanor, in their speech, in their behavior. It was almost as if, through them, France and England carried on their ancient war.

There were other voyages, organized by the Union of Jewish Students, to which Fred and Marcel, two of the trio, belonged. They were soon put in charge of these voyages.

In 1955 there was another voyage, and the whole band came together again. Meanwhile, Fred's group and my little group of former friends from Moissac had joined forces, and together we struggled to gradually reassemble the scattered elements of our Jewish identity.

It was a struggle in two phases: the first phase, becoming a *Mensch*[3] again, took place through the medium of medicine.

Recently, walking around in Paris with Fred, I saw all the places that had been the scenes of my struggle: Boulevard Raspail, my consulting-room as a pediatrician; rue d'Assas, the École Alsacienne; rue St. Jacques, the non-resident medical studentship, the hospital.

At every street-corner there were memories of incessant struggles.

I am not the only one who has had to struggle to regain this human dignity. Three generations of Jews have, in many cases, not yet reached this stage, after which it becomes possible to begin the second stage: the reconquest of our identity, which we are trying our best to achieve. Reconquering the right to one's dignity as what you are, and not only as what others are ready to accept that you are.

If so many Jews run away from their caricatural image as projected in the distorting mirror of their enemies (and which they've interiorized) by taking refuge in what they imagine to be a universalism of salvation (but which turns out only to be a cosmopolitanism void of content), it's because they haven't had the good fortune to meet a Master capable of a true face-to-face relationship with each person, a Master capable of giving back the Torah and the Jew their true image: the image of the Hebrew before or after the sufferings of the exile.

But I've had the good fortune to benefit from the teachings of Monsieur Gordin and Manitou (Rabbi Léon Ashkenazi), which for many years were transmitted via Régine Lehmann. They had the capacity to formulate the wisdom of our Sages in present-day language and to explain it as it applied to our current problems.

That's why Manitou has remained our teacher and that of our children. He has illumined with the light of Torah from Zion contemporary generations of French-speaking Jews who without him

---

3. A human being.

would have continued, like so many others, to stray in the darkness of the West.

Perhaps Israel as a state has not yet passed the first stage.

In 1955–56, when my studies were almost completed, the chapter began of engagement in active life: marriage, children, specialization... In short, all the normal problems of existence of someone who has regained first his dignity and then the right to his identity.

I was finally able to tackle the so-called "normal" problems of existence without avoiding any of them, but always with this load that I carried. And that is no small thing!

I often have the feeling of experiencing a miracle. I often say to myself: it's marvelous; it's a miracle that I was able to marry someone who was normal, who was neither sick nor deranged. It's a miracle that I was quite simply able to marry, that I actually dared to do it.

Do you know what it means to place your trust in someone, when you saw that you no longer had any real face-to-face relationship with anyone anywhere in the world? To place my trust in someone after all I had lived through? It's never easy to marry, to "give oneself," as people used to say in the days when they were still sentimental and romantic.

When you forge a liaison with someone, you board the same ship, which risks once again to be the other person's. You have to give up your protective rigidity, renounce the defense-mechanism whereby you make every effort to prevent anyone from touching it, because otherwise you would drop dead on the spot. Because the whole world, every person, is your potential enemy, and if you don't beware of them, what will become of you? The result can only be a catastrophe!

And then there's this "crazy" sensitivity that never leaves you in peace. And then, what about all that you drag around with you, which the others haven't experienced?

Who hasn't got his *packel*, his bundle?

My husband also has his. He lived for quite a while as if he didn't have one, but it is not without a reason that he boarded the same ship as myself. Although it was to a greater or lesser degree buried deep within him, he had the same baggage and the same language, with of course his own personality, his own experience.

But, deep down, we complemented one another and we recognized each other completely.

Who can imagine what this commitment meant for me? Previously, I always had to place myself in unbelievable situations. As soon as someone seemed to become attached to me, I fled to the other end of the earth. It was too dangerous. I risked falling into a situation of dependence, a situation where I would be laughed at. Or conversely, one had the reverse situation: I attached myself to someone who showed no interest in me, and then I was no longer at risk.

You have to build yourself up, to prepare yourself before you are able to achieve an encounter, which will cause something positive to spring up on both sides. It's not automatic.

I entered into these so-called normal stages of existence with an acute awareness of all their difficulties, which I thought were only mine. This sharpness of vision was an advantage.

With the passing of time, I realized that these problems were the lot of each and every person, with the difference that in my case they were multiplied tenfold and presented themselves in such an intense form that I could not be anything but lucid.

Still today, I always see difficulties coming a little while in advance. I give warning, and people say, "You're crazy, you're imagining things; it's your persecution mania again."

I say, "I haven't got a persecution mania. I've been persecuted by the manias of others!"

I've had a good apprenticeship and I see the shadow forming long before the cloud appears.

It's like this: First stage: I'm on my guard. Second stage: I analyze. Third stage: I ask myself, "What can I do?"

I don't allow difficulties to arise without struggling to prevent them from doing so.

Everyone used to say to me: "What a likeable fellow your husband is! How well you seem to get on together! What lovely children you have! How do you manage to work at the same time?"

I won't say I solved all these problems, but I attempted, on the job, to confront them, brave little soldier that I was.

I think I was very plucky, imbued with the fundamental optimism of the Jew, for whom nothing is ever impossible.

Well, one must go for it, one must get there!

Life is to live. It's go forward or perish. No one else will do it for you. It's both the good and the bad part of my story: I'd long ago learnt to manage alone. And I set about it honestly, without sparing myself, without fearing that I'd be impoverished by giving.

One is not impoverished by loving or by making concessions, providing it's not a one-way street!

It could be said that I was someone who never lost her bearings. Even when nothing went right, I was able to say to myself: "It's amazing nevertheless. Look, we have a house, we have enough to eat, we have children, there are the two of us, the kids are in good health. There's no war; nobody is killing us."

So, it's okay. It's a miracle, nevertheless. It's rather as though I didn't have the right to anything and it wasn't my due to have a husband, fine children, a family.

The Snare of Exile

When I'm in my Land
it seems to me
the obvious thing to do,
but when I'm in Exile
I lose my bearings
and I stray.
I get caught up
and can no longer break free
and make the liberating move
that would bring me home.

November 4, 1982

RE-POSITIONING ONESELF IN EXILE

Whenever a patient turned up, I said to myself, "Why does he come to me? So many doctors are more capable than I am!

I am always confronted with a fundamental self-questioning; I always go back to *Bereshit*. I always ask myself these same questions: "What am I doing here? But what am I doing here?"

At every moment, more or less, I have to look for a meaning in my life. Each new event calls everything into question. It's with all these non-certitudes that one can help young people.

Generally, one says to them, "Life's like this, like that" – "Do this, do that." And if one doesn't make a speech, one fobs them off with a drug, some piece of trash one sells to them to line one's pockets. But what do they retain of all this? "Do what I say, don't do what I do."

It's this contradiction that young people feel, and the so-called "problem children" sense it much more than others. They see at once if your words are consistent with your life.

Adults also feel this. They know exactly where you stand, and I have a thousand and one proofs of it. They are able to perceive through your words and even through your silence what you are and how you place yourself.

It's with what you are that you can do something for them, or you can't do anything. If you can listen to their questions without giving them ready-made answers, it's because you too are capable of asking yourself questions.

Basically, people are unaware of what it is that prevents them from living. They stifle themselves at every moment and at the same time stifle those around them.

But for all those people who are stifled, my story can serve as an example. And all these searches I have made in order to be able to breathe a little oxygen, glimpse a little light and to simply be able to survive and carry on – all this can be of use to many people who have passed through experiences that undoubtedly are very different, but who resemble each other in their non-right to be what they are, their non-right to difference, their non-right to their specific nature, their non-right to speech.

I've learned and experienced that in catastrophic situations no one can help you. Finally, perhaps ultimately, no one can ever really help anyone else, but one can nevertheless in a certain way be present and useful. And it is here that I have a profound faith in Jewish values, which educate people to find themselves while bestirring themselves for others.

I have come to the conclusion that everyone is alone, that each person has to take upon himself his solitude, and it is on this basis that one can help others.

When you have faced your own solitude, you can be two, three or several people, and live in society in the midst of your people, accompanied by God.

Judaism is the pedagogy of life, an age-old teaching that is embodied in all actions, even the simplest, and teaches people that they are not alone on earth.

You may think I am playing with paradoxes. Everyone is alone in face of his responsibilities, and at the same time no one is alone.

No one has the right to have the power of life and death over anyone whatsoever, or even to dispose of beings, things, the world, including himself.

All these *mitzvot*,[1] all these precepts, teach you how to set limits, how to behave towards the Creator and His world, towards others and oneself, how not to let anyone despair of life through a sense of abandonment.

To my mind, nothing could be more isolated than someone in the midst of an overcrowded city. It's unbearable. Everyone there has his psychoanalyst because one suffocates at not having anyone to talk to.

Or, instead of the psychoanalyst, there's the doctor or the hairdresser or even the taxi-driver. No wonder the cellphone and the Internet have become so popular; they lessen this solitude.

Why do people languish in hospital and why is there this medical inflation? It's the last resort.

If only you had seen how Fred was immediately surrounded with people when he lost his mother! And it wasn't just anyone and it was not

---

1. Commandments.

just in any way! It was people who had learnt to live by the Torah and knew how to behave towards someone who had just lost his mother. They knew what to do and they did it. They were present from the very first evening, and they were there every day to say the prayers. One ran to the hospital to recite the psalms. Another ran to buy the first meal for when they came back from the cemetery. They were all there – both the closer and more distant relatives and friends – to carry the coffin. They knew what they should say and what they shouldn't say.

It's a whole savoir-vivre, a wisdom of life, which can't be invented. Though in fact it *can* be invented. There are sensitive people, tactful people who do the right thing spontaneously. But I for my part believe that the virtue of humanity can be cultivated, and that of all the peoples of the earth, the Jews are the ones who have devoted themselves collectively to its cultivation so that human beings will be as human as possible, so that life amongst humankind will be good and possible, and so that they will be as alive as possible.

And Israel is the place where all these values are in the air, and hence my irresistible attraction for that country. In going there I was looking for what I already bore within me. What I bore within me was a vision of humanity and a way of living.

For example, a beaten child is unimaginable to me. It could happen that my father got angry with us, but above all we were his *kinderlech*, his beloved children.

In the midst of all their sufferings, my interned and deported parents undoubtedly suffered most from not being able to come to our aid.

Now that I'm a mother, I know that there is nothing worse than to have both one's hands and not to be able to do anything for one's children.

You, of course, are going to confront me with the image of the devouring *Yiddishe mamme*. So I'll tell you about her antidote: the *Yiddishe tatte*, the Jewish father!

Every Shabbat, I read the parasha. This week, precisely, it was *Shemot*, "Names." I've unraveled in this text the whole antidote to the maternal phagocytosis, the matriarchy and the results of two thousand years of Christian influence. When I say two thousand years, in fact the heritage is far older.

The parasha of Shemot (Exodus, chap. 1) relates how the Egyptians drowned the male children in the River Nile. In Hebrew, Egypt is mitzrayim, which means "being in a narrow place." You can see in this cramped mitzrayim a macro-uterus, which seeks to retain the embryo of the Jewish people. It's the mother who devours her child.

The book of Shemot, literally "Names" (called "Exodus" in English) is there to remind us from its very first lines of the irreplaceable role of the name of the father in permitting the blossoming of the special identity of each child.

The father, in order to be the guarantor of the child, in order to permit him to leave his mother's womb and become autonomous, must himself recognize the omnipotence of the Creator. He is then able to give him his name, his "*shem.*"

The father is not a father simply because he has given his sperm and has remained there in flesh and blood. He is the father as a bearer of values and the transmitter of a name. And the name in the final analysis is the Name of *Hakadosh Baruch Hu* (God) who is the totality, the guarantor of all life.

If there isn't a God, I don't see why I shouldn't steal or kill. I don't see what would stop me, why I wouldn't be the owner of my neighbor, my child, my father, my mother, my maid and her belongings. I'd do everything the boys who commit hold-ups do, and then I'd take you hostage and then I'd kill you, and then I'd start again!

Why not? Why should one stop? Why should I curb my appetites, control my impulses, restrain the animal that is in me?

And if secular morality seems to contradict me, what happens in the third or fourth generation?

This is where we come back to the Yiddishe mamme, who only became the Yiddishe mamme inasmuch as the Yiddishe tatte was emasculated, castrated, devalorized and infantilized due to his lack of power over the outside world and also because of his escape into a studious existence unconnected with life.

I am referring to a certain Christianized Judaism contaminated by a long stay in superstitious ultra-Catholic matriarchal countries, worshippers of the "Holy Virgin."

In that world, the flesh is sin, the body is the source of all evil and the ideal is to retire from the world and live in a monastery.

All this has nothing to do with authentic Judaism.

One speaks of Judeo-Christian civilization, of Judeo-Christianity. It's an abuse of language.

Greek philosophy fused with Roman imperialism has nothing in common with the world of the Hebrews. It's true that Christianity has borrowed its backdrop from Judaism and that Judaism in the Diaspora has been largely deformed, with the deformation varying according to the country.

In Islamic countries, for instance, there's the *mektoub*: "It's written."

It's now time to cure ourselves of all these sicknesses, to free ourselves from all these contaminations.

Our prophets have told us: "I will bring you back to the land and I will heal you of all the sicknesses you have contracted in the midst of the nations and all the peoples amongst whom I have scattered you and amongst whom you have dwelt."

And if I can state this with so much conviction, it's because I've heard a number of people tell me the true story of their lives.

Only the other day, a young woman spoke to me about her Christian father, and about the deeply Catholic milieu in which she lived: "A mother who gives birth without the intervention of a man, a child who dies so that others may live, and then one eats his body"

I said to myself: "That's what we've come out of !" And in all this I don't recognize us Hebrews. It's so little like us that many of those who deserted the *yeshivot* (religious seminaries), calling themselves "non-religious" but being profoundly Jewish nevertheless, rebuilt Israel. They regained their bodies, their hands, their physical existence, their feet planted in their soil. And I have no doubt that they will rediscover the Jewish way of looking at life and of living it, which has no connection with any Western system, religious or otherwise.

The "Hebrew" is finally on the way to finding himself again.

As for the Yiddishe mamme, she exists, as I said, because there's no Yiddishe tatte, and if there's no Yiddishe tatte, it's because the man has been devalorized as the bearer of his own values, has been trampled underfoot together with all that constituted his dignity, his virility.

Every day one can see how immigrants become like little boys again, and the woman is transformed into a "mamme" because she is forced to have both feet on the ground. She has to wash the nappies, change her children's diapers, prepare the meals. It's the same everywhere.

The woman, faced with all these tasks, has a different form of resistance to her extraneous position in society, and she preserves her own values. As a consequence, she becomes "hypertrophied," if I may say so, and she often wears the trousers. This is what happened in Poland.

During this time, the men, to escape total devalorization, shut themselves up in houses of study. And the men began to live a bit like the

Catholics, with religion on one side, life on the other, whereas Judaism is not a religion but a way of life, among other things.

Life took refuge with the "mamme," and the men avenged themselves by excluding the women from their houses of study, their "religion" and their practices. And in reaction, the mammes kept their distance, taking their beloved sons with them because they loathed seeing their mothers assume the thankless tasks of running the house and earning a living while the men were sitting around studying without any connection to reality. It was an understandable reaction in order to survive.

Thus, a matriarchal civilization came into being which certain members of this generation describe very well, especially the Jewish school of New York, which never stops talking about the phenomenon of a society without fathers. Without fathers and also, paradoxically, without a body. Without any right to pleasure, any right to the body.

In the Talmud, on the other hand, there are whole tractates dealing with the sexual relationship.

The Jewish marriage contract, the *ketuba*, stipulates, among other things, that the man owes the woman shelter, food, clothing and sexual relations, without ever making her into an instrument for his pleasure.

One can follow the history of the contamination of the Jewish people through its music.

When the Temple was destroyed and the people left Jerusalem, everyone sang the prayers according to the same melodies. Two thousand years later, the texts of the prayers are still more or less the same for everyone, but some sing them to the rhythm of a march or rather to the rhythm of a goose-step, while others make them into a flamenco or Arab chant.

When you change your country, you change your appearance. Think of the short-statured Mexicans who arrive in New York and gain ten or twenty centimeters in a generation.

When you're a minority, when you're not master of your fate, you become impregnated with the majority culture. You have only to see how the Jewish communities in France structure themselves on the model of the French institutions. That's what I call contamination.

It's inevitable and most probably to some degree necessary and enriching, but a time comes when you have to sort out what is yours and what is foreign to you, what has been imposed on you or what you've acquired from others. At a certain moment you have to sort this out.

This Shabbat, I had a young kibbutznik in my home. I said to my-self: the resurrection of the dead has taken place. He's alive, that boy! He's sound in wind and limb, he has the breath of life, he's full of the joy of living. He's not inhibited; he's not a mother's boy. In Israel one again finds the "fathering" dimension.

Together with the land, they've regained the life of the body. The body is neither dirty nor sinful. It's a marvel, made up of innumerable miracles, which take place at every uncountable fraction of a second in the smallest particle of a cell in order to snatch life away from death. So, ought this marvel of the Creator be despised?

This was no doubt one of the reasons I took up medical studies.

As long as the exile lasts, we're like encysted amoebas. On coming back to Israel, we suddenly regain our bodies. And at the same time, what had been reduced to a "religion" without connection with life looks like a series of death-dealing imbecilities. Whereas Judaism is life, the whole of the Torah teaches us how to live it.

Why, suddenly, does the series of social laws which follow the Ten Commandments end with: "Thou shalt not cook a kid in its mother's milk"?

The mother, the mother's milk is the source of life. The mother mustn't take the child and kill it or use it for her own pleasure. She shouldn't prevent it from living on its own account. This is the principle of forbidding incest.

And that is why I say to you that the Torah is the antidote for the idea of a blind fate, for that intermeshing that the Greeks called destiny, and that might very well today be called the fetters of the unconscious, among other things.

I could tell you so many improbable stories, which can be explained by the logic of the unconscious.

It's not by chance that you have the unconscious you have or the history you have or the co-ordinates you have. It's in order that you can realize in your life what you were born for.

This dimension of sublimation by means of values, which you can call the "Law," or whatever you call it, is the means of controlling an overflowing of one's drives, a control that is backed up by the father, pro-viding that he himself respects the word, which distinguishes man from the animals.

And this is not just any word. It's the revealed Word, the Torah given to the Jewish people as directions for life in its land.

I return to the exile.

Take the case of the *shtetl* as it was in Poland: a sort of Jewish enclave in a completely Christian universe.

You lived there like a cytosome (I can't even say nucleus. I'd be blamed for being "proud and dominating," as General de Gaulle called us).

You lived there like a corpuscle whose condition of life was to be completely covered: it could be said to subsist owing to the fact of being covered.

When you live in a country, you speak its language, you use its railway-system, its roads; you absorb its landscape, you breathe its air, you feel its snow, its rain. You hear people singing and shouting, "Dirty Jew, go to Mass!"

However, in France we nevertheless had an impression of extraordinary liberty and respect. It was nothing like Poland, where all the Yiddish songs and all the folklore reminded you of your condition, not to speak of what happened during the war.

If you managed to elude the Nazis, there was always a Pole behind your back who had an axe to split your skull or who would send you back into the arms of the Boche.

All this has been in existence for a long time, as we can see from the Yiddish song whose refrain goes: "*When a goy goes to have a drink, what does he do when he leaves? He beats up a Jew.*"

The problem could be stated the other way round. Perhaps the reality was that if they had this hatred of the Jews, it was because the phantasm of a people who were at once present and absent preyed on their minds, assuming incredible proportions like some alien monster that had insinuated itself everywhere.

In France, likewise, just by speaking the language of the country, by living there, by breathing its air, by seeing what other people eat even if one eats kosher, one ends by being completely impregnated with it without even noticing.

One lives at the same rhythm as the others. Even if one remains *dati* (religiously observant; pl. *dati'im*), even if one tries to avoid it, one can't help being "soaked" in it, if only through the language.

If you say "touch wood," nothing could be more innocuous, but do you know what you have said? You're touching the wood of the cross: Jew though you may be, you're talking like a Catholic. Don't you believe me?

You may not be aware of the religious connotation of this expression, but it's no less real for that. Take the Métro, see the stations as they pass: St. Paul, St. Georges, Notre-Dame des Champs, St. Lazare – it's a veritable pilgrimage! Quite apart from the calendar by which you are forced to live, and which bears no relation to yours.

After that, you have to do the work of disengagement, a constant effort to rediscover in yourself the Jew who was at Sinai. When I say "Jew," I mean the Jew in his specific character, inasmuch as I believe that a true Jew is quite simply a true man. The whole of Judaism only exists in order to teach you to be human, to make you truly human.

In the shtetl, the ghetto or the *mellah*, they succeeded as far as they could in avoiding the contamination. It was a reflex of survival, the reflex of an amoeba, which becomes encysted, the behavior of biological defense. It is able to leave its protective cyst and regain a normal membrane when it finds a favorable surrounding milieu that permits a normal interchange with the environment. The human being has the same kind of reaction as the amoeba, and so has the Jewish people.

It is said in our tradition that, ultimately, all the practices observed during the exile have perhaps only one purpose: to preserve them in our memory in readiness for the distant day when we will once again finally be in our land.

Can one undergo an apprenticeship in humanity without the mitzvot?

Rare individuals called the Just of the Nations succeed in doing so. But the Jewish people has the program of realizing the "fully human" on a collective scale.

Today, when this program becomes realizable for the entire people, they seek by every means to undermine it, to nip it in the bud. Read the papers.

We are reproached for Israel's incursion into southern Lebanon. Shouldn't soldiers be sent to try to uproot the terrorists?

How else can you defend yourself and prevent a psychosis from developing in the country, where people would soon feel closed in as in a ghetto where any Nazi could infiltrate and tomorrow come and incinerate our children, without anyone in the whole world lifting a finger?

Does one have to suffer passively? They *have* to do what they are doing. Put yourself in their skins, if only for a moment! You can't even travel quietly from Haifa to Tel Aviv or from Jerusalem to Hebron.

And if you knew how hard it is for a Jew, wherever he is, in Israel or anywhere else, to have to kill in order to defend himself! I know from my Israeli colleagues: it makes them sick.

Elie Wiesel said something like this: "Any other people, coming out of the concentration camps, would have set fire to the earth. The Jewish people planted a rose on the dunghill."

What did they do? All they tried to do was to build themselves up on a few kilometers of sand. The day you declare your independence, the six surrounding Arab states rub their hands and rush out to kill you. No one lifts a finger. On the contrary: people provide arms to your enemies and then applaud.

So what do you do on that day? You say: "Thank you, murder me? Haven't we had enough of it? Are you still continuing?"

All this to prevent us from living according to our specific Jewish identity.

If you think a mitzvah means a religious rite, I understand it as a way of behaving, of living, a style of life. When a man respects his wife, when a father is kind to his child, it's a mitzvah.

Anything that makes me put myself out for others in my daily behavior, my immediate primary actions, and stops me from taking myself for the center of the world with the right to devour everyone else, is a mitzvah.

Indeed, we live in a world where peace isn't possible, where nothing curbs anyone's appetites.

A world whose motto is: "I don't give a damn. Whatever I want, I take." (See what is happening today in Rwanda, Yugoslavia, etc.).

Remember Sodom and Gemorrah? Do you think that all there was to it was that "once, in the Bible, there was a little village in the Jordan valley where people lived"? When a stranger went there, they gave him a bed, and if his feet stuck out beyond the end of the bed, someone came at night with an axe and chopped off the part that stuck out. And if his legs weren't long enough, they stretched them.

A fine concept of hospitality!

In addition, they gave you alms, but at the same time they forbade anyone to sell you the smallest scrap of bread. They were generous: they put you in their framework. Sodom and Gomorrah – we're right there today!

And who was Amalek, whose descendant was Haman and then Hitler, and whom I think the Soviet system was heir to, as well as those who manipulate the Palestinians?

Amalek is the person who doesn't believe in anything except power relationships. Anything is therefore permitted.

He is the person who, seeing the people of Israel when they had only just come out of Egypt and emerged from slavery, attacks it from the rear.

But the people of Israel is led by "the hand of God," which is a way of saying to humanity that however powerful a state or an empire may be, however many watchtowers and concentration camps it may have, there is a superhuman power which is the true human power, the power of true values that can vanquish any kind of hostility.

Israel represents this power, and that is what the world cannot forgive it for.

When Israel came out of Egypt and went into the desert, it didn't stay in luxurious hotels: nobody laid out a red carpet to welcome it. It was expelled and then pursued with the purpose of overtaking it and killing it from the rear, with no other regret than that of losing such a cheap source of manpower, and people whom one could kill out of pure sadism.

Amalek attacks from the rear: that is to say, he attacks the weakest, those who walk the slowest, just like the terrorists.

They don't come to make war; they don't come to fight an army. They go to a school in Ma'alot and murder the children.

Terrorism is a plague which has spread throughout the whole world.

When I say "Jewish," I am speaking of eternal values, universal values, human values. We've been paid for it. When I say "paid," it is unconscious black humor; it's we who do the paying.

At Sinai, we took it upon ourselves to willingly defend God's values, because the privilege of being Jewish is nothing else than this acceptance: "I'm ready to pay the price."

How many people are willing to do this work? And when someone wants to convert, you discourage him. You tell him: "You can be a man observing the seven laws of Noah. Why do you want to take on the six hundred and thirteen commandments? It's really too difficult."

We are killed because in a certain way we've agreed to carry the torch, saying to ourselves: "The others have lost their nerve, but we can't lose our nerve or else the whole world goes to the dogs."

This isn't a state of superiority; it's a responsibility – an immense responsibility because it isn't only for ourselves. We assume it for the whole universe, and we're aware of it.

And if we've kept going, it isn't because we're better than others, but because human values, true ones, are stronger – stronger than all those who seek to destroy those who transmit them.

And because on High they don't let go of us so easily!

To carry out this task, which is a collective one, we need Eretz Yisrael. I can do certain things in Paris, but it's not Jerusalem. Not only because of my life experience, which is merely the subjective side of history. This subjective side, however, has had the effect that my house in France could never be other than temporary.

You see, I never bought a house in France; I couldn't even think of it.

None of the apartments I lived in was ever finished. Something was always missing: curtains, chairs, a lampshade. I can say that I never really settled in, in the full sense of the word.

To me, France remains France, and to the end of my days you won't take from me what I experienced there during the war. I can't erase it from my mind. I can't help it, when going to a certain chemist to buy a bar of soap and observing him – I can't help thinking: this man would perhaps have been a collaborator during the war. Perhaps he would have denounced me.

When I see someone I don't know, my first reaction is: "And if it were wartime, would he shelter me or would he give me away?"

The Other's Image of You

Through turning the other cheek
and bowing the neck
under their yoke
we have gone mad!
We think
it comes from us
and we forget
we're interiorizing
the wishes
of our hateful enemies
who everywhere and always
wish us dead.
We've got used
to this kind of solitude,
and as a result of being charged
with all the sins of humanity
and being condemned by them
for that,
we continue to play the game
and to give
ourselves
the role of scapegoat
even when it's no longer necessary,
since we, thank God,
have returned to our land.

Let us, then, be the
"proud and dominating" people
of our fears
who do not allow ourselves
to be led by the nose

in order to "please"
our fellow-humans
who only like us
buried underground!

October 2, 1982

BEING ONESELF

In Israel, there are many other problems – innumerable problems – but one can breathe!

It's Pesach; you go to the supermarket. Everything is on hand. In Paris at Pesach, you have to run to the rue Cadet or to the rue des Rosiers and order everything in advance, anticipate everything. It's a real headache.

In Jerusalem in the supermarket I have in front of me an enormous stand with all the cheeses, the yogurts, carp, meat – everything kosher.

On Wednesday evening, we decided to remain in Jerusalem. On Thursday morning I went to the supermarket while the others arranged the house. Overflowing with energy, I cooked all day without stopping, and in the evening for the prayer service we had the choice of five different synagogues a stone's throw away from us.

I know that nobody will beat me up because I go to synagogue, and moreover, the street is closed off in front of the great synagogue of Heichal Shlomo so that no car will pass and disturb you during the service.

When I think of the Shabbatot and the Jewish holidays of my childhood in Berlin, not to speak of those in le Sablet, I ask myself whether I'm not dreaming.

Do you know that even today in Israel we're being pursued? Do you know that Christian missionaries come to Israel to try and convert little Jews? What dishonesty, what mental trickery!

Words fail me to say what I think of these soul-thieves, and I don't see why, if people are put in prison for committing hold-ups, they shouldn't be put in prison for exploiting the wretchedness of the poor in an attempt to buy their souls.

For two thousand years and even more, Jews have been burned on the pyres of all the Inquisitions to prevent them from being what they are and believing what they do.

When they proclaimed their ideal, they were treated as lunatics, as sorcerers, as devils. Auschwitz was nothing else than the culmination of all these lies.

Throughout these thousands of years, they lived and died without ever forgetting that one day they would again have a country where finally they would have the right to be what they are. And there they are again hunted down.

We're accused of subjecting the non-Jews who live in Israel to the same treatment. Come and judge for yourself! Walk around Jerusalem and you'll see.

Has a Jew ever stopped a Christian from being a Christian, or a Muslim from being a Muslim? You'll see how their churches are guarded.

Go up and down the streets of Jerusalem. The dignitaries of the Greek Church aren't ill-at-ease there, nor are the Armenians. You see the clergy walking around, each in his own costume and not at all humble-looking. They possess half of Jerusalem. They're in our home, and we – we're the occupiers!

I wouldn't say that *they* are occupiers, but, after all, that wouldn't be a heresy. And when in addition they try to show me that they are the ones who are right, that I have to kneel down before their statues, like the Warsaw Ghetto survivor who told me that they were willing to save her skin, but in return she would have to pray in Latin and drag herself to Mass every Sunday.

She told me: "My adoptive grandmother certainly gave me love, but I wasn't to bring my Jewishness with me."

Tolerance is only possible where there is mutual respect. A tolerance that permits anything is no longer tolerance but laxness, a weakness that leads to joining hands with all those who put the earth to fire and sword, to aerial hijackers, to the Baader-Meinhoff gang,[1] and so forth.

They come to kill me, and do I have to open my door to them?

People like to quote the phrase from the Ten Commandments: "Thou shalt not kill." But "Thou shalt not kill" isn't what is written. What is written is, "Thou shalt not murder." There's a difference between killing and murder.

Don't you have the right to kill if the other person wants to kill you? You have to defend yourself. If the other person doesn't respect you, I don't see why I should respect him at the cost of my life.

---

1. German anarchist terrorists who were rampant at the end of the 1960s.

That's the difference with Catholics. They say they turn the other cheek, but they would kill you and the whole world with you to make people adopt their beliefs.

In the Talmud, it is said, on the contrary, that if you stop someone killing you, even at the cost of his life, you save your life and you also save his real life (that is to say, his "life in the world-to-come").

You can't be half a Jew or a quarter Jew. Either you choose to be Jewish (and possibly want to live in Israel, believing it to be your country), or you choose not to be Jewish.

I've met young people who are the product of mixed marriages. If I were a film director, I'd make a film about the drama of these children who are not half-Jews and half-Christians but neither one thing nor the other – neither Jews nor Christians.

One can't live if one doesn't create a unity in a given direction.

Jewish identity can't be enclosed within a system. Everyone has to "invent" himself, in the sense of discovering himself as he goes along.

And each Jew learns to live his Judaism in accordance with his own characteristics while respecting the integrality and authenticity of the common heritage.

What is it that makes one belong to an ethnic group? One belongs to such a group if one speaks the same language, eats the same food prepared in the same way, adopts the same religion and dances to the same rhythms as the others. There's a community of gesture, language and culture.

An identity is not just a matter of, "I put on a yellow star and I'm Jewish." That's a parody viewed from the outside in which one takes my identity card, stamps it, and hey presto! I'm Jewish.

Or, like the Russians or the Nazis, they give you the caricature of an identity, an identity à la Sartre: a Jew is only Jewish because the others say he is. That's the Jews' misfortune.

No! The Jewish condition has content. I am well aware that many Jews who live in Israel are far from having retrieved this content, but where could they find it again better than in their land?

One might say that during the two thousand years of *galut* (exile), the Jews were like the trunk of a tree with a bark that was frozen, but which nevertheless retained all its potential for life. As soon as the sap rises again with the return of spring, it again puts forth its leaves and fruits in its own way. That's the Jew.

Now we've returned to our land, the sap circulates once more and we'll produce our own leaves and our own blossoms. We shan't produce our neighbor's fruits or those which our neighbor wants us to produce.

It's in living among others that you create your identity, your "I" in relation to the "I" of others. No identity can be created except in relation to the Other, but for a relationship to exist, each one has to be himself.

To make a line, you need two points. If the two points are confused, you get an amalgam: one has swallowed the other.

Each person has his own riches providing the other doesn't stifle him.

As I see it, the Jews can only give the world what they have to give by being themselves, by realizing themselves and by realizing their ideal, which is one to which all humanity aspires.

It's not for nothing that the Jews get spat on so much, and if a Jew has a hiccup in Israel, the whole world knows about it. Why are all eyes riveted on this little country?

Why, precisely, as though by chance, does everyone support the Palestinians? Why was it precisely the Jews that Hitler wanted to kill? Why?

Precisely because this ideal, of which we have the *chutzpah*[2] to declare ourselves the representatives and for which we pay the price, is not a privilege but a responsibility, a duty to be taken on.

They make us pay dearly, for not only do they not help us but they constantly try to destroy us rather than to recognize the requirements of this ideal, which is that of the whole human race.

That doesn't mean, however, that everyone has to be Jewish! Each one has to have his own human path!

Every week, the parasha says it again. This week, it's *kedoshim tih'yu* (Leviticus, chap. 19), where the Ten Commandments are repeated in a more concrete, more detailed form, and where one of the main ideas is respect for the specialness of each person, each animal, each thing.

Each person has to develop according to his own rhythm, or it's oppression. You shall not do as [you did] in Egypt where you come from, or as in Canaan where you are going, for the day you do as they do the earth will vomit you out. You shall not burn your child to death in sacrificing him to Moloch, which has the same root as *melech*, king (*limloch*, to rule). You shall not burn your children to death in sacrificing them to power.

---

2. Cheek, impudence in Hebrew.

And today, every day we sacrifice our children to Moloch, to power and money, to the power of drugs, oil and arms for the Arab countries, with the risk of total annihilation for all, Jews and non-Jews alike, the entire planet.

When one attacks Israel, whether one intends it or not, it's all that is human that is attacked, it's the whole of humanity which will suffer sooner or later.

Hitler hunts down the Jews: at the other end of the world, a bomb goes off in Hiroshima.

Samuel Pisar isn't the only one to have considered Auschwitz a global phenomenon. It's like the first tumor of a cancer. If the first cells pass unnoticed, the metastases are fatal.

Those who, like us, have been under Hitler, can tell you where in the world it smells bad. They are told: "You are mentally sick, imaginary victims of persecution."

But they are able to detect this destructive madness because they've seen it at close quarters, and they are as sensitive as a radar screen that detects it long before anyone suspects what is brewing.

The other day, I was at a meeting at a school where I was working. They wanted to help the handicapped. They came out with proposals for another regulation, more structures, punch-cards, drawers... And where were people in all this?

They invented remedial classes, and then, when the schoolmistress says to the child, "Go and speak to the psychologist," what ought to be a breath of fresh air, an escape exit, risks becoming a source of shame.

Didn't Hitler begin by wanting to exterminate the mentally sick and handicapped?

Perhaps it's my phantasm once again. But how could this fail to revive my memories as a Jew prevented from living according to our own conceptions?

When I was able to celebrate a true festivity, a *chag*[3] in Jerusalem, you can't imagine what a victory this was over all those programmers who want to force you into their plan or shove you into their cattle-cars.

I was able to have a true feast in my own home, for my children, for us in Jerusalem. I prepared the meal. We went to synagogue, we sang. Everything was ready. Everything was on hand, both for Shabbat and for the *yom tov*[4] that followed.

---

3. Jewish holiday.
4. Feast day.

I previously had to organize everything *in extremis*

I don't know if you can imagine the work that represented. But there was also my sense of triumph and jubilation. I was no longer a refugee. Before, the approach of the feast-days made me ill.

Even in Israel until that day, I was unable to feel anything else but a refugee. And I was even more sick to feel myself a refugee even in Israel.

I went to the Western Wall. There for the first time I heard the priestly blessing as it was given in the days of the Temple.

Thanks to the loudspeaker, I was able to follow all the prayers. The swell of the sea, storms, the forests, the stars entered my heart.

I said to myself: "What my parents told me is true. They didn't lie to me."

What they presented to me as the truth, and which was half-dead to me as I was being chased, hunted down in order to make me renounce and give up. Right down to you, who asked me the question: "How, after all that, can you still believe and practice?"

It is all true. I am now at home and at peace with myself.

Our God and the God of our fathers who is also the God of my sons... That's how life is possible.

Do I have to eat with chopsticks because my Chinese neighbor eats with chopsticks? Why?

I'll wear out my tongue repeating it: dialogue is only possible if each one is himself.

What would I have to say to you if it wasn't me speaking, if I didn't have the right to have my say, the right to speak in my name of the things for which I live?

If I'm merely your echo, I might as well be silent, for it would only be the parody of speech or even a meaningless confession extracted from someone through torture.

You see, this book, like my idea of a gathering in Jerusalem of survivors who were children during the war (with possibly a collective *shiva*,[5] even if only symbolic), like the project of a school for Jewish psychologists in Paris, all these dreams which fill my head... from there to carrying them out... We would be sitting in front of the Wall with the schoolchildren bringing us our meals and listening to us.

These projects have been partly realized with many people's help. The gathering did take place in Jerusalem, but not the shiva. A group of

---

5. Week of mourning.

Jewish psychoanalysts who met for reflection also existed in Paris for a few years.

At Moissac and in all those homes in which we were placed, we were like parcels tossed hither and thither, unfortunate in being ten years too young, classed as children who couldn't decide their own fate and, still less, join a resistance network.

In this situation of helplessness we remained hyper-lucid, hypersensitive, anxious and on our guard.

That's the reason I feel such a kinship with Joseph. Thrust into your hole or unjustly imprisoned, if you're not taken out by others, it's all over. You're condemned not to be able to do anything. You can try to ask the *sar hamashkim*[6] to "remember me" (Genesis 40:14). If he doesn't want to remember you, he won't. You're not the one who decides your fate.

When I came to Moissac, I was Joseph who had found his long-lost brothers. After a time of solitary tribulation, something of my own world still existed.

All the memories I have of it are filtered through my subjectivity. But as long as you haven't got the right to look at the world with your own subjectivity, you can't reconcile yourself with objectivity.

Only afterwards can you see how subjective you had been and you are able to put yourself in other people's skins, or rather you understand that you can't put yourself in the skins of those who saved your life, and you say to yourself: "If I'd been in their place, I probably wouldn't have done a tenth of what they did."

In any case, the situation was such that nothing and nobody, however good their intentions, could give you your parents back.

I dress my daughter and my sons without any trouble, but when it comes to me I can never manage to decide. I go into a department store and I can't buy for myself, although I've made some progress. I walk around the shop, I push the door open, I go in; I'm overcome by panic, the world collapses. There's nothing for me, nothing that suits me. It's useless to insist. I leave.

If my daughter or my husband aren't with me, I won't buy anything. You don't have the right to have anything, you don't have the right to decide your fate, to choose something that would be right for you. Is it because of the alte shmattes, the old rags one had to wear at Moissac?

---

6. Cup-bearer.

You were just a piece on a chessboard. The captain of the ship made the ship go, and everyone had to be at his post and keep his place, or there wouldn't be any room for you at all.

It was "our home," and on days of inspection you had to look good and things had to have a good appearance.

In the final analysis, once you've been thrown out of your home, you no longer have a secure framework in which you could have grown up in safety. You're cast upon life like something *hefker*, an abandoned object, dependent upon others who look after you to the degree that you fit in with their standards, the things to which they are devoted, their work, their goodwill and the task they've imposed upon themselves.

I now know that all these young "leaders" had just landed there, that they were as lost as we were. They were just a few years older than we were, that's all.

They were perhaps not aware how essential it is for every child, and especially for a child who has lost everything, to have some small corner to himself with his things that nobody touches.

At Moissac, they could dispose of you and your things as they wished. You had nothing left whatsoever. For my part, I was afraid to open my mouth to say anything about myself, because I had the feeling – and I'm sure I wasn't wrong – that any of my private affairs I would divulge would be used against me.

In an institution in which I worked at a certain time, a lively discussion started up one morning because they had a meeting in my absence in which it was decided that anyone who had a piece of information concerning a child would set it down in writing and put it in his file where it could be seen by the others. I said I would have nothing to do with this.

When I arrived at this school, I almost got on bad terms with half the staff because I wouldn't agree to have the secretary present during my consultations. I refused to put my observations in the files, and I asked for a safe that could be locked.

At Moissac, I knew what I was doing, even if it wasn't understood. I was fed up with not having my corner, my own room – so much so that one day I took my bed and moved out.

There was a staircase at the back, a service staircase that nobody ever used. I took some blankets and I installed myself in the entrance on the landing. I created a room where I set up my bed, and I said: "This is where you can leave me!" This caused a real scandal. I asked: "Who am I disturbing here? Nobody ever comes here and I'm left alone."

Nowadays, I can't function without my corner. I'm only productive when there's silence and when the door can't be opened at any moment, and my vital space, my "four cubits" isn't violated. My space doesn't have to be large.

This respect for a person's right to silence, for his intimacy, for his right not to have the door opened on him, is something I have taught my children from their earliest years.

I drummed into them: "When someone is sleeping or separates himself, you don't intrude, and whatever your age, you don't rush in on someone else. You knock at the door, you ask nicely, you enter. You don't wake people abruptly.

"If someone writes a letter, you don't open it and read it if it hasn't been shown to you, and if someone confides in you, you keep the knowledge to yourself and don't say anything. You never divulge what has been said to you in confidence."

In a certain way, I've always tried, perhaps without necessarily succeeding, not to repeat the things that made me suffer.

So, during our attempt at *aliyah*,[7] I was constantly surprised on arriving in Israel: "How can you treat people who arrive in a state of total vulnerability so insensitively?"

And you call yourselves *dati'im*, not to speak of the non-dati'im with their well-tried methods of "dis-identification" with which we are familiar, and especially their disastrous consequences.

When you arrive in Haifa and you're not given a decent Shabbat, and they want to take your children away from you and put them in a treifa boarding school (we were living at that time in the Haifa absorption center), it shows they have no understanding of the motivations for your Return.

Not only have these children just left behind the country in which they were born, their grandparents, their school, their home, their room, their language and their sense of security, but they want to take them away from their parents and put them in a boarding school where their way of life isn't respected.

On Friday evening, nothing was arranged! If you wanted to pray, you had to go to a little minyan organized by some obliging neighbors, but when you came back there was no longer a place for you to eat!

---

7. Immigration ; literally "ascent" to Israel.

You were pressured to let your children go to a non-dati school, and they put them in an *ulpan*[8] where they were taught biblical criticism.

They were all sick of it in a couple of days.

You come to Israel with Jewish ideals, you've left your "golden calf" behind in France, you've decided to return home to cultivate different values and rebuild your country, and what do you find? "Objective," "scientific" analysis of the Bible!

God be praised, we've managed to make our way. If we'd wanted to chase after money, we could have raked in a great deal.

The Israelis, even those who don't seem to live according to the values of the Torah, nevertheless build up the country and make it live, but when I was in France, though I may have had fine ideals and Torah values, I did nothing for the existence of the country and so didn't have the right to criticize it.

Nobody's perfect, either in Israel or in Moissac. Ah, here I am back at Moissac! If I'd been the directress, I might perhaps have been able to have put myself into the skin of the children, but I would have been very frightened and would perhaps have been incapable of dealing with such a terrible situation and of saving so many children's lives. I see how much trouble I have in taking responsibility just for a house and a small family.

When we returned to Moissac after the war, it was in a state of total uncertainty, hoping against hope that our parents would come back, but knowing that they wouldn't.

We weren't sent to the Hotel Lutétia in Paris to see if they were there; we were kept out of it. The returning deportees were welcomed, fêted, looked after. They were heroes.

But, as for us, it wouldn't be wrong to say we were the "children of silence." We weren't anything; we hadn't even been deported. Fortunately! You were there with your guilt feelings about not having been deported, about not being dead, about having survived, about not being able to do anything, not having been able to do anything either to save others or to help yourself.

After the war, Moissac was in a ferment. The whole Resistance, all the élites, came to this great house, le Moulin, which had now become a sort of Jewish intellectual center. These included Jacob Gordin, André Neher, Régine Lehmann and many, many others...

---

8. Rapid course in Hebrew.

You could discuss your philosophy essay with Régine, Raymond Kahn could help you with your math homework, Georges Levitte taught our group philosophy and Judaism.

This was Shatta at full blast: the house impeccable, the budget balanced, things to eat, camps, excursions, games, songs and walks. Guests enriching the courses that were given there. There was a pulse of life in that place which I have to admire despite my negative inner vibrations.

I lived in my own inner world, which helped me to hold out. I had safeguarded this world throughout all those years, even when I was in hiding. I knew by heart the prayers, the Pirkei Avot and whole sections of the parshiot. I was connected day and night with the main elements of my world.

Two worlds were juxtaposed: the outer and the inner, and this has been the case until today. It's only now that I can speak about it, at my age and with a thousand precautions.

I hardly dare to open my mouth to say what I think in the depths, or how I feel. I perceive it as a danger, something that is going to come back on you, something for which you'll be made to pay dearly. That's what I felt and what I still feel.

To say what I really think is still often a virtual impossibility.

Writing seems to me impossible (meanwhile there have been poems, which have opened my sluice gates). I'll be condemned to death immediately.

You can only survive if you protect your inner self (though some people manage to shut it out!).

And I know people who were unable to marry or to live their Judaism because it meant renewing contact with the family, touching that painful inner self.

After that, one requires a long, long process of learning to gain confidence – confidence in yourself and confidence in others, for it is one and the same thing. The question of confidence is central to recovery. The sicker you are, the less you can speak to anyone.

Similarly, taking a medicine, going to see a doctor can be a superhuman effort. There's a mountain of obstacles you try to overcome and which you get through with difficulty when faced with reality; that is to say, when you meet someone stubborn enough to take you out of your system of defenses, or who shows you he's not a door shut against you.

Otherwise, why go and see a doctor? Just to talk? What could he say? He won't be able to understand anything, and in any case he won't be able to do anything, and that's it. Nobody can intervene in the chain of events and prevent the inevitable slide towards a catastrophe.

I have a horror of anything mechanized, anything automatic. You won't find me taking the R.E.R. (regional railway system) without trepidation. It's an effort to travel by the Métro, a closed bus is a major problem.

When the buses were open, it was okay; you could jump off en route. Do I seem to you out of my mind? A machine you can't escape from takes you from somewhere. You go in, and you only leave at the end of the chain when it's all over.

No system will ever be a giver of life; systems can't do otherwise than destroy you. When everything is registered, robotized, given a serial number, you no longer have the option of leaving at any time.

Similarly, I hate crowds; I can't stand traffic jams. I make a thousand detours – kilometers – in order to avoid entering into a bottleneck where everything is blocked. I don't want to be caught; I don't want to go into a tunnel where I can't see the exit, nor be closed in by masses and masses of cars.

Crowds – it's the concentration camp, it's Hitler. You're shoved into a cattle-car, and at the end of the journey you find yourself in the oven.

Medicine's a bit similar. You go into the hospital standing up, and you come out lying down with your legs forward!

For me, the hospital also conjured up the concentration camp with its chimney, its morgue, a whole system that turned you into a thing, that gave others absolute power over your body, which (with some exceptions) they used to satisfy their latent sadism; where you were a number on a card, good material to publish in a journal.

When I worked in Doctor Brissaud's department for children with tuberculosis and meningitis, I arrived before the procession of doctors and I made the children laugh because I couldn't bear to see their sadness.

One day, he arrived earlier than usual and saw me. He remained behind the door, not wanting to disturb me. He called me to his office and asked me, "What do you want to do?"

I answered, "Pediatrics, but there's no way I can. I don't know anyone."

In those days, one couldn't expect to get a place as a non-resident student in a good pediatric service if one didn't have connections. The head immediately gave me a word of introduction.

After the war at Moissac, now that we were "big," we looked after the younger children. The leaders had left and Shatta appointed me leader of a group of girls. But I couldn't play this role; I couldn't consider individuals as numbers. I couldn't face a group.

I needed a profession where I could deal with one person at a time. When I had to teach, I only saw each individual pupil, never a class in front of me.

At that time, I said I wanted to become an interpreter or possibly a teacher. So they gave me a class to take care of while doing my studies at the University of Toulouse.

In this class, all the children were of a different level and I had to teach them! So I went crazy. I saw the face of each child and "took out my *neshama*" (gave all I had; lit. soul). And when I corrected their work, I spent hours at night saying to myself, "No, it's not right, I can't give him this mark! What if I hurt him, if he no longer has the courage to work?"

I was always contesting the labels stuck on one pupil or another, saying, "He's nevertheless an exceptional person. He's got problems and they have to be taken into account."

And Shatta listened to me, which was quite miraculous, because I took the side of the children without playing the leader, and she normally gave her attention primarily to leaders and external benefactors. One always had to curry favor with such and such a notable, present the home and children in the most favorable light.

Something in me drew me irresistibly towards the suffering of others, with an infinite desire to help them. I have in fact perhaps been very fortunate in having been able in real life, thanks to my profession, to work and struggle in that direction: to help each person mobilize himself to the utmost to fight against the injustices which, whether affective, social or cultural or resulting from assimilation, have alienated him intentionally or otherwise.

At Moissac, those who wanted to go to school had to fight, to come first in class, to show themselves to be "worthy" of studying, and all this in midst of adolescence when you ask yourself all sorts of questions about everything.

I liked studying, especially languages. I had been forced to be good at languages as a result of being forced to cross frontiers with kicks in my behind and of having to use words.

Languages are life itself. Literature makes it possible to know someone without his being there with all his weight, without your being dependent on him and on the way he looks at you, which is always alien, hostile or indifferent.

At the end of my time in the senior class, seeing that I had to organize the camps, look after the girls and arrange excursions, I decided to stop going to high school a month or two before the end of the school year in order to prepare for my matriculation alone.

I was consequently denied the prize for outstanding performance. It was a scandal in the school. Although all the teachers regarded me as their star pupil, my report was worse than mediocre. They all blamed me for not going on right to the end.

So I had to present myself to the jury in these unfavorable circumstances, and I knew that if I didn't get my matriculation, I wouldn't be allowed to continue!

Matriculation, first part; matriculation, second part. I was terribly frightened. I said to myself: "I'll never make it," but I got through both parts with distinction. In the end, I was very successful. My fears, at bottom, were only a manifestation of my instinct for life.

I'm frightened, I'm paralyzed with fear, but in the hour of testing I do whatever's necessary, I go all out to be able to continue.

I foresee all the disasters, everything that could happen. Then I set out the markers and do the right thing in order not to perish.

In my opinion, this is an inheritance from our ancestors, from our imahot, our maternal ancestors. Take a woman like my mother who in the worst circumstances was able to create a microcosm in which one could live.

It took me a long time to be able to cope with daily life. It was easier for me to deal with exceptional situations, to create life out of death. Just living was an impossible task. Perhaps I now manage more or less, although I still have to struggle all the time to overcome my phantoms, the thousand demons that drag you away to re-experience all that was imposed on you and which is no longer relevant to you, at least where external reality is concerned.

So I passed my matriculation exams. In the summer, I was a group leader in the scout camps. I was two years older than the girls I looked after.

We hitchhiked down to the Côte d'Azur, and I don't know where we slept or what we ate. When I think about it today, it makes me shudder; but it was good – an educational way of doing things, a way of making young people responsible.

It was only that I was much too frightened of mismanaging things, a fear probably connected with the memory of my parents' deportation, for which I felt myself to be responsible because I had left them on their own when I knew French and they didn't. Without me they were lost!

In my phantasm, it was therefore wrong to put me in charge of the girls. Things were liable to turn out badly and I'd be unable to prevent a disaster.

I was long haunted with the same anxieties when dealing with sick children. I was frightened that my treatments wouldn't be able to prevent their deaths.

The only thing to which I was able to grant the power of survival was moral values, not physical life. For years, I was unable to "sound" patients. I had the impression I didn't hear anything. I looked into the microscope, I couldn't see; I felt someone's abdomen but I couldn't feel anything. But of course this wasn't true! I *did* feel; I was even an excellent clinician with an accurate power of reasoning. I was a good doctor.

But I was in such a panic that I always had to telephone someone and ask: "What's your opinion?" I'll never stop trying to understand all this negativity and to draw something positive out of it.

In passing through Moissac, I'd gone quite a distance from my own personal world, the world of my father, for whom Moissac was already "assimilated."

But this assimilated world had saved our lives. It was comradely, cheerful, open to the world outside, connected with nature. You felt the breath of life there, of people who lived with their bodies. For the first time, I no longer felt that a gathering of Jews was synonymous with the camp.

I've had to rebuild everything with these two elements: that of my parents and that of the scouts of Moissac. If I'd followed the world of my parents, I wouldn't be where I am today. But the assimilated world, the external world couldn't be life either because you can't be alive if you aren't yourself.

I've had to undertake a whole work of unification, putting together my deep identity and present conditions.

One Must Tell

Again and again
one must tell
of past misfortunes
if only in order to appreciate
all the benefits
which God has showered upon us,
and of which the most precious
are freedom
and dignity
in the material world as well.

August 24, 1985

ENGLAND

After the war, journeys to England were organized by the Marrainage Scheme,[1] acting in conjunction with the O.S.E. Good ladies over there looked for families that could receive child-survivors who in this way could learn English.

This was how I was one of those who had the right to make the voyage. It was in 1947: all my friends had gone, and I was left behind on the platform of the railway- station because I had no documents.

I was supposed to be Czech, my father being Czech as he was born in Czechoslovakia, a country bordering on Hungary and Poland.

But the Czechoslovaks did not recognize my right to their nationality. The Czechoslovakian consulate did not want to give me a passport. I wasn't French either, and the French didn't want to give me the identification document of a stateless person since I was Czechoslovakian.

One of the "chiefs" from Moissac had to go to the consulate in Marseilles on my behalf, declaring that I had renounced my Czechoslovakian nationality so that I could finally obtain the celebrated "accordion" (folded document) – the green identification paper of a stateless person, with my name entered by the French.

I renounced my Czechoslovakian nationality, which the Czechs did not recognize in order to have no nationality at all, as French nationality was also denied me.

The problem of nationality later came up in a very insistent and dramatic way when I began to study medicine. The *Ordre des Médecins* (Board of Physicians), with a stringency which I can only describe as xenophobic, prevented the government from granting naturalization to foreign medical students.

Nobody was enthusiastic about my decision to study medicine.

---

1. A committee set up in London to arrange for young people from children's homes to stay with families.

In any case, we weren't French, so one couldn't even register with the Faculty of Medicine because the Board of Physicians vetoed naturalization, and if you *did* do medical studies nevertheless, you couldn't practice in France.

My sister had already come up against enormous difficulties. In my case, things worked out differently.

I registered for the literature course at the University of Toulouse in order to escape the opposition of the Board of Physicians. I found it enthralling. I was dealing with the thing that interests me most: human problems.

I put in a request for naturalization and I told Shatta. France recognized the children of deportees who weren't French as war-orphans and gave them scholarships. I applied for a scholarship, I obtained my naturalization and then I registered in the medical school.

I also did the same for my brother who was in Bordeaux studying biology during my two years of literature.

Shatta had very kindly put him in contact with a professor of biology over there and with the rabbi of Bordeaux, both of whom took him under their wings.

After all these detours, there we were, all three of us, medical students in Paris, sitting on the same benches in the same school. What a fire it gave out when we three redheads were together under a street lamp! You could spot us from far off. I think we can't have failed to have made an impression on people. We weren't part of their world.

In the medical faculty, Jews who were comfortably settled in Paris rubbed shoulders with those who had just disembarked from North Africa with their brand-new suitcases, their brilliantined hair and their daily changes of suit, while we wore the same clothes all the time.

We were so glad to be able to study that we couldn't understand how the others could waste their time. Some canvassed for the Communist Party, others went out or flirted or went displaying their immaturity from one discussion to the next.

When we were in front of a sick person, something happened. The sick man was there with his sufferings, his problems, and all our efforts were devoted to relieving him, while the others often did this work in order to make a lot of money or because mother and daddy had decided on it.

We liked medicine and we had to pass all our exams, or else our scholarships would have been withdrawn. We were eager to learn, to go forward.

It must have been an unrealized vocation of my father and grandfather. Our vocation was to be present for the other person who was suffering (the other person perhaps being ourselves abandoned to our sufferings).

So I was only able to discover England the following year.

It was a whole expedition. You took the train and the boat and you were sea-sick.

When we got there, there were two lines: one for the "British" on one side and another for "aliens" on the other. We, of course, were foreigners once more.

The secretary we dealt with was a woman writer who had been partially crippled by polio. She was extraordinary. It is often people who have suffered who are able to identify with the underprivileged.

We were placed with people in a somewhat haphazard manner. My brother found himself at first with a Jewish family of German origin which didn't understand anything about anything. Discipline, first of all: "Either you come to meals on time or you take a sandwich with you!" Just imagine! After years of knocking about the world, to be treated like a four-year old!

A girlfriend of mine was with another lady. They didn't get on too well together. We met to talk about our adventures – "The woman I'm with is like this, the man I'm with is like that" – and laughter was the only way to protect ourselves in this new situation of dependence. I was lodged with an Orthodox Jewish family of German and Polish origin, where each person lived his own life. The children, apart from the last two, were more-or-less grown-up.

Each had his own program: the father went to his work, and the mother was active in Zionism. She collected funds to help Israel in its struggle against the British, received Moshe Sharett and gave herself unstintingly. The oldest daughter, a psychology student, was active in a Zionist youth movement, and the oldest son, who was studying chemistry, was never there.

As people were out at all hours of the day, I found myself with the daughter, who put together something for me to nibble. Apart from that, I wandered about all day: visited museums, walked around with my chums.

In this family, they were very nice, but they weren't present in the house, which suited me well enough because I would have found it difficult to have been treated like a small child.

In a sense, it was very good for us who came from children's homes to get a glimpse of family life while having the possibility of being amongst ourselves and organizing our own activities, visiting one another and spending evenings singing together.

I mostly went to the family where my brother was staying because there was a presence there, a quite extraordinary woman.

She sat there in her garden with her young children. We had tea; she talked. Delicate and sensitive, she was able to convey a presence without imposing herself.

In England, I once again found my uncle Jacob (the husband of my aunt Ida, my father's sister). In Berlin, they used to live very close to us.

We took refuge in their home when my mother was picked up by the Gestapo. Uncle Jacob had always been a warm person.

When we found him again in England after the war, he was very unhappy, as I've said, that he couldn't have us to stay in his home. He was poor and badly housed.

The German Jews who had immigrated to England weren't treated much better than in France. We were put in concentration camps and they were sent to mines where they worked for a pittance, and as he was a *tzadik ba'olam*[2] rather than someone preoccupied with money, he had only just enough to live on.

His wife's story had left him with some very tragic memories. When Jewish children had been allowed to leave Germany, their son left with the *Kindertransport*,[3] and my uncle also managed to cross the frontier.

His wife was expected to follow soon after, but it was difficult to obtain the necessary documents, and the very day she was due to leave, when she finally had the permit in her hands, the frontiers were closed and she was trapped in Germany.

Just imagine what I must have represented for this man! I had the same name as his wife and I resembled her. He was so happy to find me again, and at the same time so sad.

He lived in a garret, which had survived a bombing raid. He liked to tell us how one morning he woke up under a pile of rubble that had fallen

---

2. One of the righteous on earth.
3. Britain agreed to accept 10,000 Jewish children from Germany as a way of clearing itself of guilt for refusing hundreds of thousands of Jews entry to the Jewish National Home in Palestine, which was then under the British Mandate, in this way consigning them to an inescapable death in Germany.

from the roof. And suddenly, there was somebody in front of him who said, "We're from the Red Cross. *Would you like a cup of tea?*"

He answered, "Get me out of here first. Then we'll see."

So he was always in this garret, which, it would appear, once again had a roof.

This man who lacked everything had spent all his money on stamps, trying to trace the members of his family who had remained alive and to bring them together, telling each one where the others were.

He wrote regularly, and, thanks to him, we knew who on my father's side was still alive and who wasn't, and where they lived.

My aunt Ida having been deported, he was left all alone with, I imagine, a sense of guilt, as is usual with survivors.

His son was in London at that time. We had little in common with him.

My grandfather's second wife was also there with her three daughters, as well as my female cousin L, now in Israel. The only ones we got on with were those who had suffered: Uncle Jacob and cousin L.

The others were nice enough, but it was impossible to link up with that world as if nothing had happened, to start up again with meaningless little stories. We probably begrudged them that they were there and not the others.

One needed a great deal of finesse, delicacy and attention in order to make a connection with us and to be forgiven for being there in the absence of those closest to us.

The only ones capable of it were Uncle Jacob and to a certain extent, cousin L. Her parents had gone to China, to Shanghai.

At that time, one went where one could. You would have even gone to hell – anywhere except Germany!

The husband died there and my aunt found herself alone.

Later, this cousin went to Israel where I saw her again, as adorable as ever.

In England she wanted to show us the stately homes. Everyone wanted to please us, but for us, bricks, however attractive, were no more than bricks and stones.

Uncle was really the only one we visited with pleasure. I think it was due to him that we were able to renew contact with the family. Without him, I don't know if we could have done it; it was too painful.

He remarried, to our dear aunt Kitty, who, together with her whole family, struggled to take him out of his difficult situation, buy a house, get him clothes, purchase him a place in the synagogue and give him the *kavod*[4] which he so much deserved.

Among these English Jews, most of whom were *am ha'artzim*,[5] he stood out as someone who was able to study and teach, to pray and sing, who knew how to read the Torah, who could give a *dvar Torah*,[6] a *shiur*,[7] who had something to say. The only thing was, he was a foreigner!

The two daughters of my aunt in Shanghai, who had been stuck in England during the war, later went to Israel where they were joined by their mother. One of them, during this long enforced stay in England where she was in a *hachshara*[8] training center, found herself living in a hostel and had a nervous breakdown.

As they had decided to put her in an asylum, my Uncle Jacob, whose niece she was as she was his wife's sister's daughter, came to fetch her: "I've come to pick up my niece."

"Who are you?"

"It's about my niece. I'm her uncle; what's going on here? I'll never let her go to an asylum. She's no more insane than you or me."

He took her out of there immediately.

He put her on a mattress in his room, and he got her out of her condition with a little affection and attention and by providing a bit of her own background.

He saved her life, because she could have rotted in that asylum until the end of her days.

Basically, we liked London despite the government's foreign policy. It was pleasant among the English. It was a bit as if we'd found the family again, even if it was only through an intermediary.

It was also the city to which one could have escaped.

We remembered that when we had left Belgium, we had wanted to go to London...

In England today, there are places I don't like to go to and places I do like to go to. In London I feel good, as in a place which represents life and liberty and has nothing in common with children's homes.

---

4. Dignity, honor.
5. Ignorant people.
6. A brief commentary on the Torah.
7. A lesson.
8. An agricultural training centre where young Jews prepared to emigrate to Palestine.

We had a few rights of our own there, even if it was only the right to receive attention.

Our entire group was in London – at least those who were regularly re-invited by the families, like my brother and me.

My brother ended up at the Sinclairs, who are still like family to him. Before he got married, he brought his girlfriend to see them, and then to see our uncle, who said: "So we'll drink *l'cha'im*,⁹ you're engaged now!" He always did the right thing.

He wasn't able to come to my wedding; he was ill. We were very sorry. For my uncle, our slightest action or gesture was important. When we succeeded in passing an examination, he was delighted. And it seemed to me something marvelous that the marks I got meant anything to anyone.

He enhanced the value of everything, he was proud of us. He realized that nothing could be taken for granted where we were concerned. Like the cousins from Belgium, he knew how to be present at the key moments of life.

When I was expecting my second son, in the eighth month, I said, "We must go and see Uncle Jacob."

For Pesach we went there for a week. We almost weren't able to enter England. I was pregnant to bursting-point, and the British didn't want to let me in. British nationality is costly! Supposing I'd given birth over there!

My uncle gave us a marvelous welcome. He saw my husband for the first time. He gave him his tallit, he took him to shul, and Fred was called up to the Torah for the first time in his life.

After that, he always said: "It was my bar mitzvah!"

Uncle was an Orthodox Jew and Fred had come from far away.

As he was my husband, he considered him part of his own family. Appreciating his human and intellectual qualities, he knew how to set him at ease and made him feel at home. He died that same year. I believe that our visit gave him very great pleasure.

Before giving birth, I used to write to him asking the names of our ancestors (together with their meaning), to give to the children about to be born.

As my mother-in-law wanted us to give our son the name of her father, he wrote me long letters explaining that the name Mendel had come from Spain and signified Menahem: that is, comforter.

In this he played the role of the elder, and he played it well.

---

9. A Hebrew toast, "To life!"

Once he came to France with his second wife. He had a piece of wax blocking his ear, and at that time I was a very young non-resident student in the surgical outpatient clinic.

What pride, what joy he had on seeing me in a white overall in the hospital, fully empowered to treat his ear (just half a minute and he was no longer deaf), and then in seeing my room in the students' halls of residence with my name on the door, and in meeting all my chums who little by little were returning to Judaism together with me and who studied with me on Saturday afternoons.

Nothing could have given him greater happiness. We felt very close to one another.

After his death, we regularly invited his widow, Aunt Kitty, to our home. We banded together to pay for her journey. We spent the Jewish holidays together.

One day, long after her husband's death, she turned up with a magnificent pair of silver candlesticks, saying, "When young Jews get married, it's the girl's parents who provide the candlesticks, and uncle always wanted to buy you some, but he didn't have the money."

She promised herself to do what he had wanted, and saved up penny by penny until she had enough.

These things which seem to have no importance but which are beyond price!

And yet she was a stranger in relation to us. She was the second wife of my uncle-by-marriage, but she was closer to us than many others and was like a grandmother to my children.

When they were small, she'd hug them and kiss them; she ruined herself for them at Marks & Spencer.

Every small progress the children made was like a gift which she appreciated.

She saw us with the eyes of her husband whom she had loved so much. The two of them didn't have any children together, being too old.

So that was London, an alien world, but one which for once was not hostile towards us. That world opened up towards us without swallowing us.

We had escaped from Moissac with its labels and all those unmentioned things which had closed us in.

I walked around, I bought some trifle; I was happy. I went to the National Gallery, to concerts. I read in bed late into the night, and if I wanted to sleep in the morning, I did so.

A breach in the system! And for me who loved languages, it was a delight to be able to speak English.

Among ourselves we poked gentle fun at that narrow little world which revolved around cups of tea and games of bridge. And the question was always with me: how could one continue to live as before the war? How could one?

England was one stage among so many others in building oneself up and finding oneself again. A whole undertaking which I might describe as the conquest of one's identity and dignity.

I stopped going to England after my first voyage to Israel. There were also short holidays with non-Jews somewhere in France, where I felt a complete stranger with nothing to do among people who lived for good wine, good food and their good local soil, "like God in France."[10] Me, I can't live "like God in France." To live like a *ben-adam*[11] is quite hard enough.

---

10. *Leben wie Gott in Frankreich*, "To live like God in France," a Yiddish idiom declaring how well one lived in France, and the title of a book.
11. Human being.

Testimony

I love France
because of Saint-Exupéry,
but does France
like what I say?

October 30, 1983

PARIS

In 1950, for the last time, I organized the summer camp at Laversine[1] with Aviva, a friend who was an orchestral conductor and a pianist. The two of us started off Laversine with this camp of girl guides.

After that, the connection with Moissac tapered off. In 1950, I went to Paris because in provincial towns like Toulouse where each person had his own family you felt even more uprooted than in the capital. One or two girls from Moissac were already in a hostel in Paris, and said to me, "Come and join us."

Having got through my P.C.B.[2] brilliantly in Toulouse, I landed in Paris and settled in a garret where one could only lie down or sit down and where there was just enough room for a bed, a table and a washbasin.

There, despite everything, I felt happy. I could close the door; I was at home.

I had asked to be lodged in this hostel but to be given a room of my own. It was my way of setting down roots: I just had to be left in peace.

That's how I got this little place under the roof.

I was not acquainted with Paris, having been there only once or twice with the Moissac choir. I was completely lost: everything was strange to me – the endless streets, the tall buildings, the climate, everything.

If all these child-survivors didn't become tuberculous, mentally sick, prostitutes or tramps, it's a miracle.

There was no one who really cared about you, but we helped each other, and fortunately there were my brother and sister.

My sister, who had got married and was already the mother of a little boy, lived in Kremlin-Bicêtre in such an "attractive" hovel that it became a permanent symbol of all that is to be avoided.

---

1. A château in the Paris region given by the Rothschild family to house the young people from Moissac.
2. P.C.B. (Physics, Chemistry, Biology): the preparatory year of medical studies.

She and her husband were studying while earning their living. He was a tailor, she helped him, and as he was allergic to the dust on fabrics, he coughed every night.

Despite everything, their home was nevertheless a stopping-place for us.

Here I was in this Paris of the 1950s, not knowing a soul. The other students had their families, they'd done their studies in the city; they had their school-chums, they'd done their P.C.B. together, they had their homes; and me, I was lodged in this place where no one cared about me, where I just came to sleep and where there was only a gas-ring to heat up some coffee.

As in any collective, I came across all sorts of weird types, and I had more than ever to stick to my objective: study and more study. One had to grab one's time in one's little place or in the library.

There were a few girls from Moissac there, all more or less at a loss. They would come around to my place to tell me their troubles.

The days passed quickly: in the morning, the hospital; in the afternoon, practical work and lectures at the university.

I attended all the lectures. I learned while listening, the lessons being registered in my memory; but the hospital exhausted me. The world of the hospital made me sick.

You won't believe it when I tell you how I learnt anatomy. Learning by rote for its own sake is impossible for me. I can only retain things by relating them to a system, to a whole.

I went off to buy a skeleton; the price was terribly high. But there was a second channel: someone who worked at the Pantin cemetery sold students bones from a common grave.

With my delicate sense of smell, I was haunted by the stench for years.

First of all, I had to lug these bones through the Métro, then I had to stow them somewhere in my room. It was ghastly! But there was no other way I could learn anatomy. The artery goes through the hole along the muscle behind the bone... I couldn't visualize it. I must be on bad terms with space.

When I had to do solid geometry, I made use of a ruler and a sphere, and with two or three objects I put together a construction that represented the facts of the problem. Otherwise, I just couldn't visualize it.

This perhaps is like *gemara*,[3] where you always start with a concrete problem to be grappled with first and only then draw an abstract principle of conduct from it.

---

3. A compilation of the oral texts of the Torah in written form.

There is no generality where you would be such-and-such a number. You're always dealing with Yankel or Schmil, this person or that person, each with his particular characteristics, and for one the problem is not the same as for the other.

There may perhaps be a common denominator behind their problems, but you can only approach them one by one.

I lacked the ability to synthesize, but in analysis I was unbeatable. But learning by heart or giving a rapid summary were not gifts I possessed.

In order to arrive at a synthesis, I had first of all to absorb everything and analyze the smallest detail. The synthesis would only come afterwards, and, together with that, the registration in my memory.

My husband didn't function in the same way as I did. He sat with his books on the day before the exams and in one night reviewed the whole anatomy.

Next morning he got up and went off to get good marks, and then went on his way forgetting all he had learned. Me, I'd worked all year long, every day of every trimester, and I'd seen every nook and cranny.

It's true that with the letter A, the first letter of his name, which comes at the beginning of the alphabet, he'd always encounter typical questions which had been asked in all previous examinations, while I, with my name at the end of the alphabetical list, was confronted with questions that had never been asked and about which nobody knew what to say.

And I, who had gone through my entire syllabus, who had studied and thought about each bone and all that is around it, I'd succeeded in putting together an answer, describing the orifice in question and getting an average mark. And that was already not so bad!

Not to speak of the fear of not making it. If you failed, you were left out in the cold; you couldn't continue.

Return to Zion

What an immeasurable joy
to belong to the generation
of those who return to Zion,
who see their children active there
and their grandchildren growing up there.
What an infinite happiness
to be here already,
to get up in the morning
in one's home and garden
and see its flowers grow
and to be in a sovereign State
in one's Land.
When I think of our parents,
they would have given much
to have had as much,
when so very many
were exterminated in camps.

April 27, 1994

ISRAEL

After England and Uncle Jacob, one of the most important stages in my life was my stay with my uncle in Haifa.

I lived at his place; he left me in peace. In the morning, he went off to his work; he let me sleep or doze, take in the smells, hear the noises, feel all this life around me. You wake up, you hear the birds, you breathe in the atmosphere of the gardens, you sense the little horse-drawn carriages going by.

In Haifa, it was a bit like the quarter of Jerusalem where we live now, with little houses where everyone knew everyone else, as in a village. You could leave your front door open.

You went out and everybody greeted you in the street, especially when I was with my uncle who knew everyone. He couldn't walk around in the town without saying "Shalom" to all those who crossed our path. He had a shop called "Carmel Bazaar."

Uncle was a Freemason, and so were most of his friends, including one who was a chemist. He compensated himself in this way for the fact that he hadn't been able to study (and also perhaps for the fact that he had cut himself off from any religious community).

He liked to discuss the books he had read recently with all these intellectuals who were bourgeois in a German way. For my part, I wasn't going to bow and scrape or play the learned ape in front of these "fine people" who spoke German and belonged to a world I didn't want to be part of – a world of assimilated German Jews.

I wasn't able to give him the pleasure of becoming part of his group, but he didn't ask anything of me. He got worried just once. I went to see one of my chums and didn't return at the time expected. Someone was actually worried about me! I wasn't used to it.

Here I once again found the London ambiance a bit, except that I didn't feel I was in a foreign country and I could speak freely, opening my heart to any Jew in the bus or in the street, as he spoke the same language as I did.

We looked at each other, we had the same history, and I felt myself to be in a sort of haven of security.

When I arrived in Israel, it stopped my breath to find that the policemen were Jewish, that the soldiers were Jewish, that everything was written in Hebrew, that they spoke Hebrew.

The whole world that you carried within you, hidden away, had all of a sudden burst forth into reality and gained acceptance. Your dual quest for human dignity and Jewish life was realized before your very eyes.

In France, you had reached the stage of social rehabilitation thanks to your studies, but not the stage of the right to your family-and-collective identity. The Jewish history you carried within you had to die.

And suddenly, in Israel, all that had seemed dead and finished had the right to live: I saw it living in front of me. You could regain your dignity, recognize your inner language as a value freely manifested by an entire people.

All at once, you recognized the tremendous impact of the *galut* and you realized to what a degree you had been exiled.

Never before had I felt things, people, the elements, everything as intensely as I did now. I had inherited the love of the land of Israel, even if it was only through prayers and tradition.

I felt again, but this time in the land of his ancestors, my father's euphoria on arriving in the south of France, crazy at seeing the seven species specific to Israel and explaining every detail of the vegetation, although he had never set foot in a Mediterranean landscape, describing to me the pomegranates, the figs, the vines...

I always say that one can make one's history coincide with one's geography. If you "carry away your town with you on the soles of your shoes," one day you'll find your town again. You're in it. Everything you've been told is true. It's there, vibrant with life.

In Israel, at the beginning, I wasn't able to go and pray in a synagogue. I entered into communion with the landscape. The sky, the vegetation, the scents, the earth, every tree, every stone spoke to my heart.

Can you imagine what a festivity every moment was? You find again a world that belongs to you, where you're welcomed, valued, recognized, loved – a world where you have your place. I could only think of staying: living in Israel, finishing my studies there and then working there.

But when they proposed that I should go to a Kupat Holim[1] in the Negev, I rebelled. Once again, I was treated like just anybody who could be disposed of in any way whatsoever. So I went back to Paris.

The following year, it was my brother's turn to discover Israel. Then in 1955, I went back to my uncle for a vacation. I returned to France with a heavy heart, as I did later on every time I came back after spending the Jewish holidays with my children in Jerusalem.

Once, when none of my sons was in the army, we succeeded in doing some touring, covering the land from top to bottom and traveling the length and breadth of it.

After this rediscovery of places which you felt to be more and more alive, it was senseless to return to France, not only, as most people think, because you're separating yourself from your children, because you're going back to work and the vacation is over, but because in Israel you feel yourself to be in your element, exactly like a fish which is back in its water.

Put a fish from the sea in fresh water and you'll see what happens. Fresh water, it's all very well to say that... and then a bomb goes off at the synagogue in rue Copernic.

I said at that point: "We must go. We won't die of hunger over there. We have to go."

They preferred to consider me crazy rather than to confront the evidence. But those who were honest amongst them confessed to me that they felt the same way as I did but were incapable of formulating their feelings, and still less of drawing the practical conclusions.

You can't live constantly with this distressing lucidity if you don't at the same time have the courage to move, to tear yourself away from your well-appointed home, your clinic, your environment, your habits.

Why would someone who has "arrived" socially be crazy enough to put himself back into the skin of a refugee? Why should he do it? To escape what? To escape a "persecution mania"?

I was flabbergasted by certain reflexes – of denial, of flight, of repression. And *I* was the one who was accused of being delirious! When someone said to me, "You're right, but one can't live with that way of thinking," it did me good to hear it.

Not everyone can afford the luxury of doing what I do – look the cause of suffering in the face without telling oneself stories in order to stop feeling bad.

---

1.   Health Insurance Fund clinic.

I felt more in exile than ever because of the images I had brought back from Israel. On Erev Shabbat everyone goes home with flowers or prays at the Kotel, the Western Wall; you're in unity with your surroundings. It's your country.

I was able to appreciate how a French peasant felt about his land. Previously, I had never really sensed the meaning of belonging to a land. I was able to perceive how much I'd been a stranger everywhere.

But the day you arrive in Israel to live, you still feel a stranger there. Your neshama isn't a stranger there, but you're a stranger to all the dross of the galut that they want to impose on you as your collective Me, despite the fact that this isn't the case, but if you dare to resist, watch out!

My love for Israel has never wavered.

I have had the schooling of a life which wasn't a usual one for a child, but which taught me to stand up to ordeals, to struggle and to give things their proper value.

In Israel I was in seventh heaven. I learned Hebrew, I was happy, I had succeeded in bringing my children to the country.

It's said in the Torah: "Man does not live by bread alone." What makes people happy is not to have fifty maidservants and six marble palaces, to be able to afford caviar morning and evening and to possess fifty boats.

The only thing which makes people happy is to be *beseder*, in accordance with their ideals. It's the only thing which gives one the strength to overcome difficulties, and the only thing which bestows happiness in the true meaning of the word – not the pseudo-happiness of consumerism in which you stuff yourself with drugs, but the joy of following a path which you recognize as being your own and in which you go forward whatever the difficulties. As Régine used to say, quoting Camus, "Whatever obstructs the path helps one to go forward."

You're pleased whenever you succeed in taking a further step forward and advancing in that direction. That's why we were happy.

This whole story, *my* whole story could be told by following the traces of the *malach* (angel) who has been present at every crossroads of my life fraught with mortal danger, and I could thank Hakadosh Baruch Hu for all the *chesed*[2] He has shown me at the very heart of all the evil that has engulfed us, for all the help He has given me unceasingly in this mad struggle.

---

2. Kindness.

How many times was it *min hashamayim?*[3]

However much we wanted to take ourselves out of the galut, it clung to our skin, and every Jew who makes aliyah must be aware of this phenomenon.

I couldn't understand why aliyah, Israel's other front next to the IDF, was so ill supported. In the entire world, the greatest psychologists, educators, scholars in the humanities are in large part Jewish.

To successfully achieve the massive transplantation of a whole population dispersed for two thousand years, it seems to me that a committee should be set up. There are many who would be willing to do this voluntarily in order to consider the psychological, social and material problems which are involved.

Isn't one always a *holei hadash?*[4]

It's a sickness which can be treated like any other – a sickness caused by aliyah. It's a syndrome which has to be taken into account and attended to in the same way as any other pathological syndrome.

Everyone knows that once you've been received into the country, once you have your home and some work, the first stage is passed. And if everything doesn't work out for you, at any rate the situation is saved for your children.

We're a people that has been *na va'nad* (wandering) for two thousand years, and when *olim hadashim*, new immigrants, arrive, we can't put ourselves in their skins or imagine for a second what it is like for them to go into a supermarket and be unable to read the labels on the products.

Our destiny and our re-identification can only come about in Israel, but one need hardly insist on the difficulties of aliyah. The term *savlanut* not only means patience but also endurance of suffering.

In this so much hoped-for land, one suddenly finds oneself a stranger, one has a poor knowledge of the language. The culture is so different from the one in which, despite oneself, one has been immersed for decades, and one is confronted with a population preoccupied with its own problems of existence and which is not always attentive to the new oleh.

Despite the warmth and devotion of a few exceptional people, the obstacles to integration seemed to us so insurmountable at that time that

---

3.   Heaven-sent.
4.   A new sick person (a play on the words, *oleh hadash*, new immigrant).

with rent hearts and aching souls we returned to France, swearing to ourselves that it was only for the time being.

For my part, this is how I imagine an aliyah should be. The former *shlichim*[5] would come and fetch the newcomers, and would install them in a housing block and help them with the bureaucracy, while their wives would act as mother's helpers, visiting the women in their homes, explaining how the water-heater works and where and how to do one's shopping.

The newcomers would be taken by the hand like toddlers as I do in my *tipul*,[6] and as one does with small children who are learning to walk.

Shalom Wach and his wife did this with a group from Nice which immigrated with our son in 1993, and much was done by volunteers who devoted themselves to helping with the reception of olim from Russia and Ethiopia.

An oleh may appear to be an adult, but in reality he is thrown back into the situation of a small child who cannot walk or speak.

As in psychoanalysis, one makes a regression, one is small again and one reverts to one's former life. One must be conscious of this risk of regression and know that the present will be tinged with one's past experience.

For those who come from Europe and have passed through the *Shoah*[7] it will be one thing; for those who come from North Africa it will be experienced in another way, and for those who have already been refugees it will be something else again.

And for each one the present is mingled with what he has experienced in his family circle with his father, his mother, his sisters and brothers.

Why not envisage a real psychological tutelage in the *ulpanim*[8] by placing, next to the Hebrew teachers (some *morot*[9] do this work very well), volunteers who would show these brand-new Israelis the way and would be responsible for them during the transitional period, the time they need for learning to walk on their own?

---

5. Emissaries of the Jewish Agency.
6. Therapeutic treatment.
7. The Holocaust.
8. *Ulpan*, plural *ulpanim*, Hebrew-language courses for immigrants
9. Women teachers.

When a parent gives his hand to his small child who is beginning to walk, that does not mean that the child will never be able to walk. You simply give him your hand until he is sure enough on his feet to be let go and allowed to continue on his own.

And in a case where a successful adaptation does not take place, the immigrant's community of origin should receive him back warmly. What is there to be ashamed of in recognizing one's difficulties?

And if everything isn't ideal in the reception of newcomers, that is hardly surprising.

This little country of four million inhabitants obviously has to defend itself.

How can one be tough and firm with one's enemies and suddenly be gentle to someone else? It's by no means simple, and the people of the country need a true education which teaches them to behave in a suitable manner in every circumstance. They've been reared to live a hard life and they know how to put up with a hard life.

At the present time, they're tough with each other and soft with their enemies. It's the world upside-down!

In a certain way, they're contemptuous of the weak. There are so few Israelis, they have war on their borders and terrorists within, plus innumerable financial problems and all kinds of social and economic difficulties. It's hot but one has to work nevertheless.

It's true that life there is hard. There's the three years' military service – without counting the periods of reserve duty – the permanent state of danger, the claustrophobia, international opinion focused on you, the hatred of all the peoples, and all the weight of the distant past and the more recent past.

So why should they help people who have lived in a land of abundance and arrive "laden with gold and silver?"

I envisage an army of people interested in these problems who would set up teams of volunteers devoted to facilitating aliyah (this is already being done in part). Personally, I'm willing to do my bit.

And even if this idea would cost money, it would be less expensive than the failures, however few there may be.

Try to imagine thousands of Jews coming to populate a town or a village. You need a doctor, a baker, a nurse. If you discourage the first comers, the others won't come either. That's what happened with the Russians.

You have no idea of my husband's professional abilities. He's invited to all international congresses because in his field he's one of the most experienced doctors in the world from the clinical point of view and even with regard to research. He has obtained results with very modest technical means.

It's not because it's my husband that I'm speaking this way. He's outstanding in his field.

In the case of a man like him, you thank the Lord that he's come here with his goodwill and knowledge. You put him in the middle of the country and you get him to serve.

But as he's better than the others, everyone is terrified of losing their place.

We're coming home, but after two thousand years, you've become like a stranger in your home. You have to get used to the climate and learn the language, and your *hamor*[10] doesn't always follow.

I know there are few countries where such efforts are made to integrate immigrants. But however that may be, in the case of an oleh, the volcano erupts.

Ida Akerman with her two eldest children, Myriam and Olivier-Menachem, 1959.

---

10. "Donkey," meaning one's corporeal nature.

Myriam Akerman as a child.

Olivier-Menachem Akerman as a child.

Fred and Ida Akerman. Paris 1972.

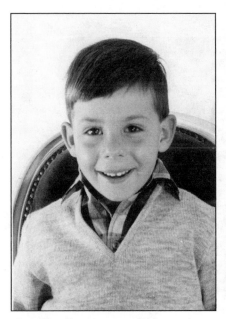

Guy-Elie Akerman as a child.

Rav Botschko, Rosh Yeshiva at Montreux, Switzerland.

Olivier-Menachem Akerman, tankist, 1978.

Guy-Elie Akerman, parachutist, 1979.

The wedding of Menachem Akerman and Manou Landau. Jerusalem 1983.

The wedding of Guy-Elie Akerman and Rina Wolf. Jerusalem 1981.

Myriam and Daniel Bauer

Return

I don't want to go to the Antilles
or to Manila,
the lovely Seychelles
or Tahiti
or Amazonia.
That's all over;
I've done it all.
I only want to go back
to my land of blessing,
for all the splendid scenes
of these places
are etched in black
in the depths of my memory.
I don't want to go into exile
even in Brazil
amongst strangers,
eating their food,
suffering their rottenness.
I've toured the earth
and all the wars
of the hatreds
and sorrows
of all the nations.
So let me go home
to Zion!

March 24, 1984

SOME EVIDENT TRUTHS

On my return to France I worked in a Jewish school. I went to the principal and said to him: "In your school I see two main groups of children, each of which has its own specific problems. On the one hand there are Ashkenazim, children of survivors of the Shoah, and on the other hand Sephardim, the children of refugees. But I don't see anywhere here where their problems could be taken into account."

So I set to work fighting to have the possibility of listening to the children. It was a whole business.

I had been engaged as a pediatrician, a school doctor. There was a male pediatrician for the boys and I was the woman pediatrician for the girls. In this way, it was "kosher."

But when I saw that twenty girls were made to wait for an hour undressed in an unheated room and that they then had to file past at a trot, just long enough for one to glance at their backs and say, " Oh yes, this one's distorted, that one's feet are crooked, that one has decayed teeth," and that moral slaps-on-the-face were then administered to the parents and the children and that this was "kosher" too, I fought once again, and I managed to get them to agree that I would have only a few children at a time, that they wouldn't have to wait completely naked in the cold, that I would conduct my visit in the way I wanted and that I wouldn't have to fill out the forms in the way they asked for.

The secretary was very kind and devoted, but when a child said, "I feel sick," she answered, "You must have eaten too many French fries." I for my part noted down the name of the girl on a list that I was drawing up as we went along.

Having requested and been granted payment for one or two extra consultations, I had a private meeting with all the children in whom I had detected a problem, either healthwise or psychological, or with their families. It appeared that the child in question felt sick because at home she lived with a number of people in one room. She hadn't had a holiday for seven years. When she went home in the evening she couldn't study, and at night they put her three-year-old brother in her bed. It was enough to make one feel sick even without the French fries!

I saw I could have worked day and night there because there was no adult to whom the children could go.

There was no lack of problems. In adolescence, things aren't straightforward. There were simple day-to-day medical problems: children who had dental decay of a kind one wouldn't expect to see in our enlightened age, when one or two telephone calls would have been enough to fix an appointment with the dentist.

Was it a lack of money? A fine excuse! There were children who hadn't had a holiday for ten years. I became active. In a couple of weeks I got together four thousand francs, and I squabbled with Tikvatenu and above all with Bnei Akiva,[1] telling them, "All the money I've collected, I'm going to give as a grant for these children, but you'll have to take along everyone without exception."

All the children went on holiday that year.

Is it such a complicated business? It's enough, firstly, to be available to hear the problems and to know how to keep them to oneself; secondly to spend a few minutes thinking in a non-routine manner, and thirdly – with a little imagination – to move into action. I don't accuse anyone.

Perhaps I'm able to act in this way simply because I don't function within a ready-made system and I haven't been caught in the snare of these stifling organizations with their empty language and their millwheels which turn without any grain to grind when they don't turn to crush those they're meant to serve.

In Israel also, I dream of seeing each person's specific problems attended to. I would like it if, instead of looking after one's patients or one's pupils, one didn't have to put out publications like the non-Jews. And if you haven't gone to France, England or America to write your thesis in the manner of these people and be accepted by them, you hardly count for anything.

Why should we have a country of our own if we can't conduct ourselves according to our own values, our own identity, and teach our children to see life from our point of view?

---

1. Tikvatenu and Bnei Akiva, youth movements.

I have a host of examples that show to what degree Israel is subordinated to the American system. And besides, it's very hard to have the diplomas of non English-speaking countries recognized here.

For two thousand years we've been impregnated with foreign cultures and we've lost our own identities. In France, still today, you go of course to a secular school, but at Christmas you sometimes receive a manger or a little Father Christmas as a present.

When you study literature, it's Bossuet, Pascal, the disputes of the Jesuits and Jansenists.

I understand why the gentiles lay all evils at our door. It's because we're not consistent with our own values. They're angry with us because we don't resemble the ideal we've proclaimed during the two thousand years of wandering. We've said to them all the time: "You're not what you should be. You can try and kill us but you can't change the Torah."

Now that we're in Eretz Yisrael, *we* don't live as we ought either. Because this state has not been built in the Jewish way, in accordance with the Torah, nor is the legal system based on our system of law.

It's Turkish law or British law, Roman law or Arab law, what have you... The State has been built on the ruins of *non-Jewish* foundations.

The whole world was against Mr. Begin, and why was that? Because he had the audacity to behave like a good Jew. When he was on an official journey, he dared to refrain from working on Shabbat.

When we proclaim our right to live in our land in our own way, Shalom Achshav[2] immediately rushes to Strasbourg and America to apologize and to see us through the eyes of our enemies or the eyes of the others.

Whatever the case, whether avowed enemies or not, they are always hostile inasmuch as they can't bear us to be ourselves.

As a result of drawing your inspiration from others and turning your back on your heritage, you reach a state of total "disidentification" or even a suicidal condition because we've become our own oppressors.

You come under the domination of a sort of *dybbuk*, a psychic parasite, which sucks you dry from within. No longer being yourself, you are no longer able to live. You end by repeating, like them, the slogans which your enemies have invented to destroy you.

The Chasidic rebbes were quite familiar with this phenomenon, and, speaking as a psychoanalyst, I believe that in order to open the gates of

---

2. "Peace Now," a political movement.

life to the "living dead," the work to be undertaken may possibly be to give each person access to his identity, to his neshama, to bring him to become what he is so that he may achieve the thing for which he is on earth to do.

And this begins with oneself. Everyone must discover himself, and that's his path for life. That's how I understand the famous saying, "Thou shalt make no image before My face": you mustn't impose on Me a model which is alien to Me, or you're giving yourself up to *avodah zara*.[3] The root *zar* signifies the periphery, that which is alien or external to you, when you need to be centered on yourself, to find yourself.

With a Jew, the collective identity and the personal identity are indissociable, and as long as an individual hasn't solved the problem of his identity, he can't solve the problem of his life.

I've often seen this in therapy. There was the case of the girl who vegetated, who never managed to have any friends. The day when, after many sessions, she succeeded in going to her father's grave (her parents having converted to Catholicism after the war), seeing the family vault and reading her father's name written in Hebrew, that very day she was able to have a boyfriend.

After the bomb was thrown in the synagogue in the rue Copernic, another patient regained her Jewish identity and realized that all her problems with the men in her life were the direct consequence of her demanding the right to be what she was.

It makes no sense to make a demand of this nature. If you ask someone else to give you the right to be what you are, he generally refuses you and uses this right you have conceded him "the better to bring you into subjection, my dear."

The root of all human problems is here, in the failure to respect the other person. One has to have reciprocity for a true relationship to be established, a reciprocity which presupposes that one has left behind the pre-Oedipal form of "fusion" and reached the messianic goal, the stage of human maturity.

Brotherhood then becomes possible. One should neither murder nor allow oneself to be murdered, but coexist, and that isn't easy because the old conscious or unconscious psychological reflexes, whereby you project onto the other what you can't stand in yourself, are tenacious.

---

3. Idolatrous cults.

This is the source of the difficulties in the relationships of couples and in parent-child relationships.

"*Ve'ahavta le'rey'acha kamocha,*" Love thy neighbor as thyself. If you don't love yourself, you can't love your neighbor who then becomes your "evil," as is shown by the root "*ra,*" which has the double significance of evil and fellow being.

Ultimately, you can't recognize the other as long as you haven't recognized yourself. Because if you haven't got a place, you have to take the other person's in order to reconquer your own.

Begin first of all by accepting yourself, after which you may perhaps be able to accept the other person (and act in such a way that the other person will accept you!). This is the opposite way of proceeding from that of certain missionary sisters or of those social workers who sacrifice their own lives in order to give them to others.

Except in the case of a few who are truly generous, it is generally a hidden sadism which, under the pretext of wanting the good of the other person, persecutes him consciously or unconsciously. I'm speaking in general, of course.

How can I judge someone if I haven't been in his place? I'm only saying that you can't do anything for anyone if you haven't done it for yourself, and the only help you can give another person is the road you have traveled.

Which is not to deny the importance of solidarity.

"As I've done it, you can do it." That's how I got the person I call "Varsovie" out of her difficulties. One day she came to me and said, "As you've done it, I can also do it."

That's why you have to see how a Rav lives, and that's why it is so important that a teacher shouldn't just be a talker. Is it enough to be parachuted into a professorship after writing a good thesis in order to be a true Master?

He turns up, he sits in his professorial chair, he makes a fine speech, and then he goes off and it's goodbye, get on with it!

I'd say the same about sex education in high schools. They send you "experts" who give a fine speech in class, and then one is surprised that practical experiments are made in odd corners.

Sex education is an apprenticeship for life, and it can only take place in contact with the preceding generation.

I don't say that the study of anatomy and physiology is without interest. One has the right to one's body as one has to one's geography and history, but that's not the question children ask.

They ask, "Is life possible?" For them it's a question of life and death.

"Is life possible? Do you have any sort of love for each other? Can you make life possible for each other? Can you make it possible for us? Are you sufficiently satisfied with your lives to make us want to grow up and do the same?

Does living mean anything to you?"

The adults have given life, but they seldom know how to transmit the keys to life.

At puberty, all questions come up at once. The generations are at loggerheads. I claim that inter-generational conflict isn't inevitable if the father or mother don't feel threatened by the existence of their son or daughter and can say to them:

"I got married; you too can get married. It isn't always easy; it doesn't go without saying that one can bring together strangers, people who don't know each other from Adam, without causing confrontations. It isn't always a straightforward matter to coexist; it's a messianic dream. One should at least try it, so go ahead, my girl. Since I've done it, don't be frightened."

And, as for the rest, God has given us the "ingredients" and the directions for use.

That's the work parents have to do.

One shouldn't stay on this side of the river and tell the child, "Go ahead, swim, I'm afraid to dive in," but the father and mother should go before him, show him the way and if necessary come back and accompany the child during his crossing if he is frightened, and even carry him on their shoulders if anything goes wrong.

Before transmitting life one has to live, accept life and make it livable, which means accepting oneself and accepting one's parents, whatever they're like.

The transmission has to take place through example and presence.

In the guilds of the Middle Ages they were well aware of this. The apprentice lived with the Master, and I, for my part, had the good fortune to have a master in pediatrics at the side of whom I learnt through "imbibition" – a method which suited me admirably.

I've always kept away from theoretical instruction, seminars and universities, only staying long enough to obtain my diploma. Not that I don't like abstract knowledge (biology thrills me), but I prefer human contact.

In the work of a psychologist, this is even more true. It's in doing the work on oneself with the help of someone else that one can help others.

Unfortunately, today, too many religious Jews shut themselves up in yeshivot as though in ghettoes, leaving the universities to the Jews who call themselves non-religious, and these, deprived of their heritage, can only ape the world outside. The main point of Jewish education, however, is to give people the means to resist so that they can protect their nucleus.

The first pioneers who set foot in Israel were in reaction against the religious because the religious were against them. If only the parents had said to them: "Go, my son, because we're too old, too tired," they wouldn't have felt themselves accused by those who remained in the yeshivot or judged by their rabbanim.

But the yeshiva's disconnection with life, already amply demonstrated in the practical world – due to the exclusion of women, amongst other things – was total.

In Israel, one has the opposite reaction. It was perhaps a necessary stage in order to regain one's physical vigor, contact with the earth – in order to get one's body back. But they nevertheless didn't have to lose their neshama and divide Jewish history into two parts, so that everything that preceded the creation of the modern State of Israel was the ghetto and consequently death. One mustn't resemble it in any way. One must be strong, be heroes if necessary of the type one finds in the Russian Revolution.

They put women on tractors. They too wished to escape the conditions which had fallen to their lot. But when they take the place of men there is no longer a place for anyone.

Physical force is necessary to carry out one's task on earth, but to exalt it, to make it into a supreme value is to act like the Greeks. Why in that case should one celebrate Chanukkah?

Football matches on *Shabbat*... Yes, it's all right to regain one's body, one needs it, it's the support of the neshama. But if a horse gallops away without a rider, where is it going? Why should we survive if we aren't ourselves? What's the point?

Sadat came to see Mr. Begin and not some Laborite devoid of Jewish substance. The Nations respect us when we're ourselves. Never forget that Amalek attacks us when we're weak, that is, when we're losing our specific identity. Our enemy is strong when we haven't the courage to fight to be ourselves and when we act as if God weren't the Master of the Universe.

A state requires institutions: a good army, financial resources, good diplomats. But it mustn't forget that all this exists in order to serve the people. It must be attentive to those at the bottom, go out to the little people, listen to their needs, be able to distinguish true needs from false ones.

When we were in Paris in our rue Georges Berger community,[4] and Israelis were visiting, I said to them, "The main thing is education, training children in Israel to become human beings." We have a pedagogical knowledge of thousands of years and it's as if we didn't know anything.

Torah is life, and some non-Zionist ultra-religious, victims of galutic contamination, have the appearance of fossils.

As a result of hanging on in order to preserve themselves, they got cramp, as Régine Lehmann so well expressed it.

Régine recalled the custom whereby a rav wouldn't begin his lesson without first hearing his pupil's latest dream.

The Jews' vital difficulty in connecting their personal identity with their collective identity is exacerbated when the latter assumes such a grotesque form.

---

4. A community founded and organized by our family.

The Struggle

You've never lost your dignity,
your humanity.
How can you understand
how much you have to learn
and struggle
in order to try
to get it back?

May 15, 1983

THE CHILDREN OF SILENCE

In the Diaspora as well there are problems of identity. Converts to Christianity or those who had married non-Jews, sometimes at the time of the Six-Day War, discovered that Israel existed and felt an ancestral connection between themselves and that people.

But their way was blocked. It was as though there was a refrain on the record of their unconscious: "You have the right to survive only if you submit to the all-powerful wishes of those who took you in. Get back into your drawer. If you don't, you'll be outside, excluded, abandoned."

That's the problem of all those who were children during the war, who couldn't go into the forest to join the *maquis* and set about defending themselves.

They depended on the goodwill of those who sheltered them, a goodwill that never goes as far as respect for the other. The other person has to be his little puppy-dog: "Come here, my dear child, and go to Mass," or "Boy, say your prayers..."

All those children who were hidden while their parents were deported have survived; but where is their life? Except in the case of a few rare exceptions, they haven't regained their identity. They have succeeded professionally; they often have a family; they've often found a marriage-partner who can offer them a certain security: often a non-Jew, for only a non-Jew could save them, and in many cases non-Jews really did save them during the war.

In effect, they have no true emotional relationships; they can't claim what's due to them and they don't possess what is truly theirs. At least they feel this way and probably induce this attitude in the others by making themselves small.

Although adults, they still have the reflexes of abandoned children: "Eat me, but keep me where it's warm. Don't put me outside or I'm alone in the world. I can't be left alone, I'm too little."

That's their reaction until the day they are able to hear: "But you're no longer a child now. The child of deported parents, that's in the past. Take your affairs in hand!"

But who is going to tell them that?

And from whom can they receive it?

Can they imagine that someone will listen to what they have to say without throwing them out, without punishing or killing them?

How can they say, "I'm called Yaakov and not Nicolas. Just let me live as Yaakov"?

The person who spoke of the "Jews of silence" when referring to the Jews of Russia had an idea of genius.

One should also speak of the children of silence! The deportees are no longer there to talk, and their children have been conditioned not to have a say in the matter.

And all this silence cries to high heaven. A few survivors are shown a great deal of respect and all the others are left in the shade.

To open these sores a bit is to risk ending in the doss-house, outlawed from society, for the sufferings they contain and the sense of guilt they arouse are unbearable. And they drag themselves around with this load, pretending that life goes on as before, and life does in fact pretend to go on as before.

The tragedy is that nothing prevents all that has happened from happening again. The demon is always there. For me who is familiar with the workings of the unconscious, the present resurgence of Nazism was entirely foreseeable.

That's why it's such an urgent necessity to speak up. One can judge the major Nazi criminals, but do they themselves confront their guilt?

When their children reach the age their parents had during the war, how will they escape the phantoms which dwell within them? Isn't everyone interpellated by their parents' experience at their own age?

The children of the Nazis don't escape it any more than ours do. They identify with them unconsciously and can only repeat what they did or run away from it, and that gives you the Baader-Meinhoff gang.

Only a small number are capable of *teshuva*[1] and *tikkun*[2] and take upon themselves the sins of the fathers by contributing today to their

---

1. Repentance.
2. Reformation, repair.

redress. The others build themselves up as neo-Nazis or PLO support-
ers, or they think that their parents were rotters, and so they can't build
themselves up at all. All they can do is to escape from any society. It's
important to study these reactions and it's an urgent necessity to explain
them both to our children and to the whole of the Western world, which
uses the Palestinians to clear itself of guilt.

It's so simple! In one's subconscious, the "poor Palestinian people"
takes the place of the murdered Jews to whom one consequently no longer owes anything.

Unfortunately, many *Sephardim* are deceived by these ready-made
formulas which come from outside, being ignorant of the fact that nu-
merous Sephardim, like the entire community of Salonika and many others, were also deported. (And today, the Israeli left has fallen into this
suicidal trap by voluntarily divesting itself of all its security assets to the
benefit of the Palestinian enemy).

Hitler didn't go especially for the *Ashkenazim*. He took whatever
was available. If he hadn't been stopped, he would have taken the Jews
of North Africa as well as those in Israel, for his plans extended to those
places also.

Today, the survivors are gnawed by feelings of guilt: the guilt of having survived when the others are dead.

And we, the children of silence, do not have the right to speak. We've
remained alive, so what would we have to say? We haven't even been in
Auschwitz, we haven't been deported.

So we just have to give thanks to heaven and earth and the whole of
humanity. Why should we ask for the right to complain? Our lives have
been saved, we've been taken in, we've been housed, we've been fed. We're
here; we've nothing to complain about. And here we are, a great number
confined to mutism.

There's the guilt of having survived. There is also the responsibility of
those who have killed us or who have done nothing to lift this conspiracy
of silence.

"Above all, don't speak to me about *that*!"

I remember that after the war, it was the first thing I wanted to talk
about when I met someone. I said to myself, "If he doesn't know about
this, he doesn't know anything about me and no real human relationship
is possible."

My intention was not to arouse pity, but I felt such an upheaval within myself. It was like an erupting volcano. It was impossible to put a lid on it and say, "Calm down," and yet you had no choice. You felt you had to keep your mouth shut.

Children have a perfect understanding of this unspoken prohibition. It's as it is when you go to strangers. You have to be very polite and not draw attention to yourself. Above all, don't show your leprosy or everyone will be afraid of getting it.

You had to be "*chic-sympa et dynamique*," pleasant, likeable and dynamic, full of humor, good company, and you had to make everyone laugh simply in order to be accepted and not to be thrust aside as a vulgar foreigner whom nobody knows, an ill-dressed person who has nothing to offer you materially and who challenges you even without opening his mouth simply by his feelings about your way of life.

People began to live again and, ensconced in their little habits, behaved as if nothing had happened. Everyone went home and was reunited with his parents and grandparents, and found his attics full of photos and old clothes, his furniture and his cherished family recipes. It wasn't the time to say to them, "How lucky you all are!"

This was one of the things that made us go to Paris. In a great city, there's no lack of uprooted people. Nobody looks at you. If I've got the blues and am alone, then I'm alone and have the blues; nobody notices it and I'm the only one to know. I don't ask anything of anyone and nobody asks anything of me. Anonymity has its good side. Everyone knows that large cities are the refuge of the uprooted.

I persist in believing that this guilt weighs upon the whole of mankind.

Hitler afflicted the whole world with the plague, and this Black Death has continued to prosper and kill a mass of humanity, having undermined its moral values.

Those values, it is true, had long ago been got around and flouted, but the façade was still there.

At Auschwitz it crumbled.

Hiroshima, Cambodia, Vietnam, Afghanistan, Biafra, the Gulags (and more recently Yugoslavia, Rwanda) and the wars inflicted on Israel which is the symptomatic child of the others' sickness, this whole avalanche of catastrophes, is the work of Amalek, or in other words anti-morality, the negation of the values of which the Jews are the bearers, the negation of God.

For a certain time after the war, it was taboo to attack the Jews. But hatred was working underground, like rivers that infiltrate a chalky sub-soil and disappear until their next resurgence.

The Pope permitted Nazis to escape to Latin America with gold stolen from the Jews, and the Great Powers helped the Egyptians to lay siege to the frontiers of Israel and to amass toxic gas in the desert sands under the guidance of former Nazis.

Today, Nazism continues through the interposition of the Arab countries.

The Grand Mufti of Jerusalem was just a beginning. It is as if an outlet were needed for a huge reservoir of accumulated aggressivity and violence because the peoples have never learnt to want and achieve something positive.

I too could say that my "failure," my inability to say what I have to say is the fault of others, and so it only remains for me to kill them. But would I be heard any better after that?

First of all I must work within myself, even when nothing changes around me, so that one day I will be able to have my say and break the universal deathly silence.

And if nobody wants to hear me, I shall listen to myself and then, perhaps, I shall be able to listen to others.

Rose-colored Stones

Rose-colored stones,
rose-tinted light
of the setting sun,
and a wisp of crescent moon
between two crenellations
of the wall up there...
opposite the tombs of our forefathers
on the Mount of Olives
and trees swayed in the wind.
How many of our children
do they dare to kill
so that we may have the right
to contemplate
our eternal interiority
here regained
in a reality
so much
and so long
desired?

July, 26, 1982

THE JEWISH WAY OF SEEING REINVENTED

Children will never ask their parents questions if the latter are not will-ing to listen to their questions.

To shatter the wall of silence, you have first to take yourself in hand and break out of your mutism. As far as I was concerned, there was no longer any partner in dialogue in whom I could confide.

It was impossible for me to divulge to anyone what I had in my heart without harming the system of protection that I had elaborated over the years. The living side of me, the sensitive side of me, to whom could I have confided it?

One day, someone asked me a question: it was a doctor who later became a psychoanalyst. I was riveted to the spot. He said to me, "Why do you always pretend that everything's fine? You don't have to."

I was obliged to smile. I wasn't going to cry in front of people who would reject me. My sufferings were no business of theirs.

Already at Moissac, there was nobody who could take my pain into consideration. Yes, once a leader was out walking with me on a hill and asked me, "Why are you so sad? Why do you have so little confidence in yourself?"

It's no small matter to lose one's parents in such conditions! It leaves traces. When my children are away, we can telephone each other or go and see them. We're there: they are not *hefker*, thank God. But I see that they carry all our experience without knowing it, and it's all the more operative because it's unconscious.

Sometimes I tell myself that I can be satisfied. I've discovered this whole linkage on my own and I have set my mind to decoding it. And then I came across a book by Bettelheim, and then Freud.

I told myself, "You're not so crazy, Ida!"

Then I came across a book by Eliane Amado Lévi-Valensi, writer, psychoanalyst and today professor of Jewish Thought and Philosophy in Jerusalem. She too had fun with Hebrew roots. I don't like to be given things that are ready-made: that's my sporty side. I like to discover things for myself.

When one looks properly, and one has the courage to go right to the end of one's own bundle of yarn, one can sometimes reconstitute the whole connecting thread.

That's the nature of true transmission, of which the Kabbalah[1] is the prototype. It doesn't teach you things that are ready-made; it allows you to go out to meet them. And the Master's there, who can say to you, when you tell him what you've found: "That's good, continue."

The things you've integrated into your experience you can understand and receive (le'kabel in Hebrew).

It's no use swallowing tons of books and stuffing yourself with abstract theories, and then enclose yourself and others in these theories in an attempt to make all problems fit into them. But at the same time one must make use of existing knowledge.

Look with your own eyes, see what's doing. Understand in your "guts," chochmat lev,[2] which doesn't prevent you from understanding with your brain afterwards.

Begin by feeling and by moving – for you have to be able to shift yourself – and in that way you won't alienate yourself or entrap others in your scheme of things. Reach your own goal and you'll join the others.

You only attain the universal by delving into the particular. That's the story of Rav Zousya who, at the hour of his death, regretted not being as great as Moshe Rabbeinu (Moses). But he was only required to be Rav Zousya – that's all.

It's also the story of the chasid who went searching under the bridge at Prague for a treasure he'd seen in a dream which was in fact hidden under his own house.

In Poland, the Jews were persecuted, but, living apart in the shtetl, they were able to preserve their identity.

In France, on the other hand, assimilation was usual and took place very rapidly.

In Claudine Vegh's book, Je ne leur ai pas dit au revoir, I was struck by the great difference between those who, like us, arrived in France at the time of the war and those whose parents were already in France.

---

1. Transmission of the sod, secret knowledge.
2. The wisdom of the heart.

The latter knew the language, had their frame of reference. I won't say their lives were more comfortable, but they at least had a cousin, a friend, a neighbor, while we perhaps had an identity, but nothing was left of our former family framework.

There was nobody who could tell me the first names of my maternal grandparents. There was no intermediary. Your language, your parents, your belongings... there was nothing left and no longer anyone to tell you about them. They at least were in the country where they were born, but on the other hand everything overtook them without their being able to integrate it into their history as Jews.

If they had a few familiar personal points of reference, I had the advantage of having received the historical perspective.

They could no longer feel themselves to be Jews except in a negative way, so they fled from their condition while interiorizing their persecutors and applying their laws, which only left the Jews with the right to die.

Most of the time they merely survive, with an unconscious sense of guilt at still being alive which consumes them. They have only just the right to work incessantly and try to please everyone, never showing the least kindness to themselves.

Me, too – you won't ever see me sitting in a café, watching time go by. If you're alive, my girl, it's in order to do something! Your life's a gift you've been given twice over: once when you were born and again when you survived. It's up to you to make something of it.

Life is given to you and you then have to deserve it, as Rav Léon Ashkenazi, otherwise known as Manitou, strove to have us understand. He was one of the chief Masters of our generation, whose teaching was essentially oral. Moshe Rabbeinu was "saved from the waters"; he became the one who saved others.

This reminds me of an encounter I had in a bus in Israel with a student who was finishing his medical studies. I had only just finished mine. He invited me to Rehovot where he lived, to visit a hospital. He wanted to help me.

Together with him, I spent a morning following the doctor making his round of attendance. It was extraordinary. Here was an old Jew, a doctor like those of the old days, who went from bed to bed and addressed each patient as if it was the first patient he had attended to that day.

And then I don't know what happened. I saw him pat the back of a little old lady – "So, mother dear, where does it hurt today?" – with such a warm presence that a window immediately opened in my neshama. I thought I was melting on the spot.

For that scene I was willing to drop everything and come running up. A doctor speaking in a human way to a patient!

I saw the realization of our messianic dream. The wolf will graze with the lamb... a world in which human relations will no longer depend on force, where strength will no longer be used to oppress one's neighbor but will be placed at the service of the person who lacks it until he regains his own strength.

Two shall graze in one pasture: "The wolf shall be side by side with the lamb and a little child shall lead them." Where will you find a more beautiful vision?

If you were in a position of strength, would you exploit it to crush the other person? Would you kill your brother like Cain and then wait in fear to be killed in turn?

I know many people who aren't observant but for whom the Torah is this concrete reality which is coming into being. They've become "anti-religious" because of all the religious people who bludgeon them with their truth as though it were Truth itself. They alienate the people from the Torah by declaring them blameworthy in relation to a certain criterion, fixing values of which they claim to be the sole representatives.

While Judaism is above all life, a respectful relationship towards the other person, *ben adam le'havero* (a man's respect for his neighbor), they make it into an obsessive and incriminating ritualism.

In our relationship to Israel and the Torah, my brother and I have always trodden a parallel path. As for my sister, she had blockages with regard to Israel and Judaism. She defended herself as best she could.

My brother represented for me something positive, linked to our genuine roots. Through him, I glimpsed my true self. With him, there was no need for self-justification; we were there for each other in life and death.

Where my brother was concerned, I was all things together, his father and mother, and he was the same for me in his way, which gave me a sense of security. You can't ask everything of your husband. He can't be your father, it's impossible. It's even a sure recipe for failure, even if you aren't aware of it.

Whenever I had a problem, I called my brother. When one of my children was sick, I called him. When I had a professional problem, I called him. He turned up. Just seeing him, I already felt better. I again became capable of doing something.

Jerusalem

When I go up
to the Temple Mount
I feel so light ...
and yet
whole generations
of mothers and fathers
go up with me
who have not had
the good fortune
to lead the dance
with lightsome feet
in freedom
in this city
so much desired,
or have known, like me,
the blessing
of resting the soles
of one's feet
on the reblossoming soil
of Zion
the eternal city
each day more fair,
which with God's help
is being rebuilt
before our eyes
and lives once more.

July 26, 1982

HOW TO RESTORE

Our old project of leaving for Israel remained in suspense. Then my brother did it in 1969.

I felt his departure as a new wrench in my life. It was abandonment, war. My brother had always been for me a sort of opening on a possible existence. It was the only relationship in which I enjoyed perfect confidence.

With regard to Israel and *yahadut*,[1] my husband and I had made our own way. From the very beginning, we impregnated our children with Judaism. We celebrated Shabbat: in addition to candles on Friday night, we went to a service. We organized an Oneg Shabbat with my brother and a few friends for all our children.

When they were still very small, I sang my children songs in Ivrit[2] and in Yiddish. I told them stories, I read them books – a high-powered transmission, but not in an academic way. On the Jewish holidays we lit candles.

I had a certain idea of what life should be, based on our family-life in childhood. When I had a family of my own, it had to be along the lines of the model I'd received.

In 1969, we made a major exploratory voyage to Israel with the children. We went to see my brother and a common friend who had gone there just after the Six-Day War, and all our friends were there and all the family.

My husband was very fond of Israel, which he knew well. Like me, he had stayed there several times and had many friends there. For a long time he had been active on a voluntary basis in the *Étudiants Juifs* (Jewish Students' Society) in organizing trips with stays on kibbutzim. There were no apparent problems on the horizon.

---

1. Judaism.
2. The Hebrew language.

You have to be crazy to be Jewish, and anyone who isn't a bit "crazy" can't be Jewish, and even less can want to go to Israel. You can't go there otherwise. Just as you have to be "crazy" to love someone enough to marry him or her and want to live with that person every day and every night. It's the same sort of thing.

And Hakadosh Baruch Hu gave the love which may seem folly to men but which is the only possible way for two strangers to go and live together and have children.

Our age-old neshama began to stir. We could no longer resist our desire for Israel. Is that madness?

It's a long drawn-out love story that makes you deaf to all those who tell you a number of things which could hold you back.

We didn't hear; we weren't capable of hearing. Some friends nevertheless managed to get us to write one or two letters attempting to obtain guarantees of work.

I mentioned the person who said to me one day, "You don't have to pretend that everything's fine." He took the floor at a farewell meeting in a school where I was working. He said, "Not everyone has the good fortune to be Jewish and to know what he has to do in a period as somber as the present."

We didn't carry out any propaganda unless you call the very fact of existing and living in identification with Israel and the Jewish people propaganda. For the others, whether Jews or non-Jews, Israel and Judaism are visible in our appearance and in our conduct. That's why the image you give of yourself is so important. Rav Botschko taught that if you call yourself dati or a Zionist you can't steal or tell lies, and above all you must behave in a humane and moral manner with others as a pupil, colleague, doctor, teacher, neighbor.

To be Jewish is to want to live in a certain way and to struggle to live in that way. It cannot be reducible to a series of ritual gestures.

I don't say that these have no value. But one shouldn't take refuge in ritual like monks or like Don Camillo who kneels down, receives absolution and then gaily goes off to rob his neighbor, lie to his wife, run after the girls of the village or plant bombs at every street-corner.

We were fortunate that our children chose a yeshiva with a human face.

When I'm told, "You sent your children to a yeshiva," I reply, "I didn't send them. They went on their own."

232

It wasn't just any yeshiva. This yeshiva, founded by Rav Botschko's father, has always remained a family affair. It was the first Zionist yeshiva in Western Europe. There you meet people who can help to reconcile you with the religious aspect of Judaism.

After the war I went through a real crisis where this was concerned. I can't really call it a rebellion: the term blockage would be more appropriate.

I couldn't stand the excessive legalism to which the Jewish religion is often reduced, whereas for me it's an integral part of the comprehensive Jewish heritage which is a heritage of life, which I received in a living manner and which is the power and the blessing in my life.

Young people of the generation after ours can't imagine what it is to be a Jew in galut without the existence of Israel as a state.

The re-creation of Israel implies a mutation, a fundamental change.

Today, a young person can't put himself into the skin of the Jews of that time, can't understand why they didn't rebel, why they didn't run away, why they allowed themselves to be led like "sheep to the slaughter," as they say.

You've crossed three or four frontiers, you've seen them all close against you; you hear on all sides that nobody wants you except in order to hunt you down, to deliver you up to your executioners, to persecute you without anyone lifting a finger.

There isn't any place for you anywhere. Do you get it? Not anywhere! Since the State of Israel has come into existence, the Jew has regained his dignity in Israel as in the galut.

The younger generation born together with the State of Israel has only breathed this air of liberation which seems to it quite natural. We, however, breathed the slavery of Egypt.

We learned our history in the galut where there was no solution anywhere but in our dreams.

I've always said that if this book appears one day, I'll call it *vehigad'ta le'bincha*: "And you shall tell your son." It's in Exodus 13:8. The people of Israel hadn't yet left Egypt when God, speaking through Moses, already told them, "And when in time to come your son asks you, you shall say to him..."

Even before sacrificing the paschal lamb, before making the first gesture towards liberation, you're asked to describe the slavery and the liberation which gives history its meaning.

Life is not possible outside your particular history and the meaning of that history.

Since I was very small, I have always known that the people of Israel descended from our ancestors Abraham, Isaac and Jacob, that it was formed in Egypt, that we came out of there under the guidance of Moses, led by the "arm" of Hakadosh Baruch Hu, that we wandered for forty years in the desert before entering Eretz Israel, and that a pact was sealed between Hakadosh Baruch Hu and ourselves concerning a third party, which is the Land of Israel, where it is incumbent upon us to take history forward in accordance with the principles of the Torah.

This promise was the motivation of your life, the reason you existed and struggled. Without it, you were lost. When someone remarks to me, "After all you've experienced, can you still remain Jewish?" I answer, "What, give up? Gratify those who kill us? Am I supposed to do the work instead of them?"

A pact has been sealed: the Jewish people will one day be in its land. To be in one's land is to be able to be oneself. When you're not yourself, that's when Amalek, our anti-self, crushes you and expels you from your land, and then you fall back into the cycle of persecution.

The whole of Jewish history consists of these relapses. We know very well that Amalek assumes various guises. At the time of Purim,[3] it's Haman; when Hitler comes to power, it's Amalek reappearing.

We somehow knew, through a knowledge handed down in each family throughout the entire people, that inhuman persecutions could recur. Every Jew knows from experience that as long as the *Mashiach*[4] hasn't arrived, every time that for whatever reason we are blind due to various circumstances for which we are not entirely responsible, there comes a time of ordeals.

You may remember the postcard written by my Uncle Goldsand from the camp of Dachau. Everyone who has received an authentic Judaism recognizes this way of seeing things.

Each one assimilates it in accordance with his nature. It's not an easy thing to transmit. When we were persecuted, our reflex wasn't to blame the other person but to ask ourselves, "What could I have done? What should I have done? What can I do now to put everything back in place?"

---

3. Holiday commemorating the rescue of the Jews from extermination in the time of Queen Esther.
4. Messiah.

When something doesn't go as it should, that means I haven't been on track and I try to get back into it. But where can one find the strength to get back on track when one's in exile?

Now that the possibility of returning to Israel is no longer a dream, we are able to struggle against Amalek.

Alas, the tragedy is that he forces us to use the same weapons as he does and to fight on the same terrain.

Our great misfortune is *Tisha Be'av*, the day of the destruction of both Temples. From that day onwards we have lamented the tragedy of a people expelled from its country, of a people which has seen the mainstay of its identity collapse and which has been delivered to the wild beasts of the earth.

Having become hefker, no longer having any possibility of being in contact with itself, it is cut adrift and wanders far from its sources.

So you remain dumbfounded, without a hold on anything. You've lost your bearings, you can't do anything; you can grasp the meaning of things only with difficulty. All you have is a reflex of survival, of flight in order to escape those who, for their part, have a grip on reality but create death where there should be life.

I've always tried to make people welcome. When I met my husband, we put our two groups of friends together, paying special attention to those who had drifted away from Judaism. Each person helped the other; it was a whole dialogal enterprise.

It's no accident that neither my brother, nor my sister, or myself married religious people, although we have these riches deep within us and we struggle to bring them to life again.

But do you think you can get back into your pair of shoes left outside your door as if nothing had happened?

We had to go back to our sources step by step, each at his own pace, and reinvent them so to speak, find a new way to bring them to life and to live through them.

At first, we just lit the candles on Friday nights and then we got together for an Oneg Shabbat for the children. We conducted the service ourselves, with my brother and a few friends, little by little, sustained by a sure emotional attachment. It was a moment of encounter where you strengthened yourself, felt supported and didn't risk anything.

We casually invented all the principles applied a little later in Georges Berger, the minyan we founded in 1973 in the street of the same name.

235

We didn't go to a shul where everyone turns round to watch you coming in like an intruder: "Who's this foreigner? Where does he come from? What's he wearing?"

On Shabbat and the Jewish holidays we went to Neuilly, to the hostel connected with Moissac, where we and families and friends would come together, creating our own community that catered for our specific needs.

At the beginning, we didn't know how to do a Seder,[5] so my brother or some unmarried friend came to do it with us. How could we have received anything from a world which we felt to be closed-in and hostile?

You may say I was a "dreamer of the ghetto," a utopian, an inveterate idealist unaware of realities. I have to prove that my dream corresponds to the truth and is realizable. Success is something of a miracle, I know, but isn't life a series of miracles?

In three areas it was given to me by God to express and achieve my desires within the limits of time and space in order to show that it is possible: in my family, in my work and in the minyan we created in the seventeenth *arrondissement*.

But what resistances I had to overcome! Not to speak of aliyah, even if that was done bit by bit.

Building a home may not look like anything special; being a couple that lives, that gradually regains its human identity and its Jewish identity is not something given automatically.

Bringing up children in a world like the present one and fashioning them into human beings on the Jewish model means having to invent every day. There is very little around you that can help you (one should remember the date on which these words were said).

We hesitated to send our children to a Jewish school. Our general policy with our children was: quantity hardly matters. It's more important to give them quality, stimulate their positive motivations, awaken their wish to learn and sharpen their tastes and desires – all this on a basis of the value of human relations and mutual confidence.

Education isn't the product of books one reads while taking notes or of making a hole in one's brain in order to insert as many things there as possible.

---

5. Ceremonial meal on the first evening of *Pesach*, conducted with the family in memory of the exodus from Egypt.

To educate is to form a human being. It's an undertaking which first involves human contact, respect for oneself and for others, attention, good relationships. It's an undertaking based on a possible identification and a warm presence.

The whole Torah is in this. If you take away this kernel, what remains? Death.

At the present time, ninety-five percent of the Jewish people search for life gropingly without the Torah, and three or four percent asphyxiate themselves with the *sefer* Torah (the Torah scroll), as they wrap themselves up in it without any connection with life (these figures have no doubt changed in the last twenty years, considering the tendency that has existed to religious radicalism).

The result is death. Fortunately, there remain the people of the "knitted *kippah*":[6] the religious who are Zionists and are involved with life.

The possibly inordinate ambition of my husband and I was to bring these two elements together with our few resources and on our small scale. In a certain way we succeeded, God be praised.

When the children were small, I would have liked them to have gone to Madame Gordin's kindergarten, but it was too far away.

We decided on a good non-Jewish school, the École Alsacienne (Alsatian School), where relationships were excellent, where the teaching was based on respect for the children and where the teachers were capable of asking themselves questions before speaking ill of a pupil that lagged behind.

However, we had to inject some "*Yiddishkeit*" into our children immersed in a non-Jewish milieu, and not being connected with the Jewish community or institutions it was a challenge for us to bring them up as Jews.

They were already quite big. There was nothing on Thursdays in our neighborhood near Boulevard Raspail (on Thursdays there was no school in France). Thanks to Irène Gozlan, I found a room with the *libéraux*[7] in rue Servandoni.

Madame Gordin sent me a kindergarten teacher. We opened this kindergarten on Thursdays in order to teach the children songs and Israeli dances.

---

6. A ritual skullcap worn by all observant Jews.
7. Liberals, the French Reform Jews.

I picked up cousins, neighbors, friends in my *"Deux Chevaux,"*[8] which served as the "school bus."

There were about ten children, and I created my own *Talmud Torah* for the under six year-olds. I did this in a living way, as I felt it, connected with Israel and rooted in life.

There's nothing mysterious about it. If you want children to attach themselves to anything, everything has to be organically connected.

Our forefathers, who coated with honey the first page of the first book read by a young *talmid*,[9] were well aware of this.

The idea of God, Judaism, Israel and the Jewish people is all expressed in the Jewish holidays and becomes tangible in family gatherings where there's good food, songs, dances, the joy of being together with friends.

I no longer remember who told me the story of the couple who had adopted children because they didn't succeed in having any of their own.

One day the woman, who was already forty-three years old, noticed she was pregnant. How could she tell them? They'd be jealous. She waited and waited. One morning, she and her husband decided to speak. They summoned the children and didn't have time to say much, but the children immediately declared, "Yes, we've noticed your tummy getting bigger and bigger. The poor little thing hasn't even been adopted, but we've made up our minds we'll love him twice as much."

Basically, all children are adopted children, and it's never easy to succeed with an adoption!

As at that period Régine came to our place to give lessons to us and a few of our friends, the children could be there, ask questions and meet other Jews.

Then the question of the premises for the Thursday kindergarten came up at the same time as they had to begin Talmud Torah.

They were now old enough to begin to read Hebrew, and above all to meet other Jews and see that we weren't the only Jews in the world.

That's how the years passed until we left for Israel. It represented a great effort of rediscovery, of reconciliation.

Rabbi Schilli recommended the Talmud Torah of V, which happened to be the nearest synagogue.

---

8. A popular Citroen model.
9. Pupil.

When I saw the disorderly children running around on tables, playing ball, throwing their satchels across the room and generally larking about, I said to myself, "My children go to a *non-Jewish* school where everything is well organized. I can't let them have *this* image of a school where Torah is studied!"

So we decided to ask the teachers from the Talmud Torah to come and give them lessons in our home.

I deliberately invited very religious girls, authentic *datiot* who taught the children prayers, spoke to them of Hakadosh Baruch Hu and not of a Supreme Being, and used a language which was familiar to us.

Every time, I discussed things with them: Auschwitz was like a bone in my throat.

At that period, we weren't really kosher or really *shomrei Shabbat* (Sabbath observant), but at the same time we felt it vital that our children should become acquainted with the positive content of our tradition while remaining open to life.

The *libéraux* had already thought about these questions and asked and even begged us to entrust our children to them, but I didn't want that. I can't adopt their ideology. I'm quite willing for each person to act according to his understanding: each person is responsible for what he does. But modify the *Shulchan Aruch*?[10] No! the Law's the Law, liberty is liberty.

Each person has his account, his *cheshbon* with Hakadosh Baruch Hu. In those days, I felt that doing things that had no meaning for you was perhaps more destructive than not doing them at all. But to suppress these things completely because they have no meaning for a few people is also destructive.

If you think that quantity is what matters, you're under an illusion. What matters isn't where you are in relation to the next man but where you are in relation to your point of departure.

The more you study the Torah, the more you see that that the slightest Jewish act is full of meaning and something marvelous for descendants of *Chasidim* like us.

To practice just one of the mitzvot isn't a bad thing. If you do it well, a light goes on in the world, for it's not the gesture that is most important, it's the human face.[10]

---

10. "Laid Table," a guide summarizing Jewish practices.

Do you imagine that the 613 mitzvot practiced at breakneck speed while trampling on the whole world, yourself included, will break open the doors of heaven for you? I don't believe it.

During these same years, I opened up my practice as a doctor and began to work. The way one practices one's profession can also be a *kiddush Hashem*.[11]

---

11. Sanctification of the Name.

My Land

With its inland
Sea
and its Father
on High,
beaches
which stretch forever
and landscapes
worthy of any country,
this is my land
whose inhabitants
have finally left exile.
All human types
are gathered here
and also
all opinions...
But, even if the Messiah
is not yet come
and if perfection here
is only in process of creation,
one should not speak
ill of my land
which
so soon
has succeeded
in existing
against wind
and tide
stirred up
by the jealous
nations.

September 10, 1982

IDENTITY OUT IN THE OPEN

My brother having left for Israel where our friend Saül had preceded him, we stopped going to the minyan organized at the center in Neuilly. For the Jewish holidays we henceforth went to Vauquelin[1] because of the presence there of Rabbi Schilli, the very one thanks to whom we were able to get out of the camp and the only person in France to have known my parents.

Each time, at the end of the service, he came up to me and said, "Hello, Ida, how are you? How is your sister? How is your brother?"

He took each of my children close to him and said *Ye'varechecha,*[2] placing his hands on their heads. Each time I was overwhelmed.

It was his way of saying, "Some people are absent, but I am there. I am doing what they would have done." It was the only place of prayer I could go to, the only one where I met a human being over and beyond the artificial smiles.

You see, it's my constant refrain: you can't give Judaism back to the Jews if you don't first show them a human face, quite apart from any doctrine, any attempt to draw them in.

So we went to Vauquelin for the Jewish holidays. That's to say, *I* went. I took everybody in my car, including Aunt Kitty, who spent most of the holidays with us, and every time I wept. I was there and the tears kept on running.

All that was in me recognized the feelings hidden in the memory of the little girl I had been, while I had nothing in common with the people sitting around me, settled, calm, who would go back to their homes after the service and with whom everything ran like clockwork.

---

1. The synagogue and rabbinic center in rue Vauquelin.
2. "May the Lord bless you," the priests' blessing over the community and parents' blessing on their children.

But as for you, you were there with your questions, your deficiencies, the yawning chasm in your heart, your impossibilities, your soul of a tramp sitting on the doorstep. You felt like a stranger.

The children continued to go to the École Alsacienne. There, too, how could one avoid problems? When *Pesach* or some other holiday came round, you made them miss classes, and each time you had to explain the reason to the teachers.

You left the house, you went to see them and sometimes you even invited them to your home.

One day my daughter brought me some forms to fill in. The children were going to a "snow class" (winter sports) and one had to answer some routine questions, including some concerning the wishes of the families with regard to religious practice.

The next day, I went to the secretary's office and saw two young ladies – the headmistress and the deputy headmistress, both adorable and highly competent professionally – with whom I had developed good relations.

I said to them, " If I understand correctly, there's a Mass and a priest for the Catholics and a pastor and a service for the Protestants, and is there nothing for the Jews?"

There was a big discussion. We looked at the pile of forms that had already been filled in. We read them. Only two families had stated that they had Jewish children: our daughter and L.F., who came from America.

But the two young ladies knew very well that a certain child was Jewish, and another and also another... I had a good laugh that day! I said, "I'm quite willing for my daughter to go (we didn't eat very kosher yet at that period), but I very much want her to have her Friday evening, to be able to dress nicely and light her candles, and I'd like the boy S who is also going to do kiddush over the wine. I'll provide the wine and the candles."

Once again a lot of talk. "But that's a very good idea. It's excellent for the others."

Then a telephone-call came through from S's parents. The mother, somewhat unenthusiastic, asked me, "What have you done?"

Best of all, it was the school that got them to light the candles and say the kiddush and the brachot.[3] And in the following years it was the deputy-headmistress who brought the candles, the wine and the *siddur* (prayer book) in her suitcase, and she thanked me.

---

3.   Blessings, benedictions.

Every time there was a Jewish holiday we invited the schoolteacher so that there wouldn't be any break between the world of the school and the true nature, the Jewish nature of the children. Every time there was a new teacher, we invited her to our home. The children showed her their Hebrew copybook.

On Pesach, they brought *matza*[4] to school.

We continually gave all the necessary explanations to their little friends and many of them came to our home and were always amazed by the atmosphere and the welcome they received.

So, little by little, our three children developed a great pride in being Jewish and a joy in being able to express it. To such a degree that one day – it was during the Six-Day War – when I went as usual to fetch my children as they came out of school, I was assailed by about ten children, all half-Jews or children of converted parents or of Jews ashamed of their origin.

I was told that in the middle of the class, my daughter had got up and asked for money to be collected, explaining that it was for Israel. She was still a little girl, barely ten years old.

The teacher, embarrassed, said, "I don't know. We'll have to ask the headmistresses." Would this be meddling in politics? Was it permitted?

And all these children plied me with questions, "What do you think? What do you say about it?" They clung to me like bees in a hive.

I was their I-don't-know-what, their identity which declared itself openly. For them it was extraordinary and for me no less so.

My daughter and her brothers enjoyed great prestige at the school precisely because they came forward as Jews, which gave rise to many exchanges of views between them and the *others*.

And this was possible for them because they had places where they could ask questions and receive something positive, either via Jewish teachers or through records, books and a few places where Jewish life could be found, like those in which they spent their holidays.

There, they found other Jews, could observe Shabbat and keep kosher. And it was there with Raphael Yelloz on snow-covered ski-tracks that they learnt their first song by Shlomo Carlebach, the "singing rabbi": "*Essa Einai.*"[5]

---

4. *Matza* (plural *matzot*), flat unleavened bread eaten at *Pesach*, when leavened foods are not allowed.
5. "I will lift up mine eyes unto the hills from whence cometh my help," Psalm 121.

I bought our first Carlebach record, and it was the beginning of *Techiat hameitim*,[6] a music which brought your neshama home.

You can do so much with records!

Already when they were small I sung them Hebrew songs day and night. I translated them into French for them, I sang to them in Yiddish and I made them laugh on walks by telling them stories.

In the evening, true to the methods of my father, we had the *Birkat Hamazon*[7] at the dinner table and *Yevarechecha* and the *Shema*[8] in bed, all these little moments of intensity, all these questions which parents try to answer – an education not of cerebral abstraction but which accompanied the thousand and one actions of life to give them meaning, so that we shouldn't be ashamed of our past, of what we have to transmit and which, in the final analysis, makes the non-Jews admire us.

Ever utopian and a dreamer, I said to myself that finally the ideal would be to create a Talmud Torah in the École Alsacienne and I actually succeeded in doing so. With the help of Irène Gozlan, we managed to open a Hebrew workshop of which my children were the actors and moving spirits.

Here again you can see the minyan of rue Georges Berger looming on the horizon. They invited little Jews – it did them no harm – and also some little *other children*.

From that moment, a great informative enterprise was set in motion with regard to Israel. I observed the difference when I went to fetch the children at school.

We were very close to the teachers, who adored our children, and with them as with the headmistresses there were lots of discussions.

I invited them to eat at our home. I'd told them what I'd seen in Israel, how Israel was gradually beginning to take shape, informed them of what was really happening and explained why the real situation, distorted by the media, wasn't known.

But nothing could replace a visit. The two "little" (non-Jewish) headmistresses left for Israel on an organized voyage, and in their suitcases were two books we had given them.

And I'm sorry not to have recorded what they said on their return:

---

6. The resurrection of the dead.
7. Blessing over food after meals.
8. *Shema*, the central proclamation of the Jewish liturgy.

"We Christians are barbarians, idolators. All the human values lie with you."

They had become unconditional admirers of Israel. They had understood.

I think that's what kiddush Hashem is, and my children learnt that very early. It's an experience of life. It's not necessary to put oneself in a ghetto and take pleasure in it. Rubbing shoulders with others won't do any harm providing one respects the principle of vaccination: the dose mustn't be too strong and one's system must be capable of producing antibodies.

Isn't that the best preparation for learning to defend oneself?

We've lived that way for two thousand years. Why, suddenly, and in Israel of all places, would that no longer be possible? Why do the dati'im have to close themselves in with dati'im?

We've resisted the *others* for two thousand years, and do we now find ourselves unable to resist our little *hiloni* (non-observant) Jewish neighbors? If they mingle together in small doses it can only be beneficial for both parties.

One is constantly told, "We have to shield our children from contamination." But isn't it through difficulty and confrontation that you build yourself up, that you come to ask yourself questions?

If you've asked them and succeeded in answering them you are much stronger, and you will no longer cave in at the slightest encounter with the outside world.

So we were the moving spirit behind the creation of the Hebrew workshop at the École Alsacienne. Children went there. We showed them photos of Israel, they listened to Israeli records and we took them out to shows.

Our daughter taught them to dance and the boys taught them to sing. Being on the giving rather than the receiving end gave all three of them a certain importance.

We nevertheless got tired of the pseudo-secularism of the École Alsacienne where, at Christmas, a crib with clay figures and carols were *de rigueur*.

And then all these children whose parents had a second residence made us look almost like tramps to our daughter.

She was getting to the end of primary school. We said to ourselves: it's alright to be coddled in early childhood, but after that it would be good for her to go to school and mix with everyone. We enrolled her in a school a short distance from our home.

There she discovered a different world. She came home and told us that the unfortunate daughter of the concierge hadn't had a holiday for three years and the little Japanese girl adopted by the woman who lived alone had never been out of Paris. Country homes and a fresh dress every day were no longer the norm. Two years later, on her return from a holiday-camp organized by the *Fond Social Juif Unifié* (Unified Jewish Social Fund, FSJU) where she met E.B., who attended a Jewish school, she told us, "I also want to go to a Jewish school."

We agreed. At that period, in 1971, we'd already decided to leave for Israel. The Jewish school seemed a good preparation.

In adolescence, one's home relinquishes its hold over you in favor of the surrounding milieu. One needs external surroundings that "take over": school, youth movement, community, Eretz- Israel. The Jewish school provided us with such a take-over point. There were no longer any problems concerning kashrut, Shabbat, the holidays. We could speak openly of our intended aliyah.

Our older son had reached the age for his Bar Mitzvah, which he prepared in a very short time, helped by Shimen where reading was concerned, and by G, who had recorded the *ta'amim*[9] for him on a tape-recorder.

His brain was functioning properly and Shimen was an excellent teacher. When he went up to the Torah to read the parasha – *Tetsavei* (Exodus 27), one of the most difficult – you could hear the silence filling the whole synagogue. He had a lovely pure voice, and he sang with the grace and simple faith proper to his age. Everyone was moved.

Something was happening. An idea was taking shape in everyone's minds: even if you don't come from a milieu that is acceptable to the Jewish establishment, you can make your way in your own manner. You could see what a miracle it was!

I couldn't stop myself crying. Through my tears, I saw that many people were crying. Rabbi Schilli recalled the memory of my parents and said what had to be said, and I was overwhelmed.

Without him, I don't know if I would ever have been able to set foot in a shul again.

---

9. Cantillations.

It's because he was a *ben-adam* that something as painful as that was made possible, and the children felt this.

We provided a kiddush, not without difficulty, so rare were kosher food shops at that period. Certain products had to be ordered from Strasbourg.

Rabbi Schilli, sitting in his office, patiently initiated me into the complexities of commercial channels which were as yet unfamiliar to me.

It was a turning point, that *Bar Mitzvah*. It was our son who stimulated us, who swept us along, who pushed us to do things that we might otherwise not have done, or that we might have done at a slower pace.

We felt the importance the children attached to these things, so we did them. They began to go to shul on Shabbat. I followed, while my husband more or less continued to go to work.

Ida and Fred Akerman. Paris 1988.

Myriam, Binyamin, Michael and Gabriel, Mitzpe Nevo.

Oliver-Menachem and Manou with their children at Naava's wedding with Sammy, 2004.

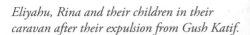

Eliyahu, Rina and their children in their caravan after their expulsion from Gush Katif.

Eliyahu and Rina's house in Neve Dekalim, Gush Katif (pre-expulsion).

Tzahal[1]

My son's
a reservist,
reservist in a tank crew,
my little Zionist
artist ....
I can hardly bear
to see him cross the border
in his antiquated tank,
there
where bloody war is rife.
May God preserve
my little talmudist
of the tank crew,
musician,
philosopher, specialist in electronics,
who takes such care
of his neighbor
and really has nothing to do
with the plight of those poor Palestinians.
But he must face the engines
of the Syrians
and be exposed to the mines
of the murderous PLO,
and, as for me, it burns me up
that they make war
precisely
on these young folk
of inspiration divine
who give themselves unstintingly

---

1. The Israel Defense Forces

to transform
this Land
into a haven of peace!

October, 14, 1982

BACK IN OUR ELEMENT

We were investigating the possibilities of aliyah. This project preoccupied us. We'd made many journeys to Israel, and aliyah seemed to us the culmination of our path, the concretization of our Jewish identity, a way of showing ourselves to be fully fledged members of our people in our land, claiming our collective heritage without having to be pigeonholed as dati or "religious," terms which don't always fit me.

Leaving in a state of being so little in the swing of things was a bit rash: the *olam hazeh*[1] isn't our strong point. One is more fragile than one thinks.

Little by little, however, we burned all our bridges. We had to reassure the patients who were not in a good state, find them another doctor and see them more frequently. We also had to hold out. We had to sell our practice, buy whatever was needed in order to leave, pack our things – me, who never knew how to pack a suitcase and can't bear either to see them or touch them!

Today, I find packing a bit easier. I can give myself a shake and say, "My dear, this isn't the war. You're not leaving Berlin or Antwerp." Even my daughter was suffering from my "syndrome."

I didn't know then what I do now, which would have helped me to understand her reactions. She was sick at having to leave her room. The boys, for their part, adapted to Israel quite quickly and they liked the place. But, as for her, her enthusiasm was not unalloyed. She was older, more aware. The family was once again split up and scattered to the four corners of the earth.

The Bar Mitzvah was one stage, aliyah another. Returning to France was a further stage. You perceive that each person has to find his own way and create his own possibilities on the basis of his impossibilities.

Whenever our children left for a place where they'd find a response, they sang the Birkat Hamazon. Everyone began to sing with them, thinking, "What our ancestors said wasn't so silly!" And things began to move

---

1. The material world, here on earth.

when they were around. Their little pals wanted to accompany them to shul. In Israel as well as in France, this is the work that has to be done.

On our return to Paris, landing in an area where I had never previously set foot, where I didn't know a living soul, where Jewishly speaking there was nothing to be found, I was on another planet.

After I had made the house livable and regained a certain rhythm of life, I went to fetch my children who had remained in Israel at my brother's.

With my brother, they'd taken on certain habits: they went to shul every Shabbat.

And here in France, we'd decided to eat kosher, to observe Shabbat and go to shul. The time of straying in this area was over.

On the first Friday evening, we set out on our way to the shul. At a street corner, a clock gave us the time. By the time we'd arrive, the service would be over.

We had a poor knowledge of what was to be found in the quarter. All the most accessible synagogues were equally Orthodox.

My husband didn't often set foot in them, but I nevertheless wanted to go with the children despite the interminable journey, the more-than-glacial welcome, all these people who chatted loudly while glancing at you sideways, and the important figures who each time were called up to the Torah.

Here again, all that counted was money. If you wore a nice hat, were furnished with diplomas and were the possessor of a sizeable bank account, you existed. If not...

And those called upon to speak were Monsieur the Professor, some celebrity who had appeared on television, someone whose book had made the headlines, someone recognized by the world-at-large.

The world upside-down!

You never have anything to say amongst your own folk. It's useless to try and speak a Jewish language to the Jews. No one will listen to you. But if you've prostituted yourself and bowed down before these idols and if in so doing you've become a big-shot in their idolatrous hierarchy, you're like a god amongst us.

We were headed rather in the opposite direction. Moreover, we carried the memory of the minyanim of young people in Israel, these young people full of life who didn't sing like Yekkes.[2]

---

2.   German Jews, so-called because of the jackets they always wore.

We'd made our aliyah in every sense of the word, both materially and morally. We'd reconquered the right to our Jewish identity, we'd finished with the Marranism of those who are ashamed of their Jewishness.

Moreover, back in Paris, I hardly had any desire to see some of our former friends. I no longer had anything to say to anyone.

What were they concerned with? Their next vacation, the price of the most recent motor-car to have appeared on the market.

I asked myself, "What planet have I come back to?"

The sales, the country residence, becoming Mr. President of this or that...

We had what we needed. Becoming a bigwig, a great lady, an important person had no meaning for us. We had a fine house, thank God, and enough to fill our plates every day. We were respected; we were no longer dogs to be trampled underfoot on the pavement.

Was that any reason to trample on others?

In any case, I still felt as small as ever, full of questions, faced with a mass of things to do, all so difficult, so onerous in every way that they had to be snatched painfully one after the other from nonexistence and non-life. It was a whole enterprise which left no room for such worldly concerns.

Every Shabbat, we went to this distant shul, and each time I came back disgusted, nauseated. It was exile to the nth degree.

When I'm told that for Kaddish people come forward one by one, the most important person first of all, I'm shocked.

It's perhaps my background as a Chasidic Jewess from the shtetl that comes to light here. I can still see my father praying in his shtiebel, a little house of worship where everyone prayed together with devotion, where everyone was *shaliach tsibbur*[3] in turn, whatever his social status, and where it was like a big family, not like a Mass where Monsieur le Curé mumbles the prayers and everyone says Amen.

I also remembered the fraternal spirit of Moissac. We learned not to chatter when someone prayed, we acquired a certain discipline.

In this shul and in the others, problems were swept under the carpet for the sake of "peace and quiet" and at the cost of all sorts of dubious compromises. It was a window dressing of *shalom* (peace)!

Where I am concerned, a shalom of this kind is tantamount to handing in one's resignation. Empty out the abscess of your heart and, afterwards, shalom will be possible.

---

3. A representative of the community who leads the prayer.

It was really with the Georges Berger community and even earlier in Neuilly, when we held services with my brother and our friends Saül and Arty and the whole band, that we had this experience of "shalom afterwards."

It was the time of the "repatriation" of the Jews of North Africa. Many of them settled in that area (Neuilly, Puteaux) and they came to pray there. We naturally allowed them to organize the service (each community has its own rite. The Ashkenazim, who were now in the minority, agreed to have the service conducted according to the Sephardi rite of the new arrivals).

They only gave Kol Nidrei[4] to my brother or to Saül.

We were very much at ease together; there was mutual respect. We had welcomed them nicely and we put the infrastructure of the service into their hands.

We liked their prayers, despite their petty quarrels about "how things were done at our place in Oran, how they were done at our place in Constantine."

They'd start to fight, even on Yom Kippur. It was dreadful! But at least the Judaism of the Sephardim wasn't sad.

Indeed, I think that only the Jews of Israel have the proper idea of the klal[5] and know what simcha[6] is.

When I went to my son's misdar – the ceremony concluding army training – and for the first time had a close view of soldiers marching together, I felt physically what being part of a klal could mean, and how much this feeling could be lacking in the Jews of the galut, including the most religious, to the point of making them unconscious of what they are missing.

When I expressed this opinion, I was taken for a militarist. Today, except in the Spartan-type countries of Eastern Europe and in Japan and China (this was written in 1975), young people have lost all sense of belonging and of solidarity with a group, whether close or distant.

However, I see this as a basic dimension, a dimension which is one of the essential components of a human being. Man is not solely an individual, though one should never deny his right to his individuality, his personal irreplaceable identity.

---

4. Introductory prayer to the *Yom Kippur* service.
5. The collective.
6. Joy.

For the Jew, the collective identity plays as important a role as an absolute respect for each person's specific nature.

In galut we can only have an abstract, intellectual idea of collective identity. It was only in Israel that I sensed how much we lacked it and were deprived of it in the gola, where each person carried the whole of Jewish history alone on his shoulders. Previously, when I said *Yizkor*[7] during the Jewish holiday services in memory of my parents, I wept alone in my corner.

When for the first time I heard the collective Yizkor composed by the Israelis in memory of the six million Jews murdered in the Shoah, I had a shock but at the same time felt immense relief.

Even if I wasn't there to say the Yizkor, the memory of my parents had been taken into account by the klal. I had discovered a new planet.

These are little things which don't seem important, like when I understood, in breathing in the landscapes of Israel, to what a degree I had not understood how a gentile can feel related to his land.

You can do psychoanalysis for a hundred and twenty years, but there are things that can only be repaired in reality. When you haven't had something, when it has been taken away from you, you can't conceive how much you miss it until the day that you regain it in reality.

It was in going out of Egypt that all the tribulations of slavery previously endured came to the surface. My parents often said at the worst moments, "*Me soll sech nur kennen dus derzeilen in Frieden*," which means, "May we be able to tell each other about this one day in joy!"

Similarly, it's only when I got this house in Jerusalem that I realized how much I'd been in a state of lacking a house, of lacking an anti-Auschwitz.

And now, even if the phantasm reappears, I can counter it by saying to myself, "I've got the house." This house has been the most effective therapeutic tool against my obstinate obsession of being an abandoned child, alone in the world, *hefker ba'olam*[8] – its mother far away, powerless, tortured, murdered; its father gone up in smoke.

Something, somewhere in my world had toppled over. The tikkun, the reparation has to result in a concrete transformation.

Psychoanalysis is very good, self-awareness is indispensable. But it's essential that there's a possibility of taking things up again in the reality.

---

7. A prayer in memory of the departed.
8. Abandoned, not claimed by anybody.

Words are not enough, which doesn't mean that if one is well backed up and sees the problem clearly one can't put things right on one's own.

In France or anywhere else, I was never able to buy a house or the smallest plot of land, or to settle in anywhere except in a provisional manner.

Everywhere a double curtain, a lamp, a bookshelf was missing. And when I go too far away from this house in Jerusalem, the phantasm seizes me again, "We'll be held up, we're going to miss the last plane."

And it's endless. Even my son told me, when he was doing his studies in Israel, that he wasn't keen to go to boarding school and that this house in Jerusalem represented his security.

When he was in the army, he only had to go to Radak[9] for half an hour and make a telephone call to us in order to retrieve the presence of his parents and feel a ben-adam again.

In the absence of this house he, like his brother before him, would have found it difficult to hold out.

My mother in her time used to say, "A bare room, a scrap of dry bread, but to be in one's home!"

After all these wanderings of refugees, these camps, these children's homes, we needed a house and so did our children.

I had begun to tell you about the sense of simcha and klal that comes about as a result of the physical *techiat hameitim* and independence. Every Jew in Israel benefits from it, and it's from this that he draws his strength.

From his childhood, the little Sabra is taught to value his liberty and his rights.

Despite all their difficulties, the Israelis convey an impression of security, confidence in life and a joy unimaginable in gola.

I've always been struck by this plenitude, this sense of having a natural, easy relationship with life and with others, perhaps because I've had the good fortune to meet exceptional people, especially in the religious kibbutzim, but also because I believe that the number of extraordinary people per square kilometer is proportionally larger here than anywhere else.

You sense that they have the feeling that they're in the right place at the right time, doing the right thing in the right way, whatever the circumstances.

---

9. The street in Jerusalem where our home is.

They're in harmony with themselves, *shlemim*.[10]

Here you find in a living form all the Jewish wisdom which has nothing in common with the Western chasing after superfluities: "Kids are a bloody nuisance," "To marry is to put a rope around one's neck," "To tire oneself for others is to be a sucker."

The whole of Jewish wisdom has been given back to us like a fruit through the manner-of-being of the shlichim. I will only tell you about one of them: David Ben Naeh, who helped us to create the Georges Berger minyan.

One Shabbat morning, coming back from shul with our two boys, I saw from behind a man with a hat, walking along and holding two little boys by the hand. I said to myself, "A man who doesn't work on Saturdays, with a swarthy complexion and a hat on his head, and who walks around with his children, can only be an ambassador from Latin America or a Jew."

While talking with my children, we came close to them and overheard the words, "*Oi, abbeleh, hana'ala'im sheli!*" ("Oh, daddy, my shoes!"). Immediately, we exchanged "shaloms" and began to discuss the problem of these long forced marches on Shabbat to a place of worship, which seemed to suit him as little as it suited us.

A shaliach who had recently arrived in Paris, he had taken up lodgings in a street near to ours. "Supposing we organized a minyan in our neighborhood?"

He said, "Find me the place and the people, and I'll do the rest."

The idea had formed in my mind since we first set eyes on this "desert" of a quarter, and now someone had fallen from the heavens who would carry it out.

In record time, before we'd even finished moving into our home, with a telephone call here and a telephone call there we were provided with a premises, and a Sefer Torah was put into my hands by Rabbi Schilli, who immediately grasped the importance of the project.

Once again, he was able to support us in this adventure in which there was a series of seemingly improbable coincidences which made it possible.

And a short time afterwards, there we were with the Sefer Torah in our living-room, waiting for the premises to become available with a twinge of anxiety in our hearts: Would we be able to get a minyan every

---

10. Whole (in the plural). It has the same root as shalom, peace.

Shabbat? For communal prayer to take place, ten men at least have to be present.

Fortunately, our children's friends were always willing to walk kilometers to our home, which every Shabbat was transformed into a youth hostel.

David Ben Naeh proved to be the man for the situation. He had a genius, which didn't seem to be anything special, for being able to bring out the best in everyone. Thanks to him, the connection with Israel was maintained. He took our younger son next to him to say the *Mi sheberach*,[11] and gave him – at the age of thirteen! – the function of *gabbai*.[12]

Our boys, much encouraged, said the *tefillah*[13] in turns and prepared the *kriyah*.[14] It was wonderful. This practice of giving children responsibilities we later retained, as a principle in running the minyan, for other people's children.

As I went to all the services, the women felt encouraged to come also. They sat there without talking too much although they didn't understand Hebrew, and they hastened, after the service, to set out the kiddush which they brought in turns.

The little old people of the quarter who would never have been able to cross the whole of Paris to find a place of worship, lost no time in joining us, and with beaming faces surrounded the young people, happy to feel useful, in a milieu in which they participated fully.

Having become more or less resigned to their fate of being uprooted after the repatriation from North Africa, and seeing their children drifting away from Judaism one by one, regarding their parents as fossils, they found a familiar element in the minyan and gradually regained their dignity.

They saw my husband and me, Monsieur the doctor and Madame the doctor, with our fine diplomas which their children would have given anything to possess, bending over backwards to embody and bring to life the very things their children disdained.

In this shul, there were nothing but miracles. Whatever was lacking always turned up. There was always a minyan, even on the fifteenth of

---

11. A blessing said on someone who has just been up to the *Torah*.
12. The person who "carries" the *minyan*.
13. Prayers.
14. Reading of the weekly passage from the Torah.

August when Paris is deserted. You can imagine what a joy it was, but I won't say it was easy!

There were rabbis living in the quarter who appeared and immediately wanted to take over, and legalistic pseudo-rabbis who found fault with everyone and tried to engineer a putsch. There were also confirmed diasporists who walked out demonstratively when the Israeli shaliach said the Yizkor for the Six Million victims of the Shoah and the *chayalim* (soldiers) of Tzahal fallen in the wars, and who began to talk loudly when the prayer for the State of Israel was being said.

There were also those who wouldn't agree that the sum offered by the person going up to the Torah should not be publicly declared. It was a quiet revolution, but not as quiet as all that!

Every living thing is like a flower planted in the soil. If you don't water it enough, it dies; if you water it too much, it dies.

Prayer and song are for us what light and water are for flowers. The Hebrew letters read and sung have a real physical effect. They are the food for your neshama.

A person who can't sing can suffocate, but you can't sing all alone or just anything.

A good shaliach tsibbur raises up his kahal. If he prays according to your own *nussah*,[15] you naturally vibrate more easily; but even if he prays according to his nussah, he opens the gates of tefillah for you if he prays in an authentic manner.

As with flowers, you have to be there all the time, extricate a leaf caught between branches, create a support for too weak a stem, and above all pull out the weeds.

When there are too many people in a group and I can't distinguish the face of each person, I can no longer manage. Humanity is like a plantation that is cultivated through human warmth and the attention given to each one.

Of course, there was no lack of problems, and each time a problem came up, I had to find a solution.

Who else would have done it? Nobody budged. People didn't even see the problem. You have to be trained to see the detail that's wrong before it does any harm.

---

15. Rite.

As I've knocked around a bit and, as far as I'm concerned, it's "Go forward or perish," there's no question of not going forward. A problem emerges; a solution has to be found. One searches, one finds it.

One had to fight everyone: the FSJU, the Consistoire (the religious administration), the Jewish Agency, the high-ups, the little people, fight for women to come with their children and for the children to be quiet and come nevertheless and get what they needed.

While the shlichim were there, all the nostalgias of the past were channeled towards the future. Their dvar Torah, rooted in life, was nourishment for the whole week.

At the same period as we had the George Berger minyan, and no less important, there was the yeshiva of Montreux. It was the children who wanted to go there.

They'd heard about it through Bnei Akiva, at Morgins where we had spent a holiday shortly after our attempt at aliyah. A Bnei Akiva camp had been set up nearby in a house occupied by the O.S.E., and they ran there all day long, participating in all their activities.

So when the camp paid a visit to the Montreux yeshiva, my older son went along also.

Much later, Rav Shaul David confessed to me that, without knowing why, he had run after him and insisted that he should come to the yeshiva. That is something he had never done in the case of any other child. He didn't know, but God in heaven knew what He was doing.

I could tell you my whole story from this perspective – that of the malach present at every intersection – and thank Hakadosh Baruch Hu for all the chesed He has shown me in all misfortunes and for all the help He has given me in this mad struggle.

When he returned, my son was bubbling over with enthusiasm: "Papa, papa, you must go and see Rav Botschko at Montreux."

Put my children in a boarding school? All my phantasms of abandonment crowded together at the gateway of my memories.

One Monday, we rang Montreux to announce our visit on the following Thursday. On Thursday, we rang up to excuse ourselves for not coming. Every day we said, "We'll ring tomorrow." One day passed and then another. We finally reached a decision: we'd go and see my brother who happened to be on holiday at Murren and on the way we'd make a detour via Montreux.

I inspected every nook and cranny of the yeshiva, on the lookout for the slightest suggestion of those "children's homes" which I knew too well.

We asked questions, examined everything. Not only was there nothing to find fault with but we had seldom encountered such excellent human relations.

When you speak to Rav Botschko, you speak to a ben-adam.

"Our home" was *his* home, a house placed entirely at the disposition of one and all, where no one took advantage of anyone else and where the Rav still had a hand in the family business in order to ensure his financial independence and sometimes, perhaps, in order to balance the yeshiva's budget.

Moreover, children who were not wealthy were accepted in the same way as the others, and nobody knew who was paying or how much.

All of a sudden, all that I'd desired and which couldn't be accomplished because "you're a dreamer of the ghetto, a utopian with ideals suitable for the *yemot ha'Mashiach*[16] and now it's *ha'olam ha'zeh*, and that's all that can be done" had come to pass!

All of a sudden, when you meet people like Rav Botschko, who not only think like you, feel like you but also succeed in doing what you dream of, it's a healing of your wounds, a real tikkun.

He said, "Take a couple of weeks. Think it over." We, for our part, could only act in accordance with our usual attitude to our children: "You decide. If you want that, we'll go along with it."

It was no business of theirs if I'd been in a children's home; they had the right to live their own lives: 1972 wasn't 1942. We needed to separate their present reality from our past reality.

We parents must help our children to run on their own railway tracks and not keep them on ours, in addition hitching our cattle-cars onto them.

Our elder son decided to go to Montreux. It was the beginning of an extraordinary relationship: "Rav Moshei does this, Rav Moshei does that... You know, Rav Moshei..."

Everything was based on exemplary human relations, confidence in the pupils and respect for the special personality of each one.

The following year our second son joined our elder son at the yeshiva.

I no longer heard them telling me that in the *kodesh*[17] class they made paper darts while they were taught about Chasidism in Poland, or

---

16. The Messianic age, literally, "the days of the Messiah."
17. Judaism; lit. holy.

that *Shema Yisrael* had become a punishment to be copied out a hundred times.

I no longer said to myself, "I'd prefer my children to be in a field, grazing like cattle. Then at least they'd look up at the sky and wonder, 'Does Hakadosh Baruch Hu really exist?'"

In that case, they'd still have their questions, and one would have a chance of being able to give them something. Whereas there they were permanently put off and any hunger or thirst was taken away from them. Their appetite was ruined.

A teacher of kodesh must first of all be a teacher of life. He's the parents' representative. He must be able to take into consideration the personality of each pupil with his specific problems.

For our sons, Rav Botschko was the anti-guru who helped them to make their own way. He knew how to refrain from giving advice ("You're quite old enough to find the answer for yourself"), while providing the information necessary for making a decision.

He was one of those people you learn from simply by seeing how they behave. You'd never see him let someone else carry his suitcase, and you'd see him doing the shopping for the yeshiva himself.

Before meeting him, I'd never really understood why a special prayer is said for those who teach Torah to their generation. A true Rav is someone who can put himself into the skins of a large number of people, as a result of which he can support each one in his attempt to achieve autonomy, *atzma'ut* – the capacity to have access to himself. The root of the word atzma'ut – *etzem*, meaning essence, bone – denotes the strength to stand upright.

This capacity to adapt himself to each individual case was revealed to the full on the day he gave out the diplomas. He gave each pupil his diploma with a variety of facial expressions corresponding to the state of soul of each one, while shaking his hand.

Rav Botschko knew how not to exclude any area of life. The pupils could dive in the swimming pool rented by the yeshiva once a week, do judo, go on excursions on Tuesday, a day set aside for that purpose, or even go skiing.

He let them play football when they were on edge or even run upon the benches in the Talmud class just prior to taking their matriculation.

He was capable of changing the subject of a lesson in accordance with their preoccupations of the moment and their capacity to absorb.

None of the problems of the klal were neglected. When a demonstration was held in support of the Jews of Russia, the whole yeshiva traveled to take part, headed by Rav Botschko wrapped in his tallit.

Already at the end of the war, the survivors of the concentration camps passed the word around: if you don't know where to go, take the train to Montreux, cry "Botschko, Botschko!" and you're sure to be heard.

He corresponded with all the figures connected with politics and religion in Israel and read his letters and articles to his pupils, together with their replies.

The results of this education were splendidly visible at weddings. You saw the pupils of other yeshivot moving their bodies mechanically whereas the young people of the Montreux yeshiva each danced in accordance with his inspiration, with all his body and soul.

And today, the Rav's pupils teach Torah just as they danced. They know how to bring out its life-force ever renewed.

Our older son wasn't suited for going to a "*dinim*[18] factory." He has such a desire for perfection that he might have been snapped up by the ultra-Orthodox.

In the year when the Georges Berger minyan started up, before we'd even unpacked our luggage, he pestered me, fearing that I hadn't koshered my dishes properly for Pesach. I finally told my children, "You may know the Halacha[19] better than I do, but the things you're demanding you can do yourselves, because if *I'm* doing it, I'll do it in the way I can."

In the course of his apprenticeship with Rav Botschko, he came up to me and said, "You know, you were right. Such and such a thing wasn't necessary." It's very easy to be *machmir*,[20] but to make life livable for a Jew, one has to have studied a lot and understood a lot. The Torah isn't made for angels. It isn't given in order to imprison people in books.

The Rav didn't condition his respect for his pupils' parents on the pounds of mitzvot they displayed.

I was happy to find in him the living embodiment of one of my dreams: an institution on human lines. As long as I can look each person in the face and see if everything's all right (or not), it's okay. Otherwise, beware! It's a danger in store for the State of Israel, which finds it difficult

---

18. Laws concerning rituals.
19. The body of Jewish laws (literally, "the way to go").
20. *Machmir*, someone who makes things complicated.

to avoid the example of the Western states, always eager to replace human beings with numbers, to value quantity over quality.

Swallow a hundred pages of Gemara, okay. But, as for me, what if a single line is enough to nourish me all my life?

And what if the whole world has only been created for the sake of a single real ben-adam?

Thanks to the minyan, thanks to the presence of Rav Botschko via our sons, thanks to Eretz Yisrael via the shlichim, a joyous Jewish life again became possible. Yom Kippur was no longer wandering as before, Pesach was no longer the absence of family, the holidays were no longer the torrent of tears unleashed by my brother's kiddush.

Tears still flow quite easily in my case, but they resemble the dew in springtime since my children and grandchildren gave my past a whiff of the future.

When I see my sons praying like my brother – that's to say like my father – I know the connection has been made. In coming up to Israel, they have taken the voyage of my grandfather, a *talmid hacham*,[21] to its final conclusion.

---

21. Lit., pupil of the Sages.

Fifty Years After

Fifty years after the war
we've had the good fortune
of having returned
to our Land.
One should give thanks
for having been saved
from our enemies
and for having
reached this place
alive.
Many are those
who so much desired it
but to whom
it was not given.
One should give thanks
at every moment
and not be distressed,
for Hakadosh Baruch Hu
leads his people
forward
despite all blunders
and the failure
of some of His children
to remember.

April 27, 1994

EPILOGUE

My husband always says laughingly, "We're good parents. We've followed our children."

We've finally, with God's help, realized our project of going up to Eretz Yisrael, and this time to Jerusalem. And it has worked out as if by magic that each problem in turn has been solved in the best possible way for us.

This time, our sons were there to receive us as adults well integrated into the country for some fifteen years.

Our family and friends expressed a joy at our return which was commensurate with their distress at our past difficulties.

We were surrounded with affection on every side. This was evident on happy occasions and especially at our children's weddings when everyone came to rejoice with us in double measure.

Meanwhile, my husband discovered in the country some cousins on his mother's side, although his mother had thought she was the only survivor in her family! This helped to strengthen his sense of belonging and aided him in striking roots in the country.

In short, the recompense of arrival was proportionate to the difficulties of the journey. Nothing is ever a defeat... Things can only be a detour.

In this case it proved to be a profitable detour, as we've had the privilege, on our way, of experiencing and doing unlooked-for things for ourselves, those near to us, our patients, our community and our children, in order that they would become what they have become and continue to sow that which we have already had the good fortune of reaping in part.

Fred left us before the appearance of this book. He accompanied it, however, throughout its writing, as he accompanied me.

He passed away after a severe illness on the 8th of Tammuz 5755 July 6, 1995.

This book is dedicated to him.

Fred

He had taste
and his own way
of doing things well
to the end.
He saw things correctly
and knew what had to be done –
whether buying gifts for his grandchildren
or clothes –
in a second.
He knew at what angle
a photo should be taken
and how to pose an object
so that it would look good...
He could quickly separate
the wheat from the tares
and had the grace
to face up to things nicely,
not fearing the hard work.
He was a builder
who didn't look for honors.
He was our tree of life,
the loved and respected
head of the family.
With him is gone
our supporting pillar, our cloud of glory,
our manna, our wellspring.

May his strength, his courage,
his well-organized mind,
his willpower,
his concern for others,

his absolute taste for life
and beauty
and for recapturing true values
inspire and accompany each of us
with the help of Hakadosh Baruch Hu
in continuing the work
which he accomplished
with so much courage.
May Hakadosh Baruch Hu
preserve our children
whom he loved so much
and give them the strength to go forward:
May He deliver our people
from its oppressors
– these were his dearest wishes –
and may his blessed memory
help us to remain alive.

July 9, 1995

My Husband

My good husband's left us.
He was big, he was strong,
he radiated health
and no one expected
this premature
demise...
He loved life
with all his being
and gave himself wherever
life stirs...
He was there with his children
and grandchildren
in the "territories,"
with the "Hidden Children"
and their memory,
in the Civil Guard
with his cronies,
and he used to go down to the hospital
to lend a helping hand.
He loved this country
and he loved the sea
in which he liked to swim.
He advanced courageously
on the precipitous slopes
of the return to his identity,
joyfully rediscovering
the so beautiful landscapes
of his land,
giving rides to all the soldiers,
sweating over his
ancestral tongue,

and trying to struggle against the evil
that threatens the future and morality
of our society.
He was happy to live at one
with his nation
and to have the privilege
of being in his home
in Zion
which he hoped would be open and attractive
close to the Western Wall.

July 24, 1995

I Give Thanks

I'm no longer in the camp
delivered up to the wicked
and cohabiting
with all and sundry.
I'm no longer shut away
separated from my father,
sleeping on straw
In the midst of a shambles.
I'm no longer down there
in the huts in winter
with rats and lice
running hither and thither,
floundering in the mud
and tearing my little summer dress
trying to cross
the barbed-wire barrier.
I no longer have
to go walking on the jetty
in the cold and wind
with the waves of the sea
splashing against me
and drenching my light canvas shoes.
I'm no longer dying of hunger
running after scraps of bread
or have holes in the ground
for performing my elementary needs.

I no longer read suffering
anxiety and despair
on the faces of all these people
reduced to helpless misery.

I run in freedom
to our little neighborhood garden
where, sitting on a bench,
I watch my little grandson
at play.
Then I return to my home
in the midst of my garden in Zion,
so laden with blessings...
Clean, bright, shady, pretty,
with all the marvelous comforts
one could desire.
My home so quiet
yet connected with others –
with clothes, shoes,
good food,
books, friends,
the necessary
and the superfluous;
Shabbatot and holidays,
classes in abundance,
my children and grandchildren
not far away,
worthy and respected,
serving my people and God,
happy in my land...
All that is generally
taken for granted
or which one prays for
when one is wretched
but which to me seems so miraculous
and the gift
of Heaven's bounty
alone.
For one has to have been
in that absolute exile
and to have experienced all that evil
in order to appreciate the good fortune
of deliverance

and continually to say "Thanks,"
"And I beg You
spare our little ones
these horrors.
May they be happy
in their place
and work
to bring it justice, joy and peace
according to Your plan,
O Holy One, Blessed Be He."

June 30, 2004

Our Young People

One must give thanks for everything
Even when one doesn't understand
anything at all.
The ordeal imposed
On the cast-out children
Of Gush Katif
Cannot be forgiven.
It is enough to make one weep
Without end!
But to see their strength revealed
To overcome in all simplicity...
Their seriousness,
Their faith,
Their sense of responsibility
Towards the Nation,
Their creativity
Worthy of Zion,
The superior quality of this generation
Fills us with joy...
They are attached to their land,
To their brethren,
To the Torah
And to Hakadosh Baruch Hu
With an optimism and a vitality
Never known before.
How is it that we
Have deserved
To see such things?

AFTERWORD

With God's help, our little tribe has been blessed by an increase in the number of its members with the arrival of several grandchildren:

To Myriam and Prosper was born Gabriel Moshe Yitzhak.

To Olivier (Menahem) and Manou were born Moshe Yehuda and David Zvi.

To Eliyahu and Rina were born Atara, Moshe Shlomo, Yehuda and Natan Aharon.

Our daughter was finally able to make *aliya* with her family, so joining us in this country. Since then, she divorced Prosper and was remarried to Daniel Bauer, which added his four grown sons to the family. Myriam has integrated well into the country, living in Mitzpeh Nevo and working as a gynecologist, specializing in psychosomatic gynecology and sexology, in which occupation she finds much pleasure and has much success.

Menahem is a teacher of Jewish Studies at Machon Lev (Engineering Training College), devoted to his students and appreciated by them.

Eliyahu is a gifted and sought-after psychologist in charge of the psychological services in Kiryat Arba.

All three of them are truly devoted to serving others, which they do with much dedication, love and competence, each in his or her own field.

Our oldest granddaughter, Naava, the daughter of Menahem and Manou, married Sammy Belisha, who studies Torah in the Old City of Jerusalem. They are a wonderful couple, very beneficial for the family. Naava is studying to become a psychological counselor to schools.

Her sister Avital is studying psychology at the university. She is a courageous and hardworking student.

Yehoshua, our oldest grandson, the son of Eliyahu and Rina, has finished his military service. He took a course as a guide and is studying psychology.

Yedidya, their second son, studied in a yeshiva for three years. He is an officer in the army in a combat unit, where he is liked and appreciated by his soldiers, representing the new model of those officers who are full of faith and Torah through which they radiate love of their fellow man and their responsibility to them. He married his sweetheart Judith Belgrad on the anniversary of the "disengagement" from Gush Katif, truly the most tragic event of recent years, and they live in a caravan in Karmei Tsur!

Seeing Eliyahu and Rina's marvellous family expelled by the army from the magnificent home they built for themselves in Gush Katif, from their garden, their community, their landscape... all of it violently destroyed by our own government, which made no preparations to re-house them or see them reinstalled... seeing them suffer for eight months, crammed with their eleven children into four rooms of a hotel, brought back to me other nightmares from the past described in this book.

What a trial, this prolonged stay in the hotel (which even ended with a good week "on the streets"!) while waiting for the caravans – provisional accommodation, which never seemed to be ready – to become available... the failure, to this day, even to envisage construction of a future home for their family!

Since this period, they have lived in a temporary caravan in Amatzia for nearly five years with the expelled community from the moshav of Katif. In spite of the inefficiency and bad will of the government bureaucracy in charge of resettling them with dignity in a reasonable space of time, the power of their confidence in life and faithfulness to our collective ideal took over and allowed them to recreate a familial and communal life which is an example and illustration of the vitality of the people of Israel and its genius to rebuild on the ruins which have been imposed on it. I never dreamed that what I related in this book concerning my personal journey would have to be relived in another form by my children and grandchildren in our own country.

What a suffering is this tendency to self-destructiveness in a part of our people!

This self-hatred, that is to say the hatred for those who embody our "ideal selves"!

This illusory, death-dealing search for "peace" with our murderous neighbors, who want nothing better than war and our destruction, and who take our generosity for weakness!

This wish to be loved by the nations, who hate us despite our efforts to resemble them (and in so doing, losing the core of our being, and our raison d'être in the world and in the land), and our zeal to carry out their orders to make "unilateral humanitarian gestures" that endanger our basic security in the most suicidal manner!

But our history continues, and with the help of the Holy One, Blessed be He, and of all of us, who have to go forward, it will end in a better world for us and for the whole of mankind. Each one of us brings his little building block. Thus, my book came out in Hebrew, and it is on the point of appearing in English.

Poems continue to spring forth, and I try to make use of them.

We are happy each day to have the unbelievable privilege of being finally in the Land, and the joy of living in Jerusalem surrounded by family and friends, and attending marvelous courses that bring us into an ever-deeper knowledge of our age-old wisdom.

It is an immense happiness to live thus in harmony with our collective identity now regained, and to be able to share it.

May we be delivered from the many hostile forces, and may we, the entire nation, finally bring ourselves to work on earth, in the service of the Creator, for the maximum benefit of all humanity.

"May the world be set right in the kingdom of the Almighty!"

GLOSSARY

Aliyah	Immigration, literally "ascent" to Israel
Ashkenazim	Jews originating in Germany and Central Europe
Avodah Zara	Idolatrous cults (*zar* is "strange" or "foreign" in Hebrew)
Bar Mitzvah	The religious coming-of-age ceremony of a Jewish boy who goes up to the Torah for the first time at the age of thirteen
Ben-adam	Human being (etymologically, "son of Adam")
Bettgewand	Eiderdown
Birkat Hamazon	Grace, a series of blessings said after meals
Bnei Akiva	Religious Zionist youth movement
Chad gadya	A little lamb to which the people of Israel is compared in a liturgical song sung at Pesach
Chag	Feast, festivity
Challah	Braided loaf for Shabbat
Chametz	Yeast, leavened dough, not eaten during the holiday of Pesah.
Chanukka	Feast celebrating the victory of the Judeans over the Greeks and the miracle of the flask of oil in the Temple
Chasid	Follower of a spiritual movement connected with Jewish mysticism
Chayal (pl. *chayalim*)	Soldier of the Israel Defense Forces

Cheder	Jewish religious primary school
Chesed	Goodness, generosity, compassion
Cheshbon	Account, bill
Chochmat lev	Wisdom or intelligence of the heart
Cholent	A dish put on the fire before the entry of the Sabbath and eaten hot at Sabbath midday. The word is derived from the medieval French, *chault* (hot)
Chumash	The Pentateuch, the first five books of the Bible
Chutzpah	Cheek, effrontery
Dati (pl. *dati'im*)	Religiously observant
Eretz Yisrael	The Land of Israel
Fisch	The Yiddish term for fish and more specifically carp
Fleisch	Meat in Yiddish and German
Galut, gola	The Jewish exile
Gemara	The part of the Talmud commenting on the Mishna
Goy (pl. *goyim*)	In biblical Hebrew, nation; in Yiddish, non-Jew
Hagaddah	The narrative of the exodus from Egypt read with a commentary on the evening of the Passover Seder
Hakadosh Baruch Hu	The Holy One, Blessed be He (in Hebrew)
Halacha	The body of Jewish law (literally, "the way to go")
Hefker	Something abandoned
Ivrit	The Hebrew language
Kaddish	Prayer extolling the glory of God, also recited by mourners
Kasher	Kosher, fulfilling the requirements of Jewish law with regard to food and drink
Kashrut	The Jewish laws with regard to food and drink

Kavod	Honor, dignity
Kiddush	Blessing made over wine on Shabbat and the Jewish holidays
Kiddush Hashem	Sanctification of God (lit. "sanctification of the Name")
Kippah	Ritual skullcap worn by observant Jews
Klal	The collective
Kol Nidrei	Prayer sung at the beginning of the Yom Kippur service
Kotel	The Western Wall, a relic of the Second Temple
Kupat Holim	Health Insurance Fund, clinic
Lag Ba'omer	The thirty-third day after Pesach, commemorating the death of Rabbi Shimon Bar Yochai
Malach	Angel, messenger
Mashiach	Messiah
Matza (pl. *matzot*)	Unleavened bread eaten on Pesach when leavened bread is forbidden
Midrashim	Allegorical narratives
Minyan	The quorum of ten Jews required for communal prayer
Mitzrayim	Egypt, in Hebrew (it has the same root as *tzar*, narrow)
Mitzvah (pl. *mitzvot*)	Divine commandment
Mora (pl. *morot*)	Woman teacher
Na va'nad	Wanderer, vagabond
Neshama	One of the words for soul in Hebrew
Niggun	Melody
Nussah	Rite (Ashkenazi, Sephardi, Yemenite, etc.)
Olam hazeh	The material world, this world
Oleh (pl. *olim*)	Immigrant
Oneg Shabbat	Delight of the Sabbath. A festivity for children on Saturday afternoons

Parasha	The weekly reading from the Torah
Payes, payot	Locks of hair beneath the temples, which in the case of men are never cut
Pesach	Passover, holiday celebrating the exodus from Egypt.
Pirkei Avot	*The Ethics of the Fathers*, a tractate of the Talmud
Purim	Holiday commemorating the rescue of the Jews from extermination in the time of Queen Esther
Rav, rebbe (pl. *rabbanim*)	Rabbi
Schmattes	Rags (in Yiddish)
Schnorrer	Beggar (in German).
Seder	Passover meal celebrating the exodus from Egypt
Sefer Torah	Torah scroll
Sephardi	Jew originating in Spain, North Africa, etc
Shabbat	The Sabbath, the seventh day of the week, celebrating the creation of the world
Shaliach tsibbur	Representative of the community who leads the prayer in turns
Shalom	Peace. A term of greeting which is also one of the names of God
Shema	The central proclamation of the Jewish liturgy
Shidduch	Arranged marriage
Shiur	A lesson of Torah
Shiva	The week of mourning
Shlemazel	Clumsy, unlucky person who does everything wrong
Shlichim	Emissaries charged with a mission
Shochet	Ritual slaughterer of animals for butcher's meat
Shomer Shabbat	Sabbath-observant
Shtetl	Jewish village in Central and Eastern Europe

Shtiebel	Small place of worship (in Yiddish)
Shul	Synagogue (in Yiddish)
Shulchan Aruch	Rabbi Joseph Caro's codification of religious observances
Siddur	Jewish prayer book
Simcha	Joy, joyful celebration of a happy event
Ta'amim	Cantillation marks in biblical texts
Tallit	Rectangular prayer shawl bordered with fringes
Talmud	The oral law
Talmud Torah	Classes in Judaism for Jewish children in the *gola* (in France two half-days a week)
Techiat hameitim	The resurrection of the dead
Tefilla	Prayer
Tefillin	Phylacteries. A religious object made of leather containing the Shema, which men place on their arm and on their forehead during morning prayers
Teshuva	Repentance
Tikkun	Repair (of the world and of oneself)
Torah	The written Law revealed to Moses on Mount Sinai
Treif, treifa	Food forbidden according to Jewish law
Ulpan	Rapid course in Hebrew
Yahadut	Judaism
Ye'varechecha	May He (God) bless you
Yeshiva	Talmudic academy
Yizkor	Prayer in memory of the departed
Yom Kippur	The Day of Atonement, the most solemn day in the Jewish calendar (a day of fasting)
Yom tov	Jewish holiday
Zemirot	Traditional poems sung by the family at the Shabbat table

ABOUT THE AUTHOR

Escaped from Germany
Escaped from the camps
Parents deported
Left alone
Hidden to survive
From there to the reconstruction
– of a family,
– a profession,
– and a social and community life...
– from Exile to Israel
All my life was a struggle
to pass from the register of death
to that of life.

Ida Ackerman-Tieder wrote this book as a synthesis describing the process of a passage from death to life, using her own personal experience, and the experience of all the people she came across in her practice and private life, with the help of her professional knowledge. Ida believes that this enables the reader to identify with this process when facing his or her own difficulties and, in spite of past ordeals, to build one's present life, in a positive way.

Apart from that, Ida is a poet and has previously published three collections: *Poèmes Roux*, Paris, 1984; *Poèmes Roux Suite*, Paris, 1988; and *Evidences – Poèmes Roux (Autre Suite)*, Jerusalem, 2009.